Evil Eyes

www.cherylann-thomas.com

Cherylann Thomas (signature)

Evil Eyes

A Daughter's Memoir

Cherylann Thomas

To order additional copies of this book, contact:
Xlibris Corporation
1-888-795-4274
www.Xlibris.com
Orders@Xlibris.com
99801

Contents

Prologue

This above all: to thine own self be true

—Shakespeare

Imagine growing up without a parent's love. What happens to your psyche, your emotional well-being, and your self-esteem? How do you cope with life's little and big hardships when you have been trained to *not* love yourself enough to get through them?

This book is about my experiences with the sociopathic personalities of my parents and the effect they had on me. I have a strong feeling siblings of mine have pathological challenges as well, but I am not a doctor and won't conjecture other than to share what has happened to me and let you be the judge. I don't mean to sound bitter. The whole point of this book is to help others who have encountered sociopaths and as a result are left standing sick and weak and wondering why their world seems upside down.

The public would be amazed to know just how many sociopaths are out there under different names and pathologies. My book will focus on psychopaths (Ps), malignant narcissists (MNs), and sexual predators (SPs).

There are similar traits between psychopaths and malignant narcissists, and it's not uncommon for comorbidity. This is kind of where malignant narcissism comes in; although MN is an extreme form of narcissism that mimics psychopaths, it has a different root cause, internal factors, etc. The *malignant* pretext can be best described as meaning the narcissist goes far beyond self-centeredness and is *dangerous* to those closest to him or her, using seriously harmful emotional tactics to their "supply" to achieve their own ends without thought or empathy to their target(s).

One of the basic assumptions of psychotherapy is that the patient needs and wants help for distressing or painful psychological and emotional problems. The psychopath and the malignant narcissist do not think that they have any psychological or emotional problems, and they see no reason to change their behavior to conform to standards with which they do not agree. They are well satisfied with themselves and their inner landscape. They see nothing wrong with the way they think or act, and they never look back with regret or forward with concern. They perceive themselves as superior beings in a hostile world in which others are competitors for power and resources. They feel it is the optimum thing to do to manipulate and deceive others in order to obtain what they want.

I remember my mother going to an alcohol and drug center to find out more about her alcoholic second husband. She never went again saying, "Those assholes think I'm going to have to change my behavior as well! He's the fucking drunk!" I think the counselor made the mistake of confronting my mother, leaving her feeling less empowered and important than she liked to feel.

We should visit our ideas about psychopaths with a slightly different perspective. One thing we do know is this: many people who experience interactions with psychopaths and malignant narcissists report feeling "drained" and confused and often subsequently experience deteriorating health. Does this mean that part of the explanation for why psychopaths will pursue "love relationships" and "friendships" that ostensibly can result in no observable material gain is because there is an *actual* energy consumption? In my experience, I think so.

What is a psychopath?

Nothing is as it seems.

Psychopaths are good imposters of being a person. They have absolutely no hesitation about forging and brazenly using impressive credentials to adopt professional roles that bring prestige and power. They pick professions in which the requisite skills are easy to fake, the jargon is easy to learn, and the credentials are unlikely to be thoroughly checked. Psychopaths find it extremely easy to pose as financial consultants, accountants, ministers, teachers, psychological counselors, and psychiatrists (several years ago, we read about a Vancouver psychiatrist who turned his female patients into submissive mules to his sadistic ways).

My father was a diagnosed psychopath, pathological liar, and habitual criminal when he was twenty years old. Ps are masters at observing people to determine their weaknesses and use this information later on to use against them. There are many Ps who go through life without giving any sign of their sociopathic personalities. But do not be fooled; they are masters of deceit. Liars who refuse to ever give it up unless it suits their purpose are just one hint when you are dealing with a P. Most Ps live on the edge of the law, if not right in the hell of chronic criminal activity. Prisons are filled with psychopaths for crimes ranging from serial murder to minor crimes such as tax evasion, theft, fraud, and the list goes on.

Psychopaths are unable to feel compassion, or love. They are empty souls. Casey Anthony, the mother who allegedly murdered her own daughter, is a psychopath. She is on the extreme end of the psychopathic range. As most of us watched with our eyes glued to the television, we could see how she lies with an artist's precision. We saw how her own parents walked on eggshells around her as she lied and dared them to doubt her. Her eyes practically bulged out of her head in rage when confronted by her parents about the stories she was spinning. In addition, most of her attention was about her, about how hard things were on her in jail rather than the fate of her two-year-old daughter, Caylee. (Caylee was found in a garbage bag with duct tape wrapped around her mouth and nose, tossed away in a bushy area fifteen houses away from the Anthony home.) Casey is a classic psychopath who knew no bounds even toward her daughter. Although I am alive, I know the feeling of being tossed away like garbage.

While watching the court TV on this case, I listened to Dr. Drew, the television psychologist personality, describe psychopaths as

- monsters in our society,
- unstoppable predators,
- and plan violence.

And he goes on to describe sociopaths (I have read that malignant narcissists fit this bill to a tee) as

- more insidious,
- superficially charming,
- having a controlled behavior, and
- having shallow emotions.

Sociopathic behavior shows up at around the age of five or six years and includes acts such as pathological lying and manipulating, and they already consider people as objects to use and abuse. Whether that person turns to having psychopathic or malignant narcissistic behavior depends on their adverse behavior. For example, if they are killing animals or setting fires, the odds are this person is a psychopath in the making.

Psychopaths have just what it takes to defraud and bilk others: they can be fast talkers, they can be charming, they can be self-assured and at ease in social situations, and they are cool under pressure, unfazed by the possibility of being found out and totally ruthless. And even when they are exposed, they can carry on as if nothing has happened, often making their accusers the targets of accusations of victimizing *them*.

The study of the psychopath reveals an individual who is incapable of feeling guilt, remorse, or empathy for their actions. They are generally cunning and manipulative, and they know the difference between right and wrong but dismiss it as applying to them. They are incapable of normal emotions such as love and generally react without considering the consequences of their actions and show extreme egocentric and narcissistic behavior.

The following characteristics of a psychopath, defined by Hervery M. Cleckley in 1941 in the book *Mask of Sanity*, include the following (I have added an asterisk to the list which indicates additional traits that I have witnessed in my father and are clearly psychopathic in nature):

1. Superficial charm and average intelligence.
2. Absence of nervousness or neurotic manifestations.
3. Unreliability.
4. Occasional outbursts of rage often causing bodily or property harm.*
5. Inappropriateness when talking to children.*
6. Lack of boundaries; that is, when asked to leave, he stays.*
7. Nonverbal threatening, such as putting a knife on a table without saying a word.*
8. Ruthlessly sadistic even to his own small children.*
9. Untruthful and insincere.
10. Lack of remorse or shame.
11. Antisocial behavior without apparent regret.
12. Poor judgment and failure to learn from experience.
13. Pathological egocentricity and incapacity to love.
14. General poverty in major affective reactions.
15. Specific loss of insight.

16. Unresponsiveness in general interpersonal relations.
17. Easily drops friendships.*
18. Excessive behavior with drink, prescription, or street drugs.
19. Incapable of being trusted on any level; pathological liar.
20. Desire to be feared and willing to go to extreme lengths to instill fear.*
21. Suicide threats rarely carried out—the main purpose was to manipulate.
22. Sex life is impersonal, trivial, and poorly integrated.
23. Uses alluring charm to get what he wants from *any* unsuspecting source, including his own family, children, or strangers.*
24. Operates outside of the law.*

In short, psychopaths are deliberately evil and get their thrills from it, where malignant narcissists are thoughtlessly evil. Either way, both hurt others deeply.

The fact is that when psychopaths do get exposed by someone who is not afraid to admit that they have been conned, the psychopath is brilliant at painting their victims as the "real culprits."

My father once admitted to me his inability to love and that he often faked emotions because he simply did not have them and had no idea how to react to situations without looking to someone else for cues on how to behave in certain situations. They just do not know.

What is a *malignant narcissist*?

"Narcissists—do your kids a favor—don't have any" (Unknown).

My mother was a malignant narcissist. Although I am not a doctor, I do have a bachelor of life with both MNs and Ps. The term *malignant narcissist* was first coined by Sam Vaknin, a self-professed malignant narcissist and psychopath—and author of a very boring and poorly written book called *Self Love*. Since his book came out, others have followed his term of *malignant narcissist*, and to me, it suits perfectly the behavior and the actions of my mother and other members of my family.

We all have varying degrees of narcissism, but the malignant narcissist is the sibling of the psychopath. There are so many similar traits it is difficult to separate who is who. However, it is the psychopaths who are usually found in prisons, and I often wonder if it is not because the malignant narcissists are better liars and can get themselves out of trouble with ease.

My mother was as cold and bitter as a blizzard, and it was rare to see her laugh in the home. She was a raging maniac for minor infractions of her children (her supply), and if outsiders saw what we experienced, their eyes would blink out in shock since her cloak of secrecy was so well refined. She was well versed in covering up the turmoil and toxic drama she created within the home. Mostly she would blame someone else within the family if some secret leaked outside.

Malignant narcissists are brilliant at hiding their raging verbal abuse to the confines of their immediate family. They are cunning, deceitful, passive aggressive, and liars. If you asked a cousin or an aunt or a friend of hers about my mother, or any other MN, they would have nothing but good things to say about her (or him). To outsiders, she was simply a victim of circumstance, especially having to put up with the psychopath my father was and her four ungrateful brats (as she referred to her children). Mother thrived on the attention she received for her imagined victimhood. She sucked her divorced psychopathic husband's cruelty upon her for all it was worth all the way until she died. It was easy to be bitter and angry at a diagnosed psychopath. It is also easy to prey on the most vulnerable citizens of society, such as your own child or children.

I was good supply for my mother; my wrongdoings were power for her to tell the insensitive friends who would listen to her demolish her own child's character. This is especially frustrating when they do not know me in person! I have not seen many of my relatives or family friends for years, and yet they somehow believe the worst of me. MNs hate weakness. I was a very weak child in spirit and even weaker as I aged. I think the MN can literally suck the very life out of their supply as time goes by.

MNs are relationship destroyers. And people who are willing to sit and listen to a parent's nasty and ugly gossip about a child must be incredibly thickheaded. I would go to a relative's house with Mother, and it was not hard to pick up on the fact the people did not like me. How anyone could not like me without knowing me was weird. It took me years to figure out Mother had been character assassinating me all along behind my back. What kind of mother does that? A malignant narcissist would. What kind of person listens to this? I have no idea, and I don't care anymore. To me, if I hear someone gossiping about their own child, I know damn well they have a serious personality problem themselves.

Misinformed and sensationalistic people would gush about how my MN mother had such a tough and terrible life, especially escaping the damage my P father put her through. Mother thought nothing of telling anyone who would listen, including her young children, about her ex's horrible treatment of her and on how my father ruined her life. My MN mother was incredibly bitter, and she screamed this bitterness down my throat until I truly gagged. Throughout my life, she was on a character assassination rampage about Ivan's (my dad) influence on me. When that got boring, my MN mother would say I was just like Ivan. I was a cheat, thief, and liar—and I had his very same evil eyes.

I was often very confused at her assessment of me and wondered where all her hatred came from, but I had to believe her—I must be a horrible person—as she was my mother after all. Now I understand that what she was doing was shifting her own personality defects onto me to ensure no one saw her own sociopathic behaviors within her home and toward her family. Mother always had to have someone to blame and attack in her household. Forty-five years after her divorce, she continued to berate my father. For all of my life, I was her scapegoat when Ivan was not around to pound on.

I found several traits of the malignant narcissist in the Internet and have put an asterisk to the behaviors I witnessed and was subjected to by my own mother. I notice that my MN Mother kept her severe personality disorder within her immediate family and was rarely witnessed by outsiders.

1. Constantly envious of others and seeks to hurt or destroy the objects of his or her frustration.*
2. Punishing personality via *The Silent Treatment*; sometimes for years until her supply submit to her demands.*
3. Suffers from persecutory (paranoid) delusions, as he or she believes that they feel the same about him or her and are likely to act similarly.*
4. Projects his or her own thoughts onto others, as if it is *they* holding the bad thoughts.*
5. Feels entitled. Demands automatic and full compliance with his or her unreasonable expectations for special and favorable priority treatment.*
6. Devoid of empathy. Is unable or unwilling to identify with, acknowledge, or accept the feelings, the needs, the preferences, the priorities, and the choices of others.*
7. Behaves arrogantly and haughtily. Feels superior, omnipotent, omniscient, invincible, immune, "above the law," and omnipresent.*
8. Rages when frustrated, contradicted, or confronted by people he or she considers inferior to him or her and unworthy (or if the housework was performed inferior*).

9. Feels grandiose and self-important (e.g., exaggerates accomplishments, talents, skills, contacts, and personality traits to the point of lying; demands to be recognized as superior without commensurate achievements).
10. Causes traumatic drama to bring attention to herself at all of her children's milestone events including graduations and marriages.*
11. Requires excessive admiration, adulation, attention, and affirmation or, failing that, wishes to be feared (narcissistic supply).*
12. Shamelessly and openly prefers one child over another.*
13. Makes slaves out of her children including heavy housework, errands, babysitting, and running for her coffee or beer on demand.*
14. Is "interpersonally exploitative," that is, uses others to achieve his or her own ends.*
15. Seeks out a particular type of friend or friends who will listen to her put-downs of her family, especially the parts of the family she holds with contempt for challenging her behavior.*
16. Easily prefers to believe her lovers to her children's claims of sexual/physical abuse.*
17. Exaggerates the failings or perceived failings of her clearly unloved children (those born to Ivan and herself). Removes herself completely from any responsibility.*

The Psychopath versus the Malignant Narcissist

1. There are some important nuances setting the two disorders apart: psychopaths are either unable or unwilling to control their impulses or to delay gratification. They use their rage to control people and manipulate them into submission. Psychopaths, like narcissists, lack empathy, but many of them are also sadistic: they take pleasure in inflicting pain on their victims or in deceiving them. They even find it funny! Psychopaths are far less able to form interpersonal relationships, even the twisted and tragic relationships that are the staple of the narcissist.
2. Both the psychopath and the narcissist disregard society and its conventions, social cues, and social treaties. But the psychopath carries this disdain to the extreme and is likely to be a scheming, calculated, ruthless, and callous career criminal. Psychopaths are deliberately and gleefully evil while narcissists are absentmindedly and incidentally evil. We find more psychopaths in jail than narcissists.

I would be kinder about my P father than my MN mother. I'll tell you why. My father never put me down. Of course, I saw him very little since my parents divorced when I was four years old. It was easier for him to fool me into thinking he loved me than my mother who saw me daily and used me as her supply for abuse. Not once did I feel loved by my MN mother. I remember only one hug from her. I was about seven years old, and she just got a phone call from a company offering her a much-needed job. I was the closest thing around, and she picked me up and swung me around. Oh, how good that felt! My mother hugging me stuck with me forever. I do not remember a hug since.

I remember many times, even as an adult, watching the parents of children holding their hands, playing with them at a playground, sticking up for their child, and otherwise showing positive love examples and having feelings of loss and regret, that kind of love was never extended to me by my own parents. I did not know why and could only surmise I was not worth the love.

*　　*　　*

Ps and MNs are out there—destroying lives and making people around them feel they are the problem and needing mental help or wishing to jump off a ledge somewhere. The truth, when twisted by good liars, can always make an innocent person look bad, especially if the innocent person is honest and freely admits his mistakes. The psychopath and the malignant narcissist are both pathological liars by nature. They twist your words or actions and project their own evil thoughts onto you—as if you are the beholder of such thoughts. Even the simple act of giving testimony under oath is useless. If a person is a liar, swearing an oath means nothing to that person. For most of us, swearing an oath acts strongly on a serious, truthful witness. Again, the advantage is placed on the side of the liar. Most psychopaths can easily pass a lie detector test, and that, I believe, is why lie detector tests are not allowed as evidence in court.

There is no limit to the numbers of victims these human parasites create. Almost every time I turn the television on to see Dr. Phil, I recognize his guest to be either a psychopath or a narcissist. Yet I have never heard Dr. Phil say that this was where the problem may lie in a dysfunctional family dynamic. I often want to shake the television to tell Dr. Phil that there is no curing that husband, wife, father, mother, or even child. They would always be the manipulative and self-centered people the viewers were witnessing; they will never grow a soul. Dr. Phil's lack of insight got so frustrating I finally stopped watching the show.

I saw one statistic state that as many as 20 percent of our population have P or N traits in varying degrees. Interestingly, you will rarely find a P or an N in psychiatric wards; to these people, there is nothing wrong with them!

No, their victims are too "sensitive" or just can't "let go" and thus are the ones needing psychiatric help. Sadly, we find far too many *victims* of Ps or Ns in mental wards and given all sorts of labels and pharmaceuticals by psychiatrists. These poor victims are drained. Rarely do we find a mental health specialist take the time to delve into the childhood or relationship history of his or her patient.

Mentally ill people with sociopaths for parents, I believe, need to be deprogrammed from their parents or spouse completely. However, it is easier for psychiatrists to see the psychosis of the emotionally beaten victim of the P or the N and call it some mental health name like borderline personality, bipolar or manic depressive disorder, major depressive disorder, and the list goes on. I have met psychiatrists who themselves exhibit signs of sociopathic behavior and therefore lack empathy to their patients' needs, and so it is no surprise the mental health profession continues to fail their patients.

I myself come across crazy at times when I could not cope with an emotional abuse episode from my MN mother. Often when I'd I go for help from the mental health community, I have been diagnosed with several of the above diagnoses after seeing (numerous) psychiatrists over time who interviewed me for no longer than ten minutes. I was looking for help in how I was feeling (completely unworthy and unloved and wanting to die). Since I didn't know my parents were sociopaths and emotional abuse was normal for me, I could not articulate the situation other than to blame myself as I was trained to. Therefore, I always came away with pills and pop psychology about how mentally ill I was for no particular reason. It amounts to added disempowerment of the victim of the sociopath and is no less than medical malpractice for the doctor's failure to perform at an acceptable level of medical care. However, of course, what court would believe a diagnosed so-called mentally ill person?

I had no idea how to cope with the intense self-hatred feelings leading to suicidal thought after an "episode" with one or both of my parents. Intense self-hatred feelings leading to suicidal thought was my complaint. Clear symptoms of a mental case. Of course, the ignorant medical community would rather lock me up rather than give my parents a good going over to empower me back to reality. In their defense, since I am the one with the outward symptoms of craziness, it is hard for a medical professional to react intelligently to what he or she sees in front of them. I can't help but feel sorry for the medical establishment for their ignorance. However, nothing should take away their culpability in adding to the problem rather than fixing good people who simply want to understand why they want to die or cut themselves or starve themselves to death or stick needles in their arms, etc. Ps and MNs are very good deceivers and would not hesitate to throw their loved ones under the bus to avoid being caught as soulless creatures who use their own families as easy prey, leaving them emotional basket cases. Malignant narcissists, in particular, get their "supply," watching their young squirm. It is like oxygen for them. Some Ps actually laugh when seeing their supply in fear or pain. Hard to believe but true, as you will see in the upcoming chapters of my life.

You may also be surprised that being born to a diagnosed psychopath, habitual criminal, and pathological liar that my father was a walk in the park compared to the childhood imprisonment and emotional torture I endured while living full time with my undiagnosed MN mother. Even after I ran away from home at the age of sixteen, her venomous cruelty followed me until the day she died in 2009. I far preferred my absentee psychopathic father to the in-my-face-abusive narcissistic mother. I can't say the same for the spouses of Ps, however, and would never underestimate the pain they go through being married or associated with these well-disguised monsters.

*   *   *

My P father started his criminal career at a very young age. Stealing purses from his mother or sisters or any other victim who was unfortunate enough to be with him is one example. Later my dad became a fraud in that he would write bad checks back in the day when check writing was as popular as debit cards are today. He had no money in his bank account but thought nothing of writing checks to anyone who would take one from him—and too many to count did. I am ashamed to say my father's criminal activity escalated to bank robbery and rape. And these are just the horrific crimes I know about.

My father did a lot of prison time for his criminal offenses, and in between his absences, he would visit me and my older brother for short periods. To hear my mother say it my father only wanted to visit my brother and me to get close to her. Could be. She did put out a lot of peace bonds and restraining orders out on him, so perhaps she did fear him. But oh, how I loved my dad's visits! He would always bring me a present of Cracker Jacks or crayons. My dad would pick me up and squeeze me as if he were truly happy to see me. One thing that I was in awe of was his ability to pull quarters out of my ears! My father was an extremely good-looking man and could charm anyone who encountered him, myself included. No matter what Mother said about him, I was in love, and the more she called him names, the more I loved him.

For some reason, people wanted to be around this man even with his serious personality disorder. He was funny, exciting, happy, full of life, and mysterious. He made you feel special and good about yourself, and even after he robbed people blind, many continued to want to associate with him. Of course, all of him was a charade, but most people, in my experience, didn't care or were so in love they couldn't help themselves. People tend to take people at face value. When I see spouses where one is a P or MN, I am alarmed at how much abuse the victim will take and continue going back. I am alarmed at my own willingness to continue relationships with both my P father and MN mother for as long as I did—until they died.

My MN mother was one I kept going back to throughout my entire life to try and earn her love. Much to the chagrin and often anger of my friends who knew of the abuse she inflicted on me. I sometimes lost friends over my insanity. The fact is I craved her love and was willing to listen to her verbal assault on my soul to gain her love. Mother had zero sense of humor. A word to the wise: do not try to correct an MN—you will be sorry and likely verbally whipped into submission within seconds. In my case, she would ruin my reputation with extended family and her friends with lies about me or my character. She would make things up to make herself the victim and cry that her ungrateful child or children were out to get her in some way.

I suspect that the psychopaths and the malignant narcissists are siblings in their inability to love or feel remorse. Many people have one parent or another who is a P or MN, and either can be male or female. I was unfortunate enough to have both parents incapable of giving me what any child needs, love. And the sad part for me is I believed my mother when she told me what a terrible daughter I was. It's like a tape playing over and over in my head. I have to catch myself now, at age fifty-one, to ensure I do not carry on her abuse within my own head.

*   *   *

The neglect, the verbal attacks, the lack of love, and the blame and the shame my mother placed upon me almost killed me. This is why my memoir must be written. I want to save any soul going through the same shit I did before they do jump off that cliff. I want to let people know they are not alone, and no one deserves to be abused in any way whatsoever. The hardest part, I know, is saying good-bye to our abusers. We are masochists. We get use to the maltreatment and feel like we are in some empty void without their painful treatment of us. But we must say good-bye to save our lives.

If our P or MN doesn't psychically kill us, many of us will do the job for them.

While a psychopath may be the most dangerous person to the world at large, a malignant narcissist is the most dangerous type of personality disease within a family. Ps and MNs can be spouses, children, uncles, men, women—anyone. MNs are toxic and will usually destroy the weakest person within the family. I was that child. Growing up, I was "too sensitive" or as my mother preferred to call me when I cried, "manipulative." Projecting her own sick self onto me was a common denominator in her abuse.

I was her easiest target. I have my dad's eyes, which most people find beautiful, but Mother called them "evil eyes" right to my face from the time I can remember as a child. Later on, when I gave birth to my first and only son, she looked at his eyes and said he too had Ivan's eyes. When my son, Trevor, had his son, my grandson, she also saw these "evil eyes." By this point, I really had to wonder, *Was my mother projecting her own evil eyes onto me and my offspring?*

I'm going to try to write this book as objectively as possible. I will tell you the facts that I know to be true. I will not exaggerate or try to make you feel sorry for me. I don't want your pity. What I want is to warn you that if you come across a psychopath or a malignant narcissist, you will recognize them immediately and get help. I am hoping to help others feel some sort of relief when they see they were simply victims of a P or an MN like I was and then begin to heal. I pray victimized readers will learn and feel deep within themselves the term *no contact*, which is the only cure to save yourself from these life drainers.

The point of this book is not to bash my parents or siblings, or myself. I simply want to educate readers by writing my very personal and unabashed story, which hopefully will help others recognize if they are involved in a psychopathic or malignant narcissist relationship and on how they can get help to regain a healthy, happy life as soon as possible.

*   *   *

With the exception of my ancestors, due to the serious nature of my story all names accompanied with an asterisk (*) have been changed to protect their identity when first introduced. I have provided very few last names for the same reason.

Before I go any further, I researched accurate details of my ancestors/families and want to share some of this history which I find to be fascinating stuff and to show that I am not *just* the child of sociopaths.

Genealogical Background

To our children, we give two things, one is roots, the other is wings.

—unknown

There are good and bad souls in every family—we just may not have heard about them all. I wear my heart on my sleeve and try very hard not to keep secrets that could potentially hurt others down the road. My memoir is an important one, which I pray will give strength to readers to stretch their own wings and fly proudly in spite of adversity caused by monsters in their families or the evil associates of their loved ones.

This is the beginning of my story.

I was born in North Vancouver on September 11, 1959, to Ivan and Eleanor Groseclose (nee Oie). I am Norwegian by decent on both sides of my family.

My mother's maternal family immigrated to the United States in 1857 from a farmstead in southern Norway called Gundal to Coon Prairie, Wisconsin, and later settled down on their farm near Viroqua, Wisconsin.

Most of the information I do have about my mother's maternal side was found by family genealogical loose-leaf papers and books I have had in my possession for years. I learned that Thomas Bentson married Thora Tollefson in 1891. Thora was born on January 20, 1891, and died of the flu on October 21, 1918, at the tender age of twenty-seven, leaving five motherless children, including one three-month-old baby named Chester.

Thomas never remarried, and so Eunice Almira Oie (my grandmother), the eldest of these children, who was born on April 4, 1909, took on the responsibilities of taking care of the house and raising the other four children from the very young age of nine. Her siblings' names were Victor Joslyn Bentson (1911-1923), Gladys Ester Bentson (1912-1969), Evelyn Marie Bentson (May 31, 1914-), and the baby of the family, Chester Bentson (July 8, 1918-?) (My mother never told me he died, but I believe it was in the 1990s). I remember all of my mother's maternal great-aunts and uncles, with the exception of Victor who died at twelve years of age of what I do not know.

The records show my maternal grandmother was a beautiful pianist and was the musical delight for a Lutheran church as well as a Sunday school teacher.

Chester Bentson is the great-uncle I remember most. He married a beautiful woman named June Dryden, who was a nurse from England, and they issued two children they named *Steven and *Elizabeth, my second cousins. They later divorced, and Uncle Chester remarried and became a millionaire after winning a lottery. June also remarried a wonderful man we lovingly and appropriately called Major Tom (Quirk). June and my cousin Elizabeth (Beth) will figure more prominently within my story in later chapters.

*   *   *

I remember Mom telling me her father (Edwin Oie) was a finishing carpenter in North Vancouver, where her parents had settled, and that he was very strict. That was about all she ever said about him. I found out through records that his family too emigrated from Norway, from a place called Slatsboggden by Trondhjen. When they immigrated to the USA, they settled in Lanioure County, North Dakota, and lived there until the family moved to a homestead nine miles northwest of Invermay, Saskatchewan, in 1905.

Edwin had nine brothers and sisters, all born between 1888 and 1904. He was born on September 17, 1893, and died in 1953 when my mother was thirteen. He was sixteen years older than his wife, Eunice, when they were married in 1940; and my mother was born on Friday, December 13, 1940.

My mother's parents were quite old for the time when they conceived their only child, Eleanor Mae Oie, in 1940. Eunice was thirty-one and Edwin was forty-seven.

After Edwin died in 1953 at the age of sixty, the family lived with mother's maternal grandfather, Thomas, in a home in North Vancouver. It is said Eunice took in boarders to help pay the bills, which I believe. Mother told me they were *not* boarders; they were her lovers. Was there some jealousy or resentment there? Why would my mother tell me such a thing so many years after her mother had passed away? Was this why Mother said so little about *her* mother? The only information I could gather from my mother was that her father was very strict and her mother took in lovers after he died. Really? Remember, you cannot believe a malignant narcissist, and so I just don't.

My mother did tell me her mother was very passive and couldn't control Mom's behavior after her dad died when Mother was only thirteen years old. (I guess that's why she met a boy named Ivan Gilbert Groseclose and conceived my older brother at fifteen years of age.) There was a small wedding, with Mother wearing a pink lace dress several months before Gus was born.

Around the time my mother became pregnant with me in 1959, my maternal grandmother contracted breast cancer and had a terrible time with it as it spread to her lungs. My MN mother told me that when her mother moaned in pain in the middle of the night, my P father (Ivan) would "mimic" her cries loudly, frustrated with the dying woman's painful screams. I don't know about you, but if my husband was behaving mercilessly to my dying mother, he would be out the door in a second. But when my mother told me this story, I realized she was famous for blaming others for their actions but failed to see her part or responsibility in anything. Mother let her psychopath husband be cruel as her mother lie dying. I have fallen victim to my mother's closed eyes myself as a vulnerable child and can believe without a doubt she just didn't care.

*   *   *

My paternal grandmother's family emigrated from the Lofoten Islands (the northern point of Norway). For generations, the family lived in a small fishing village on a place called Vall. Grandma was eight years young when her parents purchased ship tickets for the family to arrive in the Port of Halifax, Nova Scotia, from Norway. While our family name was Ingebrigtsen, it was common practice for emigrating families to take the name of their place with them to their new land. My grandmother's family name became Vall for the Vall Place they lived in Norway.

Canada became a self-governing country on July 1, 1867, and thus was only approximately forty-five years old when my great-grandparents and their children landed here on June 28, 1911. Iver and Amalie Vall (Ingebrigtsen) moved to Star City, Saskatchewan. They brought their son Peder, daughters Annie, Margaret (my grandmother), Minnie, and Hilda as well as their oldest son Kildal's girlfriend (Borghild Jensen). Kildal had already immigrated in 1910 and filed a homesteading claim in the Chagoness district two months after his arrival. Father Iver and younger son Peder had homesteaded one week after arriving in Canada while the family stayed with cousins until 1912.

Grandma went to school for one year and was then brought back to help with the younger children and running of the household. You would never know my grandma did not get an education because she taught herself how to read and write, and she was one of the most literate people I know. Every letter I received from her was written with perfect form and no spelling errors.

My grandmother's family had many tragedies in their early immigration days including the burning down of their farm home and the death of the youngest child, Hilda, at the tender age of twenty-one years of spinal meningitis.

I am unclear of how my grandma, Margaret Marie Vall, met my grandpa, Gilbert Levi Groseclose, but I know he lived in a small border town on the United States side close to the Canadian Chagoness District. It seems to me that Grandma said she attended a dance where she met Grandpa, but don't quote me on that. Grandma became pregnant with my auntie Pearl and immediately married Grandpa, who soon held Canadian and United States citizenships. They decided to reside in Canada.

Years ago, when I was helping a distant aunt by typing the family tree, I saw the year discrepancy about my auntie Pearl's birthday and my grandparent's marriage date and asked Grandma about it. She said, "Oh, how naive you are! Even my own mother got pregnant in the barn before she married my father." Wow—that would be like in about the 1860s! And here I thought all old folk were puritans who would consider such a thing as an absolute shameful sin. I loved my grandma because she was so open—she didn't hide family secrets any more than I do.

My paternal grandparents were married in 1923 and lived three miles west of Chagoness until 1934 when they spent a short while on the Steele place. That same year they bought land from the Hudson Bay Company. My grandfather cleared the land and built a log house. Bert joined the army and was stationed at Regina Saskatchewan, Petawawa, Ontario, and Prince Albert, Saskatchewan. When he got his medical discharge in 1943, they moved to Vancouver, British Columbia. He worked for the shipyards and built homes in North Vancouver. Later, he worked for the city until his passing on March 28, 1971.

My grandma said that out of all of her siblings, she was the "ugly duckling." I could not believe this because I saw nothing ugly about her. She was so sweet and beautiful to my eyes. I remember Grandma and Grandpa's house, which was so homey and warm and just a wonderful place to visit. It was a yellow ranch style, with flowers blossoming along the house and driveway. I fondly remember the treelined sidewalks of the newer city my parents and I was born and lived in for several years. North Vancouver is situated on the side of a mountain with much of it overlooking the Pacific Ocean and the famous Stanley Park in Vancouver, and this suburb soon became a very wealthy part of Vancouver.

When I was older, Grandma and my dad (at separate times) drove me around North Vancouver to show me the houses Grandpa built and the houses I lived in after being born. I loved that—to know where my grandparents, parents, and I lived. When I heard the history of my family and saw the houses built by the hands of my grandpa, I felt a comforting sense of belonging. Mother never showed me the houses her father had built, and today I wished I had insisted she teach me more about her family. It wasn't that I wasn't interested, as my mother accused me of years later, but that she just shut down when the topic came up.

Later on in my memoir, I will tell you a most fascinating story of the paternal (Groseclose) side of my family. I know more about this side of the family than any since I ventured to find the *town* named after my ancestors—Groseclose, Virginia!

Chapter 1—Childhood Confusion

Conspicuously absent from the Ten Commandments is any obligation of parent to child. We must suppose that God felt it unnecessary to command by law what He had ensured by love.

—Robert Brault

This is hard. I am about to open up my heart and share some things that I know may cause others to disbelieve or hurt me in some way for telling my story. We live in a society where we don't talk about certain things, and I am about to talk about some very personal issues—loudly. Of course, I have fear, but I have nothing left to lose. Writing my story, I hope, will help people see the light beyond the dark world of sociopaths, namely, psychopaths and malignant narcissists. No matter how much I may be hated for opening up this unpleasant can of worms, I'll go ahead and take that chance. May more good than harm come from my words; may people involved with Ps or MNs find peace in knowing they are not alone and that there is light at the end of this frightening and lonely tunnel.

* * *

It has taken me over twenty years to tell my story, and I always wondered what was taking me so long. Now that I am fifty-one years old, I know a little bit more about myself and the parents who conceived me, so I am glad I waited. Since my father died in 2007 and my mother in 2009, I feel safer putting into words what my childhood and later life were like being the daughter of parents incapable of love. Truthfully, this memoir would be torn to shreds if they were alive, especially by my MN mother. She would discredit me in a second. She was very good at contradicting me and projecting her own psychosis onto me as being deceitful and conniving. My mother scared the shit out of me until she died, and now I can be me, the real me, and tell it exactly how life was *for me* as the daughter of a psychopath father and malignant narcissist mother.

*　*　*

Before I begin, I can't help but offer my sympathies to all survivors of psychopaths and malignant narcissists. I know I am not alone and understand the suffering victims of sociopaths go through. My story must not be for nothing, I insist. At the risk of sounding cliché, if I can help just one person in sharing my shameful history, then it has all been worthwhile.

My experience as a child of a psychopathic father and a malignant narcissist mother is quite different than that of a spouse or another adult caught in the web of these empty souls. One difference is that I was raised from birth to believe I was unworthy of love. I had nothing else to go on—I had only my parents to look to for the truth about love. For many years and decades, I didn't know love was kind and compassionate and unconditional. It took me almost fifty years to realize my natural instincts were right—that something was terribly wrong with my parents and that I am a loving and giving person so much so as to risk my own life by continuing on trying to gain their love back in return. My parents were very wrong about me, and I'm about to scream that truth from the rooftops!

*　*　*

This memoir is my story, but I am prone to memory problems most likely because of the extreme emotional and sexual abuse I suffered as a child and the added shocking traumas I experienced as an adult. Everything I am writing is the truth as I see it. My perceptions of certain instances may be skewed, but nothing I am writing is a deliberate lie or fabrication. I know certain events took place, but sometimes I ask you to not try to pin me down to a specific time or place because I will have difficulty figuring it out for you. Sometimes people have filled in the blanks for me, and I can tell the whole story of certain events.

I used to be called a liar for these gaps of memory emptiness in trying to tell an adult something that happened to me, but now I am okay with simply not remembering. Some say my memory gaps are a result of posttraumatic stress disorder. I don't know. As much as I do not like labels, this reason does make sense to me.

*　*　*

My very first memory was of standing up in very large iron crib. There was a single bed across the floor in the sterile room. I wanted to cry in fear but didn't. Soon, a redheaded boy walked into the room carrying a bag of Cheezies. He went over and sat on the bed. "Can I have a cheezie?" I bravely asked the boy. He walked over and pulled out a great big fat one and passed it through my bars. I realized I was very hungry as I chomped away on that cheezie and ignored the extreme pain the salt was causing on my raw and bleeding lips. I asked the boy where I was, and he said the hospital. Again, I wanted to cry because I didn't know why or how I ended up there and wondered where my mother was. I remember feeling a little pissed for being trapped in a crib when the boy could roam freely. I was way too big for a crib! And where was my mother? But even by then, I already had low expectations and could handle the lack of attention without too much fuss.

I later learned I was playing on the alleyway road behind our apartment complex when a car hit me. I was told I was thrown fifty feet and skidded on my face. I was unconscious, and Mother later said they thought every bone in my body was broken. Fortunately, I only bore a minute gravel scar above my lip, and my smile is somewhat lopsided as a result of the accident. No broken bones. Thinking back, I can remember waking up in the backseat of a speeding car with a cold cloth covering my face. I don't know who was holding it there. I was five years old at the time of the accident. I was later told I spent ten days in the hospital. I don't remember any visits from my family, but there were plenty of abrupt and no-nonsense nurses. I remember often wanting to cry but I didn't.

*   *   *

I loved Kindergarten. It was the only year of school I did like. I was a good girl then. I remember a boy jumping off the countertop in the classroom and wondering how he had such nerve. I had many friends, and since it was a private kindergarten within our apartment buildings (called Parkwood Terrace), the friendships flowed over to after school and weekend fun. I remember going to many birthday parties. This was so long ago a tear comes to my eye remembering I did have some good times as a small child.

My parents had recently divorced, and Mother was having a hard time of it. We often ate dark rye bread spread with yellow mustard for supper. As my older brother and I ate, Mother sat at the kitchen table saying nothing. Just staring off into space and then sometimes going into a rage about nothing. What was she thinking to suddenly blow her top at her five—and seven-year-old children? The kitchen table was my mother's favorite place. Right up until she died, she was still sitting at her table. Just sitting there thinking. In later years, she brought her television to the kitchen table so she could sit and watch TV from there rather than the comforts of a living room or bedroom.

Mother was now a single parent, and welfare was almost unheard of. I remember she took a job in an office. I think it was called the Electra. (Why do I remember that?) The company had annual Christmas parties for the children of the workers, and I remember Santa Claus being there and handing out gifts—really neat gifts!

We never knew what mood Mother would be in when she walked in the door. Mostly it was hostile and hypercritical. I escaped my realities by having fantasies in the alleyway to our apartment complex about a holiday tent trailer being my home. I would imagine furnishing it with pretty things in my mind's eye and having a family who would all be nice. I still remember the smell of wild mint still from those days. I had a particularly close friend and we often got a blanket with some dry cereal and had a picnic outside of my makeshift tent trailer house. I still love picnics!

*   *   *

My P father visited from time to time, and each visit was very exciting for me. He would pick me up and offer his gift of Cracker Jacks or crayons. Once he brought me what I really wanted—a pink crayon. Pink crayons were rare back in the day, but sure enough, my dad found a box with a pink crayon in it! Sometimes my uncle Hilliard would be with Father. Oh, how I loved my dad's older brother! He was even more handsome than my father and just as funny. When Dad and Uncle Hilliard came over, it was as if I was complete. I loved the music being played on the record player: the Mama's and Papa's, Tammy Wynett, Loretta Lynn, Elvis Presley, and other country rock music.

I do not remember one fight between my mother and father. However, from a very young age, Mother told me stories, horrible stories about my dad and the terrible things he did to her when they were married. She said he made her eat raw eggs; beat her to a "pulp," and worse. As she was telling me these things, my eyes glazed over; I had no idea what to do with this information. When Mother didn't get much of a reaction from me over her stories, she became furious. I had no power to say anything back, so I just stood there with a blank look.

Mother wanted me to hate my father as much as she did, but I never could. For me, he was a much-needed relief to the turmoil I felt in our house when he wasn't there. All that I knew and experienced was that Dad was fun but absent. He hid his psychopathic ways from me until I was much older. MN mother, however, was a raging maniac more often than not. She dripped with a hostile tone of voice throughout her entire life toward me. I do not remember any kind words or offers of support from her.

I can't remember how young I was, but it was in these early years Mother told me how much my father hated me. She said when I was two years old he put a gun to my head, threatening to kill me. She said I was lucky she saved my life. Her efforts to get me to hate my dad continued to fail. While I am sure she was telling the truth about him holding a gun to my head, I could not understand why she was telling me these things. She didn't realize that a child can never hate her parent just by telling a child to. I'm not saying a child can't hate a parent. But if one parent is pitting another parent against the other, chances are the child will end up hating the berating parent more. Just ask me.

Another horror story Mother told me was that when my older brother was a baby, my father "accidently" sat him on the hot woodstove. Mother said she was not sure if he did this on purpose or not, but now that I know my P father, I can believe it was on purpose. I never thought to ask my brother, *Gus, if he has any burn marks on his butt, or was this just another made up story trying to get her children to hate their father? You never know with a malignant narcissist.

Gus and I (he was two years older than me) often found ourselves sitting in a car outside of a bar. I've heard it be said that this was normal in the 1960s, where parents left their children in cars as they drank in hotel bars. Normal? I don't think so. I can't remember who told me that. Looking back, I can now see the neglect and the complete disregard for our safety with these "outings." Our parents' selfishness was a common event in our little lives, but it was all we knew.

*   *   *

It was late October in my grade 1 class when we were going to be having a Halloween party. I wanted to be a princess. The party was only for one hour during lunch. I could hardly contain my excitement! Mother told me she would be at the school with my princess outfit (which I had not seen yet) in time for the party. When the bell rang, Mother was not there. I waited in agony as my classmates dressed in their costumes, and time ticked by with nobody there to dress me. Finally, with fewer than fifteen minutes left of the party, she showed up with a ghoulish outfit I was ashamed to put on. Especially after I bragged to everyone how beautiful my dress would be. My mother's lack of empathy for my feelings was a constant throughout our relationship.

Later that year, I remember Mrs. Harris (my teacher) telling us that we were all going to have a test that day and whomever finished must go outside and play until all the children were done. Yea! I didn't even look at the questions since they were all multiple choice and just scratched any circle I felt like so I could get out of the class and go play. Later I learned these were our mandatory IQ tests taken on the first and fifth grades. I can just imagine how stupid my test counter must have thought I was. I now know these IQ tests carry on with you and your grades all through school.

I remember Mrs. Harris not being nice to me. Several times when I was working in my booklet I would feel a hard slap on the back of my head and told to sit up straight. I was beginning to hate school as much as I hated being at home.

We moved to a new apartment called Marathon Court after I finished grade 1. The lady living below our apartment babysat us after we got home from school until Mother got home from work. I loved Diane. (Yes, I remember her name!) She gave us snacks after school and didn't make us clean or do anything. I think we spent a lot of time watching her television, which was a novelty back then.

*   *   *

I was prone to sleepwalking. Late one night, I found myself at the bottom of our indoor stairs and heard Mom's voice yell over the railing, "Where the hell do you think you are going?" I looked up in confusion and said I didn't know how I got there. In my mind, I think I was going to get some candy at Diane's suite, but it turns out I was simply sleepwalking. I was a sleepwalker much of my childhood and occasionally as an adult.

I became my mother's personal slave at a very early age. I remember, at Marathon Court, which means I must have been about seven, already running errands to the grocery store for ground round meat or cigarettes or ten pounds of potatoes, etc. Mother had me do the ironing, dishes, dusting, cleaning the bathroom, etc. One day, I had a brainstorm (such as it was) and decided I could save a lot of time by shaking the dirty bathroom mat into the bathtub rather than taking them outside to beat on a post. I was so proud of my invention I ran and told Mother right away. I didn't get the reaction I had so hoped for (I was always trying to please Mother and usually failed miserably). She went into a screaming rage that could be heard miles around. I was dumbfounded.

The screaming didn't stop for the rest of the day and into the night. Later, as I was sleeping, I felt myself being pulled from my bed by my arm as Mother screamed at me to clean out the grit from the bathtub.

There I was, a seven-year-old child scrubbing out a bathtub at two or three in the morning. Mother had an incredible stamina for staying angry. It wasn't the last time I was awakened by one of Mother's rages since she always had to have an audience or someone to verbally take out all of her frustrations on. "You're Ivan's daughter and have his evil eyes," or "You stole my talcum from my dresser. You are just like Ivan—a thief, a cheat, a liar. I can't stand liars!" She often brought her pitch to deafening levels, and I sometimes wondered if she wasn't ashamed that the neighbors would hear her. I learned later that malignant narcissists are rarely, if ever, ashamed.

Bringing Mother coffee or a beer was common from the time I could walk I think. I don't remember when this job started. I could be in the middle of something and that never mattered—her need for a coffee or beer always came first. I served my mother and her second husband hand and foot until I left home at age sixteen.

*   *   *

The day Mother brought Dave into our lives, I had a sinking feeling. I did not like him from the start. Part of my distain could be that I liked it just fine with Mother, my older brother, and me. But another thing bothered me; he seemed creepy. Mother made me sit on his knee and say good night with a kiss. I was young but sickened by his big fat lips. I don't know why Mom made me do this because I certainly never sat on her knee and gave her a kiss good night. She would think I was nuts. Soon after he moved in with us, Mother made us call him Dad. By then, visits with my real dad were nonexistent. I think either he was in prison or Mother had a restraining order on him. Mother said she and Dave were married now (they were not; they did not marry until I was thirteen years old), and he was my new father. To call this Dave guy "Dad" hurt me very much. I wanted to cry, but I didn't. Eventually the kisses stopped, and life carried on with Dave barely saying a word to either my brother or I. He was just a part of the furniture as far as I could sense.

The first Christmas we did spend with Dave was fantastic! I never saw so many gifts in my life, and I was thrilled to pieces. Unfortunately, Mother and Dave got drunk that Christmas Eve, and we woke up to half-wrapped gifts; Mother and Dave passed out on the sofa, with drinks still in their hands! This was the year I realized there was no real Santa Clause.

I remember I got a beautiful silver watch from Dave. Mother looked it over very carefully and said it was indeed a special gift. She asked me if she could wear it just for that day. I found her request strange, but of course, I never said no to my mother. Later that evening, when she was washing the turkey dinner plates, she accidently immersed the watch in the water and ruined it. She never apologized or replaced it. Funny the things we remember.

* * *

A terrifying event happened in grade 2. I was given a detention for some classroom infraction, and after school was let out, I was told to sit at my desk with my head down until the teacher returned. It seemed like forever for my release. My neck and back hurt so badly for a long time after that. Finally, a janitor came in the room and yelled at me for being in the classroom after 4:00 p.m., which was against the school rules. It was 4:30 p.m., and my teacher had forgotten me! The janitor went to get her, but he came back and told me she had gone home! The nice janitor told me it was okay if I went home now.

When I did get to my place, I thought I would be in big trouble for being so late. Mother was already home from work and cooking something in the kitchen. I remember being shocked that neither she nor the babysitter seemed to know I was missing for almost two full hours! I was relieved, actually, because I thought I had done something wrong. I was always feeling like I was the cause of trouble, and I walked on eggshells around my mother my entire life for reasons I cannot remember. To expect Mother to stand up for me at school or anywhere else was just unheard of and never expected.

* * *

One day, it must have been a weekend day, I was at the apartment complex next door to Marathon Court. There was some construction going on in the basement, I think to add more apartments. Anyway, I found a Tonka Truck and was playing with it outside of the building. A few minutes later, a man approached me, and I shook violently, fearful I was going to be in trouble for playing with someone else's toy and be called a thief. The man didn't say anything about the truck but told me he had never seen a young girl before. I began to get really nervous. I pointed out another young girl about a hundred yards away walking up the driveway. He said no, he wanted to see me.

The man took my hand, and I obediently followed him into the apartment down the stairs to where all the construction had been going on. There was no one there now; I guess the workday was done, and it was just me and the man standing in one of the unfinished apartments. I know this is going to sound strange, but it is the truth as I remember it: The man said he would give me $2 *if I let him pull his pants down!* Even at my young age, this didn't make sense—anyone could just pull their pants down if they wanted to.

Anyway, my answer, of course, was no. I did not want to see him pull his pants down. He begged me for a while, and then he said *he would give me a quarter if I pulled my pants down!* Now I was really confused that for me to pull my pants down, I'd only get a quarter, but for him to pull his pants down, I'd get $2! I was only seven, but I knew the man made no sense. I said no once again, and he threw me a quarter and told me to get lost. I ran up the stairs to the freedom of the outdoors and hurled the quarter in the grass close to the Tonka Truck. I continued to run all the way to my own apartment complex and up the stairs to the so-called safety of my own home.

I didn't know what to do. Would I get into trouble if I told my mother what happened? Dave was sitting on a chair reading a newspaper, and Mother was in her bedroom putting on her makeup. I sat on her bed and just stared at her. There was no relaxing time if you were in sight of Mother, and she immediately gave me a chore of taking a letter to the mailbox for her. I began to shake at the thought of going outside and potentially meeting up with that man again! I reluctantly took the letter and ran to the mailbox as fast as I could. I was back sitting on Mother's bed within one or two minutes.

Because of my fear to go outside and knowing Mother would send me out again for some other errand, I decided to tell her. Mother's reaction was what I expected: anger. She turned away from her mirror and shook me so hard I thought my head would fall off. She could not conceptualize that the incident did not happen when I went to the mailbox but that it happened before! But she kept saying my story was impossible and therefore a lie, as I was gone for such a short time.

After a while, she finally listened long enough to hear that the incident with the man was *before* I had gone to the mailbox, and I was simply afraid to tell her at that time when I first came home. Mother did call the police, and I remember the policeman coming back after a walk around and said there was no man out there. I felt like a liar, another feeling I often had for no particular reason. End of story. Nothing was ever said or done about it since. A counselor later told me my mother's indifference had set me up for what was to come in my years of puberty.

*   *   *

My parents, Ivan and Eleanor, met at high school and married in North Vancouver, where my older brother and I were also born. Apparently, my parents lived in rental suites and rarely paid their rent. One item my MN mother never forgave my P father for was causing her to have to leave all of her books at one suite they failed to pay rent on.

My P father was a popular charmer and girl magnet from the mid-1950s to the 1980s, and he and his older brother were able to have any girl they wanted. After high school, they could often be found at the Army and Navy Club or the Legion, popular hangouts of the time. They danced the night away with pretty girls, forgetting about their families at home. My P father and uncle never changed their ways and Uncle Hilliard can still be found having a drink at the Army and Navy Club when someone takes him there.

Unfortunately, my paternal Grandpa was also a "run-around" husband who had several flings with various women throughout my grandparents' marriage. He didn't drink a drop of alcohol, and he went to work every day, but he had this one flaw that Grandma could not tolerate and after forty years of marriage and an unknown hairpin in her bed, she finally divorced him. At sixty years of age or so, she took positions with wealthy families in the growing "rich" upper North Vancouver area to either housekeep or be a nanny full time. At least she always had a rich house to live in! Sometimes Mother took us to visit Grandma at one of her beautiful live-in homes.

After my grandparents divorce, I saw very little of my Grandpa. I remember him as being a little more reserved than Grandma and very gentle with us kids. He later married a woman named Hilda, and visits with Grandpa became almost nonexistent until he died in the early 1970s. Grandma and Grandpa had five children: my aunt Pearl (the oldest); Uncle Hilliard; Auntie *Thema; my dad, Ivan; and lastly Auntie *Eve. All of my aunts and uncle had large families, and as young children, we cousins were all very close even after my parent's divorce. Mother was friends with her in-law sisters well beyond her divorce from Ivan. Hanging around my cousins (at their houses) was a highlight of my childhood. It offered a much-needed escape from the torture I was experiencing at home with my own mother. Mother was on her best behavior when we visited, well, anyone, and so I could always count on some freedom from her wrath for as long as we were with my cousins.

*   *   *

One day, during a visit to one of my aunties, where everyone gathered in the kitchen, I was playing on a musical toy in my cousin's living room. The toy was one where you had a pong and you hit certain colors on the music box and correct tones came alive if you hit the right key. In a short afternoon, I learned how to play childhood songs such as "Mary Had a Little Lamb," "Jingle Bells," "Twinkle Twinkle Little Star," and all just by ear. I was four years or younger at that time. When my aunts and uncle overheard my song making, they were very gleeful about this accomplishment and told Mother she must get me a piano because I clearly had talent. I remember Mom's unsmiling face as she nodded. I knew I'd never get a piano.

A few months later, she told me she had registered me to learn how to play the accordion! I couldn't believe it—I hated the accordion. It was too big for my tiny frame. It was far too complex with several movements needed while playing the melody keys. I went to three or four lessons and quit. This gave Mother the ammunition to say I was *not* musically inclined and I would not be getting the piano. I wanted to cry but didn't.

This is a typical MN behavior. Mom was jealous of me even as a child. She wanted the attention to be on her, and when others gave me positive chatter, it infuriated her and I always paid for it later in some way or another. End of story. I never learned how to play the piano and always felt emptiness over the way my mother took this (and other) dreams away from me.

*   *   *

Here is a bit of (fun) gossip: After my grandparents' divorce, my three aunties got together and urged Grandma to reply to a personal ad in the newspaper where a man in his late sixties was seeking a wife to help care for him and his home and garden. My grandmother moved from North Vancouver to Penticton, British Columbia, and married this Russian man named Mike Kacenia. He owned a very nice little home in this resort town with two beautiful lakes close by.

My grandmother loved the gardens and the room in the basement, which she filled with cots for her grandchildren to visit. All of us cousins visited at one time or another. We all grew to love the ruff and gruff Mike, and the younger cousins (and my half siblings on my Dad's side) called him Grandpa, as he was the only grandpa they really knew. Grandma filled the basement up with sleeping cots because she loved it when her family came to stay a while and she wanted to be ready for us. At this house, I realized what a perfectionist my grandmother was: even her silverware was fanned out in a perfect flair.

I don't know how she did it—I tried but failed, and my silverware ends up thrown in the tray with no flair at all.

Grandma and Mike were married for some thirty years, so if you add the forty years she was married to my Grandpa, she was married for a total of seventy years!

My grandmother was always my love savoir until the day she died on March 18th 1996 at the ripe old age of ninety-four. She was a huge positive influence on me. She calmed me when I needed calming, and showed me that unconditional love I craved so much. She was a very religious woman but never judged me or tried to push her beliefs on me. She did, however, show me how to pray and was an influence on me as I watched her read her Bible every night. I knew my Grandma's prayers *always* worked!

Once my Grandma bought me a manicure set which I savored. One day, I had a friend from the place we lived at (Marathon Court) who came over, and I saw her take my precious manicure set! She put it in her pocket, and I told her to give it back. She said *her* grandma gave it to her, and it was not mine! I went to my mother crying about it, and her reaction was to tell me to ignore it and not make a scene. Mom could not stand crying. As time went on, it became a common theme where my MN mother would prefer to let her children suffer injustices than to offend company in the house. She had to show herself to be perfect in front of guests of all ages at the expense of her own children's feelings. Or she simply didn't care about a silly manicure set my grandmother had given me.

* * *

I failed grade 2. I can't help but wonder now if it had something to do with those IQ tests I took in grade 1. I think from there on, the teachers felt I had a serious learning problem. I remember being sent to the remedial room for added tutoring. Failing grade 2 was a nightmare for my self-esteem, and I spent the entire summer worrying about how all of my friends would be in grade 3 and I would be stuck with a bunch of babies in grade 2! Lucky for me, Mother and Dave decided to move to a house far enough away where I would be in a new school with kids who wouldn't know that I had failed grade 2 the first time.

When we moved to that nice house on Suncrest Drive, I was so happy at first. There were many kids around my age, and I loved to play outside with them when I could. One house across the street from us had a large crab apple tree in the front yard. I remember how many times the house owner, an old lady, came outside with her broom to shoo us crab apple thieves away.

Just down the hill of Suncrest Drive, my brother and I attended a sort of makeshift Sunday school in the basement of one of the homes. I loved going to the Sunday school, where I learned many children's Christian songs and memorized parts of the Bible, which I have not forgotten to this day. When the father, the Sunday school teacher, died, we stopped going to that Sunday school.

From then on, I went to Sunday school with one of my aunties and her six children, my cousins. She would pick me up in my uncle's crowded dry-cleaning van, and I remember thinking that this Sunday school located within a richly decorated church was very strict and it turned me right off of God and Jesus, and I became a non-believer for a long time.

I learned around this time that Mother was pregnant with my half sister. Dave was a long-haul truck driver and was gone for a week at a time. He was not home when Mother was ready to come home with the baby. Her girlfriend, Linda, and husband, Fred, and two kids, *Donny and *Sheri (long-standing family friends), picked her up from the hospital. All of the adults were in the front seat, with Mother holding *Shivey, my new sister. I kept trying to lean over and see my new sister, but Sheri and Donny pushed me away so they could see the baby. I complained about not being able to see her and remember Mother screaming at me to sit back—I would have plenty of time to see the baby when we got home. It was like a slap in the face for me as I sat back, and Sheri and Donny cooing over my sister made me feel humiliated and invisible.

It was around this time that my memory is very limited about my brother Gus. I remember certain childhood games, such as boxing in the front yard with our cousins, and the time I threatened to tell Mom he had Ton O Gum (brand name) if he didn't give me some. I was a typical bratty sister to my brother, and he was a typical mean tease to me. Other than that, I don't even remember him being in the car to pick up our new baby sister. He was invisible in the house for years to come, and I think it was him protecting himself from the constant drama and domestic turmoil going on in our house. I remember he often soothed me when I cried about Mother's cruelty, saying everything would be okay. How he could stay so calm and unaffected was something to be admired, I thought. I eventually changed my mind about why he was so calm, cool, and collected and will explain in a later chapter.

* * *

The introduction of Shivey to the family was the end of any happiness for me in our home. I think it is around this time, in grade 2 the second time, when I began to feel depressed. I remember the teacher having all of us stand up to sing the song "Sing, Sing a Song" by the Carpenters. The words were supposed to be happy words, but there I stood, tears streaming down my face and just wishing I could run away as far as possible. I could not help the tears and was frightened the other kids or teacher would see me cry.

*   *   *

A highlight of my young childhood was that my P father married a beautiful woman named *Sunny who was my new stepmother. She was so beautiful, with her long auburn hair teased up very high, and how kind she was to me. At that time (for some reason), I was allowed to visit them for some weekends while they lived in New Westminster. I remember they had one child at that time, a baby named *Gilbert. I remember Sunny being pregnant with her second child. The visits to their apartment in New Westminster made me so excited I thought I would pee my pants! Sunny gave me her change to go to the store to buy whatever I wanted! I met a friend my age, and we played outside gleefully and without worry. Sunny paid attention to me and seemed to really care about my comfort while there. My father was hardly around during my visits, but Sunny more than made up for his absence—and I was used to not seeing him so much anyway.

Going back home after those wonderful weekends was always a sad occasion for me.

I had a bad habit until I reached the age of thirteen. I sucked my finger. I did not suck my thumb as most children do, but I sucked my finger, and this habit infuriated my mother. I remember one night, as I was going to sleep, she brought a mirror over to me and pushed it into my face, telling me how ugly I looked with my finger in my mouth. I was about nine years old at that time because I remember my new sister watching Mother bully me from her crib across the room. I had other odd habits. I felt most comfortable with my arm reaching to the sky as I went to sleep! You'd think that would be an uncomfortable position to be in, but it was not for me. I also gently backhanded the cool pillow over and over again like a safety blanket.

Mother was often unable or unwilling to give my sister her middle-of-the night feedings. At eight and a half years of age, I was responsible for getting up in the middle of the night, preparing my sister's bottle, feeding her, changing her diaper, and singing a song for her to go back to sleep, which she always did.

Much of the responsibilities caring for Shivey were mine, including folding and putting away her mounds of laundry, sterilizing her bottles, holding or playing with her while Mother was busy (with what I do not know). I was rarely allowed outside to play unless all of my chores and other duties were done and if it suited the mood of my MN mother. One day as I was boiling bottles for my half sister the steam burned me and caused a huge liquid bubble on my arm. When I went to school a boy sitting next to me called it gross and punctured it with a lead pencil. Why was I boiling bottles at eight years of age?

I began losing friends from school. I remember being crushed when not invited to birthday parties of kids I used to play with. I remember feeling very lonely at school during recess and lunch. I played tetherball by myself and watched the boys play marbles to pass the time. I felt ashamed at school and unwanted just as I felt at home. I hated the feeling of shame, but it was my most frequent feeling, along with sadness and loneliness for the rest of my school years. Shame of what? I can only guess shame of being me. The tapes of my mother's hostile voice of contempt were constantly going on in my head, and if my own mother didn't like or want me around, how could I expect anyone else to want to be my friend?

I remember Donny and Sheri, the children of Mother's friend and her husband came to visit. Donny was teasing me terribly, and I suddenly lashed out and called him a "stinky." For this violation, Mother shoved a bar of soap down my throat in front of our company. More shame. More pain.

*   *   *

As I think back and remember, I must have really craved the sensation of touch. Sometimes in school, we would have an auditorium speech by the principal, and all of the children sat on the floor with legs crossed. I almost always asked the child behind me to scratch or tickle my back. I looked forward to these auditorium events for the sole reason of having the opportunity for someone to touch me. I learned that all children and people need touch and later raised my own son to enjoy the touch of his mother. I continue to sense very strongly that *appropriate* touch is important to everyone, as important as air to me.

*   *   *

Little did I know that the next seven years of my life with my MN mother, stepfather, and absent P father would only get worse. My childhood journey was about to get very ugly. I began attracting *real* shameful, ugly things. Things we are not supposed to talk about.

Chapter 2—Puberty Mayhem

Live your life from your heart. Share from your heart. And your story will touch and heal people's souls.

—Melody Beattie

My memory gets very poor from this point on. The best way for me to remember something is to figure out the house we lived in and the grade I was in.

I remember my baby brother, *Dylan, being born to my MN mother and stepfather, Dave, when I was ten years old and how much I loved him, but I do not remember the house or school I attended the day he was born. I remember moving from our house on Suncrest Drive to a house on 144th Street in Surrey. I then remember moving to a brand-new duplex rental house in North Delta when I was halfway through grade 4. While living in North Delta, I remember finishing grade 4 at a small school next door to our house, but the name fails me and has since been torn down; then I attended another school called Hellings Elementary for grade 5 and then to my final elementary school called Gibson's Elementary, where I completed grades 6 and 7. I attended grades 8, 9, and part of 10 at Delview Junior High while living in this house. It was the last grade and place I lived in with my family.

*   *   *

My precious baby brother was a highlight of my life when he was born so sweet. He was born with a mild case of cerebral palsy, and he needed exercises for his legs, which I noticed Mother doing without complaint. Later he needed several surgeries to correct his eyes, which wandered.

My mother indulged Dylan and Shivey like they were the only children in the house. I noticed my sister especially got away with a lot of bad behavior. One day, she was walking along the kitchen countertops opening each cupboard door. I was shocked that my mother was right there and not telling Shivey to get down! I asked my mother at that point why she let Shivey get away with so much. My mother's response (I was twelve at that time) was "Cherylann, you turned out so bad I am going to raise Shivey and Dylan differently than I did with you." At twelve years old I had already turned out so bad? No kidding? I could not fathom why I was so bad; I just knew I was according to my Mother.

My babysitting days increased to daily events. Stepfather Dave took a local trucking job and was home by dinnertime (rarely). There was a typical routine that would occur daily where my MN mother would go into a fit about Dave not being home and scream out loud, "He's probably at the damn Druids Inn again!" The Druids Inn was a pub about five blocks from our house. I always found it funny (in a sick sort of way) that she would then dress herself and go "bring him home" and yet neither would return until after 11:00 p.m.

I had my work cut out for me after school, and I envied the kids on the street playing games and yearned to join them. Even if my mother and Dave were home, I was essentially never allowed outside to play, and I remember looking out of the window and feeling utterly alone.

For some reason, my older brother, Gus, continued to be invisible to me, and I have little memory of him throughout much of my life at home. I do know he was learning disabled and had great difficulty in school. I had trouble in school as well because I could not concentrate (so most of my report cards say) and I was constantly bullied. I put very little effort in my schoolwork because I hated school and feared the children who were my peers. My self-esteem at this point was extremely low, and I had a lot of anxiety just walking to and from school. I was caught between a rock and a hard place—home and school. Both were very unhappy places to be in.

*   *   *

It is at around twelve years of age that I began to realize my mother had a severe problem on her face. She did not just have pimples or acne; her face was covered in quarter-sized pussy boils! It was horrible, and I always wondered how she could stand it. Or go out in public like that! She never complained about them. I know her doctor put her on an antibiotic called tetracycline. This treatment never worked and yet she continued to take the medicine for some twenty years while going through the obvious pain and discomfort. To my knowledge, she never asked her doctor for a different method of treatment. It is like she resigned herself to those boils, but I am not exaggerating when I say they were shockingly horrible to look at. All of her four children dreaded inheriting her boil problem, and we often talked about it among ourselves as we grew older. Just getting one pimple would scare us to tears. Mother lived with these boils for thirty years. They started at age twenty-two and finally subsided when she was in menopause.

My mother had a philosophy about teeth. She believed in keeping all of her teeth and never getting false ones like my P father and other family members did when they were around their thirties. I guess back in the day, dentistry was rare and many of the baby boomer population suffered later and wore false teeth after having all of their natural teeth removed due to untreatable decay.

But not Mother. She allowed her teeth to turn black and gray, which did not add well to her appearance. She went to the dentist often, but she would only come home with a different color to her front teeth. I remember once she came so happy about getting her front teeth fixed and yet they were gray—and horrible! No one ever had the nerve to say anything to her about her appearance.

Another feature about my mother at this time was she refused to change from her polyester housecoat until it was time to go to the Druids Inn. Her hair was almost always greasy-looking, and once she bought herself an ash blond wig to throw on to avoid washing her hair. I swear this just about put me over the top! That wig looked gray to me and did not match her red face at all! My P father told me that when Mother was young, she was absolutely beautiful. She was thin, with light, fine blond hair and stunning facial features. I remember thinking, *How come you [Mother] are making yourself as ugly as possible?*

Mother's appearance was always an embarrassment to me and that is likely my shortcoming. But still! She was only thirty-one when I became twelve, and I just cannot imagine giving up on my appearance like that at such a young age.

The screaming hysterics never stopped. My mother would always find something that either I or my older brother did to bring her to the brink. She often said she was going to end up at Crease Clinic (a well-known mental institution in our area) if we did not toe the line better. Nothing I did was good enough and to expect praise or love in any form was like asking the moon to not show up.

> *If you want your children to improve, let them overhear the nice things you say about them to others.*
>
> —Haim Ginott

One day, I walked in the front door after a particularly bad day at school and overheard my mother, who was on the phone, saying in a dripping hostile tone of voice, "Oh, here she is now!" I wanted to cry but I didn't. Obviously, my MN mother was giving one of her typical Cherylann bashes to one of her many friends who sucked up all of her noise concerning me and my behavior. I do not know if any of her friends tried to shut her verbal abuse about me up, but since they continued to hang around her, I am guessing not.

I just dumped my books on the bed and sat there until my mother got off the phone and screamed at me to get upstairs to finish dusting this or cleaning that. I hated this routine so much, and it was hard to have no say or control—especially as I grew older.

One day, while sneaking my way around a park after school to avoid running into other kids, I bumped into Kelly Flemming, a very large girl who was one of my most fearsome bullies. For some reason, she was being really nice to me on this day. She pulled out a package of cigarettes and asked me if I wanted one. Every adult I knew smoked back in those days, and so it wasn't too much of a big deal. But I didn't want one—I had never smoked before, and I was petrified my mother would find out. I got out of the dangerous situation with Kelly by thanking her for the cigarette and saying I had to run home to babysit. I put the cigarette in my pocket and, when I got home, hid it in my bedroom.

Some months later, I found this cigarette just before I was going to bed. I went upstairs and stole some matches and went back to the comfort of my bed to prepare myself for this new experience. I was wearing a nylon nightie when I lit the cigarette and tried to smoke it. To my horror, little specks of burning ash dropped down onto my nightie. I quickly put the cigarette out and changed my nightclothes. I hid the nightie way back in my closet and vowed to never wear it in case Mother saw the little specky burn holes in it.

Time always catches up with you. One night, I decided enough time had passed and I could wear that nightie. No one noticed the burn specks while I was wearing it, and I felt even safer. Then I made the biggest mistake ever—I put the nightie in the laundry! That night, I heard Mother's famous stomping up the stairs from the basement to the main area of the house and her screaming rampage about my being a liar, cheat, and thief—just like Ivan. She found the nightie and knew I smoked. I tried to tell my mother it was just that one time, but of course, I was never to be believed. She would have gone on, but she had to go to the pub to "pick up Dave" and would deal with me later.

Mother and Dave came home earlier than usual because Linda and Fred, their friends, were coming over for drinks. I was sitting in the living room when Dave and Mom came in, clearly a force together regarding my "smoking habit." This is what they said, and I am not kidding: "Cherylann, if you are going to smoke, we want you to smoke *in the house*, not in the street, where you will look like a little hood!" What the hell? I was *not* a smoker, but here my guardians were giving me permission to smoke!

The next day, I caught up with Kelly and asked her if she had any cigarettes, and together we promptly went "on the hill," which was the official high school smoking area, to smoke. I choked at first, but with Kelly's teaching, I was soon a full-fledged smoker (in and outside of the house). Today I have chronic obstructive pulmonary disease (COPD) as a result of heavy smoking throughout my life. I was twelve years old when I started smoking. My MN mother's morals and values were way out of whack.

*   *   *

My P father was coming to our house to pick me and my brother up and drive us to Kelowna (about a four-hour drive through the mountains) to visit our stepmother and their three children, our half siblings, *Gilbert, *Danny, and *Shenay, for an extended stay of two weeks. Kelowna was about four hundred miles away, so we rarely saw my dad's new family. Dad arrived and I was beside myself with excitement to get going on the long journey. Unfortunately, my mother and Dave were home and drinking. I should have known that my P father would join in, and for hours, the three of them talked, argued, and drank the night away. It was midnight before my Dad said his good-byes and put my sleepy brother and me in the car.

I noticed almost immediately the pungent smell of alcohol on my dad. In addition, every time we passed a store, he would get a bottle of 7Up and have my brother or I drink half of it for him. I didn't understand why until later on down the road, I saw my father pour alcohol into these half bottles of 7Up. The drinking scared me but not as much as the following horror show!

As we were driving through the curvy mountain roads, Dad's lights suddenly began to play tricks. They would go off for short periods of time and then back on. I moved to the backseat of the car in total fear. It got worse when we were driving along Highway 3, which has large cliffs, and as my dad told it, it was 3,000 feet to the bottom!

The entire trip was a torturous nightmare. I could not go to sleep as those lights continued to go on and off as my dad drove the twisting mountain roads. I ended up on the back floorboard, covering my head, sure that we were going to die that night. My P father was laughing and said don't worry, he's a good driver, and although it was now 6,000 feet below us, he has driven these mountains for years and knows every curve on the road. This is a memory I'll never forget. But it brings home exactly how perverted and sick a psychopath can be.

Thirty-five years later, I was talking to my half sibling, Shenay, and I told her that story. You can imagine the look on her face when she said that the lights going off and on were a common theme in *her* childhood! This meant my P father was turning those lights on and off *himself* in an effort to scare the shit out of his children. He thought his joke was funny! This is a typical psychopath trait—to scare his victims for his sadistic play and laugh in glee as his children screamed in terror.

*   *   *

Out of the four children my MN mother bore, I was her least favorite. Almost as soon as I turned twelve, I began to behave badly at home and school. I was acting out and not really caring about anybody or anything. I stole money from Mother's wallet and got caught and grounded for two full months (big deal, I was always grounded as far as I was concerned). I started to hang out with the wrong crowd at school (*crowd* meaning one or two friends). I began to hate my younger sister for all of the indulging treatment she received.

Both Dylan and Shivey were A students, and while I may be blowing my own horn here, I spent hours in the basement playing school with my younger siblings (I always wanted to be a teacher, and this was a fun activity for me). By the time they went to kindergarten, they already knew their alphabet and how to read. It really irked me, however, that Shivey spent more time at home watching TV than going to school. She always had some silly excuse. I was baffled at how little parenting my MN mother did with Dylan and Shivey. Mother cared little about how often my sister missed school. My sister was already beginning to run the roost, so to speak, since my MN mother indulged her so.

Both of my younger siblings seemed to have a healthy self-esteem. My half sister was very hyperactive and got into things constantly, which were never corrected. Shivey was particularly mean to me. She was witnessing my MN mother's verbal abuse toward me, and as soon as she could talk and walk, she often parroted Mother to me. Often she said she would "tell on me" if I stepped out of line in any way—like sneak a friend over to play with while

Mother and Dave were at the bar. She was mean and manipulative toward me starting at the age of about five. She laughed at me when I got into trouble with Mother, which was often.

* * *

One particularly horrible day, which I will remember until the day I die, was when I found blood on my panties! I didn't know what to do with them, so I hid them behind the furnace near the laundry area. I was coming into puberty and had no idea what that meant. My mother found these panties one day, and my story just got much worse: we had relatives on my mother's side, a great aunt (June) by marriage and uncle (Major Tom), her second husband, living a few blocks from us. Sometimes I stole away from the house to visit my aunt, who always seemed very nice to me. I remember loving her very much.

On this day, my cousin, Beth, was there visiting her mother. She had several of her friends with her, male and female. My cousin was about four years older than me, and I felt great hanging out with these "teenagers."

About an hour into my refreshingly wonderful visit, my aunt June, who was later diagnosed with bipolar disorder, came down the stairs into the recreation room, where we were all talking, and said loudly and in front of everyone, "Cherylann, you are a pig! I cannot believe you put bloodied panties behind your furnace! What a stupid girl you are!"

I died. Or wished I could. There I stood in front of all of these older teenagers completely undressed and humiliated by my aunt. I quickly made my exit and went home and cried into my pillow for hours. I learned later that Mother phoned my aunt while I was visiting and told her of my "disgusting behavior." I wouldn't put it past my mother to have arranged for my aunt to humiliate me into submission that day. My MN mother was upping the cruelty ante by bringing others into it. This new method of employing others to join in her abuse by direct humiliation or silence toward me became a familiar theme throughout my mother's life.

Airing my dirty laundry (no pun intended) to my MN mother's friends was no news to me. But now I was getting older and feeling extremely sensitive when my aunt joined my mother in this sinister method of abuse. I truly did feel I was a pig and worthless.

Puberty seemed to have an effect on my breasts as well. My boobs and nipples were growing, and it was becoming obvious. I had no bra, and Mother never mentioned that I should have one. One Halloween night (I don't know why I remember that), I was leaning against a wall in the kitchen, involved in a conversation with I don't know who. My stepfather, Dave, came by me and twisted my nipple and said in a "teasing" way that I was going to grow bigger boobs than my mother! I ran away from him and the kitchen and everyone very humiliated and shamed, once again. Mother didn't tell him to stop or try to sooth my cries. She hated crybabies.

My therapist in later years said my mother was continuing to set me up for what was to come.

Dave started tickling me at around this time. Every time he had a chance, he would throw me on the floor and pretend he was just roughhousing with me as he tickled me while his hand landed in places it shouldn't have. The whole family could be around and no one would say a word about this. I never laughed at the tickling; it sickened me. I didn't want Dave anywhere near me. It was funny to others, however. Here was this man who rarely looked my way as I was growing up now playing games on the floor with me. It doesn't take a genius to know he liked pubescent girls in a sexual way.

MN mother and Dave met new friends named Tom and Maggie at the bar, and they happened to live directly behind us, separated by a fence. Occasionally Maggie would have me pick plums from their tree for my mother. Once she asked Mother if I could go over and help her clean the house. Mother sent me over without question. I cleaned that house spick-and-span, and Maggie rewarded me with a dollar, which admittedly was a lot of money in my view since I received no money from home for all the work I did there.

Mother was a sewer and she loved it. She could often be found in the middle of the night sewing one outfit or another. Unfortunately, the patterns and fabric she chose were downright ugly! She had no sense of taste in either her home decorating or the clothes she sewed for us to wear. Once she made me a long "gown" of avocado green polyester with tight and ruffled arm elastic. MN mother wanted to show off her achievement and told me to go over to Tom and Maggie's to model it for them! Little did I know that Tom and Maggie had company, male company, who made very crude statements to me, but they let me have some of the alcohol they were drinking, so I let the comments go. No one phoned to tell me to come home like I wished, and I was stuck at Tom and Maggie's for hours, wearing that hideous "gown."

The next day, Tom and Maggie came over to our side of the fence for a barbecue when he suddenly picked me up by the crotch and back of my head and threw me in a child's pool. I went into the house and avoided the party, completely humiliated. Once again, the audience, my mother and Dave, thought the event was very funny.

*　　*　　*

Back to my wardrobe, one outfit I remember well was a pair of pants made of a thick avocado green fabric with wavy orange stripes. There was no zipper; instead it adorned that large wasted stretchy elastic. I remember the day I wore those horrible pants to school and a boy commenting on them. He said, "I used to have a pair of pants like that—when my dad was on welfare!"

Mother paid the absolute minimum amount of money for my clothing and it showed. There was no reason for the cheaply made and out-of-style clothes she had me wear. Dave made good money as a truck driver, and she had recently taken a job as a World Book Encyclopedia salesperson. When I entered grade eight, the clothes I was wearing became unacceptable. I often borrowed clothes to wear to school from the few friends I had. I never had an allowance, but sometimes I had enough babysitting money (from other families).

I used to wonder if my MN mother dressed me poorly on purpose, but as I learned more about malignant narcissists, I learned they are not evil on purpose, just utterly thoughtless and indifferent to other people's feelings. Only her feelings mattered, and to challenge her on anything was a recipe for a long drawn-out screaming fit, so nobody in the house dared to, except Shivey, who was a brat and even had the nerve to scream back at Mother.

*　　*　　*

One day, when my P father came to pick me up for a quick dinner (I do not know where Gus was), we parked behind McDonald's and ate our burgers. Without warning, my father told me that he knew the story of the guy who wanted me to pull my pants down at Marathon Court all those years ago. He told me he found the guy while he was in the New Westminster Penitentiary, a maximum facility for the most-hardened criminals. I was sitting comfortably eating my burger and fries when my father suddenly said out loud that he and his buddies found the guy and cut his balls off!

I stopped chewing and looked straight ahead. There was a very long pause before I said anything. I don't know what my response was, but I knew I could stand a lot with my psychopath father—but this story was unforgivable in my mind, whether it was true or not. I never told my MN mother about this conversation since I didn't want to give her more ammunition to go into a rage about Ivan (or me). I just wanted to be left alone.

* * *

Life carried on as I continued to take on more of the housework and raising of my half siblings. I was often summoned to bring Alka-Seltzer (a stomach relaxant for comfort after a night of heavy drinking) to Mother or Dave, as well as the usual coffee when they woke up. When they were in the living room, I would be told to go get a beer for one or the other of them.

The babysitting increased since Mother's new job as an encyclopedia salesperson. She had many seminars to go to and leads to get for her sales. Sometimes Mother's seminars went late into the night.

One night, as I was ending my twelfth year, I was sleeping upstairs with my baby brother who was in the crib. I do not remember where my sister, Shivey, was since I was in the single bed in their bedroom that particular night. Maybe she wasn't home, although I can't imagine why. Anyway, I woke to the sensation of someone's fingers inside of me! My eyes popped open, but I stayed very still. I knew it was Dave and was so embarrassed I crossed my legs and pretended to sleep. But he could tell I woke up and just asked, "Where's Mom?" I said I didn't know, and he quietly left and closed the door.

And there it was. Dave was simply waiting for me to enter puberty before he made his move on me. And he knew my MN mother wouldn't do a damn thing about it—or that I wouldn't tell.

Oh my god! What was I going to do? I now felt so unsafe in the house during the day and night whenever Dave was around. My constant anxiety reached a new level. I knew without a doubt my MN mother hated me and would never believe me. Or if she did believe me, I would tear the family apart. I thought it was my entire fault. I felt guilty and ashamed and wished Dave didn't ruin everything. I made the decision to say nothing. It was too risky, and I was already always in a lot of trouble and I didn't want to make Mother worse.

I avoided Dave as much as I could. There was the odd tickling session, which carried on, and once he asked me to go into the bed with him to rub his belly. He had me sit on top of him and rub his stomach, and he guided my hand to go lower and lower to the point I felt his pubic hair. At that second, I jumped up and ran out of their bedroom with some excuse of having to get something done. I continued to say nothing to Mother. What is to say? I knew I would get no support or safety from her. I had been set up to take on the responsibility of my own molester just like the therapist said years later.

I remember I put a strip of scotch tape across my door and doorframe so that I would know if Dave came into my bedroom and I didn't know it. That was my greatest fear—that Dave would molest me without my knowing.

From that point on, I wore a coat that would cover my body—no matter what the weather was. One day, I was walking past the school office and a secretary came out from behind the counter and ripped open my jacket! I was naked (well, not really but it felt like it). She said, "Cherylann, you are so pretty. Why do you always hide behind that coat?" I didn't answer her, of course, and just tightened my jacket around me and ran down the hall horrified at what she had just done. I felt utterly violated and naked.

*   *   *

I did have one friend who lived on our street. Her name was Debbie McAllister, and together we decided we needed money for our cigarette habit, so we got some Windex and paper towels and set off for a local trailer park to ask for the job of cleaning the outside of their windows. We were shocked at how many residents said yes! We made a lot of money washing trailer windows and were never short of cigarettes or candy for a long time.

We were running out of trailer windows to wash and didn't know how we were going to support our bad habits. We stole our parent's records and went door-to door, selling them to anyone who wanted them. I do not remember my mother ever noticing the records being gone. I never took the good ones; the records I knew were played at house parties on a regular basis.

One day, Debbie told me about a way we could make a lot of money. She wouldn't say how but just said to follow her and I did. We walked down Scott Road, a heavy traffic road, and turned left on Eighty-eighth Street. There was nothing there other than some construction going on, so I was getting nervous and insisted she tell me where were going. She said she knew a guy who worked in security at this new Hydro building they were constructing. Debbie went on to say he would give her money, and so I reluctantly followed.

When we got in the secured area, a huge dog started to bark and a man came out of a small work trailer. He hushed the dog up and motioned for Debbie and me to come over. I couldn't believe it; the man was really, really old. He was scruffy-looking, and once again my antenna went up and I judged him to be creepy. As creepy as Dave. I told Debbie I wanted to go home, but she said wait, wait until she gets the money.

We walked into the work trailer, and suddenly Debbie pulled her pants down and the old guy went in between her legs with his face! I grabbed a wooden board and told him to stop or I would hit him with it. He looked over to me, and both him and Debbie told me not to worry about it—everything will be fine. After a few minutes of this scene, I witnessed my twelve-year-old friend being given oral sex while I held a board over the two of them until they finally stopped.

The old man, who later said his name was Randolph, took out his wallet and passed Debbie a ten-dollar bill! *Wow!* I thought. That is where she got her money from. We left that day, and I thought long and hard about the situation. Debbie said earlier that I could make good money doing the same thing if I wasn't such a baby. The whole idea of it made me sick. But not too sick as to stay away.

I don't know what switch was wrong inside me as to agree to do the same thing Debbie did with this old guy but I did it. And more than once. I went back time and time again, and the one regret I have in this whole ugly experience was that I brought one of my friends, (Linda and Fred's daughter) Sheri, who was two years younger than me, to do the same thing! End of story. I can't go on writing about it, but for sure, it took a little something out of me. I finally believed my mother. I was a horrible wrench and slut of a person.

Later, when I was an adult, a therapist asked me if a twelve—or thirteen-year-old girl came to me to say this was going on in her life, who would I blame? This one question by an outside observer was a lifesaver. Of course, I would blame only the security guard! That little girl was innocent. It was like a ton of bricks fell from my shoulders since I had spent most of my youth feeling like a whore, on top of all the other names my Mother called me.

*   *   *

I was in Mother's bedroom for what reason I do not remember, but I remember she was angry, but not over the edge. She said, "As soon as this bedroom suite is paid for, I'm going to leave that asshole!" Again, something inside of me knew she was wrong to talk like that about her husband to her twelve-year-old daughter and even more wrong to use him financially like that. I was an anxious, nervous, sensitive waif of a girl, but I was not stupid. My internal morals were intact. I was glad I was not like my mother.

She never did leave Dave until a few years later, much to my disappointment.

For Christmas, one year, I bought my mother a bottle of perfume. It was in a very pretty blue bottle, and I thought she would like it a lot. She accepted the gift, but about a week later, when she was raging at me for one infraction or another while we were in her bedroom, she picked up the bottle off her dresser and threw it at me as hard as she could, saying she hated the smell. The bottle didn't break but landed at my feet. I wanted to cry but didn't. I picked the bottle up and brought it down to my bedroom. I took the bottle to school the next day and gave it to my friend, Vicki Cawlishaw.

For the first time I can ever remember, Mother showed some sort of remorse over her actions. About two or three days after that upsetting incident, she said she wanted the perfume back. I told her it was too late, I had given it to someone at school. What the hell?

*   *   *

Mother's extreme narcissist behavior was a well-kept secret to be kept within our home. As I write this, I realize that all of Mother's cruelty toward me was always behind closed doors. No one dared tell anyone on the outside what was going on in our house. The only witnesses I had were my siblings, and we often talked about Mother to support each other. I remember my sister once saying she will dance on Mother's grave! I was horrified anyone would say such a thing, let alone the favored daughter of my Mother. However, years later, way later, they too (my siblings) would turn their backs on me and deny how bad it was with Mother, and the incident with Dave, well, just never happened. My MN mother had something over us. Mother never had any siblings and perhaps she didn't realize that pitting us against each other the way she did would create problems in our adult lives. None of us speak to each other to this day.

We were constantly walking on eggshells in fear of Mother's wrath. In her later years, her money or inheritance enticed my siblings into submission. MN mother always had a carrot on a string to keep her supply obedient and her secrets intact.

I noticed my MN mother and younger sister both had a fascination with money and both projected onto me that I should care as much as they did. This was one carrot I did not bite on and never would even until my mother's dying days and thereafter.

* * *

I do have one witness to how abusive mother was to her children: My malignant narcissist mother was on the telephone with one of her friends, Joyce. After she hung up the telephone, she went into one of the worst rage outbursts even I have even witnessed. Her screaming and verbal abuse toward me, I'm sure, could be heard for miles around.

It was about six months later that I was over at Joyce's, and she told me that Mother hung up the phone incorrectly that day. As a result, Joyce heard my mother's terrifying abuse as it was going on! She said she was so afraid for us she almost came over to our house. But she didn't. As far as I know, she never confronted Mother either. But it was nice to know someone else outside of the family was on to Mother, and her "perfect" status came down a notch.

* * *

I often wondered why my sister and brothers never supported me and my pathetic life with Mother later in life, and it came to me that I bore the brunt of Mother's rage and perhaps the siblings were just blind and deaf to my circumstance within the family. There may be another reason for their indifference, but I will get into that toward the end of my story.

My thirteenth and fourteenth years were pretty much the same. I don't remember anything different standing out in my memory other than the bullying at school reaching new heights. Bullies tend to pick on people who do not fight back. I was not one to fight back as trained by my mother. Oh, how I wanted to drop out and run away from home! I think but I cannot remember any details that Dave molested me in my bed again when I was fourteen. I only remember it happened; I do not remember the circumstances at all.

* * *

One time around Christmas, I had the flu, but for some reason, Mother allowed me to come along with her and my aunt Eve and Mom's two younger kids to an evening shopping event in New Westminster. The Army and Navy Department Store, which was a warehouse type of depot that didn't have anything in it I wanted to buy, so I walked across the street to the Metropolitan Department Store. I was walking around and feeling very light-headed and sick. I brought my gifts up to the counter where a long line made for a slow exit. Suddenly I collapsed unconscious. I woke up near the café in the store, and the staff was asking where my mother was. I told them she was across the street at the Army and Navy. They paged her, and after some time passed, Mother and my aunt showed up. Mother held her tongue, but I could tell she was really pissed off at me.

We drove to the hospital in silence until I overheard my mother whisper to my aunt that she suspected I was pregnant! This is just one example of way too many where Mother projected her life onto mine. My mother got pregnant at age fifteen. I was still a virgin, and it never occurred to me that I may be pregnant!

I was fourteen or fifteen and had my first vaginal check at the hospital that night. I remember being very self-conscious. Nothing made sense. Mother knew I had the flu, so I shouldn't have gone out—it was as simple as that as far as I was concerned. But my malignant narcissist mother had to make a big deal about me and sex, and all of this in front of my aunt Eve and the hospital emergency staff. God forbid she be wrong for taking her deathly sick child out on a shopping excursion! No. I had to be faking it or pregnant.

After I healed from this flu a few days later, Mother was sitting at the kitchen table and suddenly (it was always suddenly until I got to know the symptoms of an upcoming abuse session) went into a rant about the consequences if I ever got pregnant. She said she would make me have an abortion. She was positive I was sexually active, and I know this because she often called me a slut. I remember being cheeky and told her I would never tell her if I did get pregnant, and her reply was to say she knew of places that gave abortions right up until the ninth month. I wanted to cry but didn't. Instead, I ran downstairs to my bedroom and wrote in my diary that I was going to become a slut. I was beginning to really hate the view my mother had of me and thought it might be a good idea to live down to her expectations. That would show her!

* * *

I had just turned fifteen when I was babysitting for a family directly across the street from an acquaintance friend from school. *Doreen saw me and came over. She said she was having a party and would I like to come over. I was babysitting, and so I said I couldn't. I don't know how it came up, but I told Doreen I was a virgin and didn't want to be anymore. Later, as I was watching television while looking after the sleeping children, a guy showed up on my doorstep and said Doreen told him I was a virgin and didn't want to be anymore and if he could come inside. I was so flabbergasted and ashamed I said no and shut the door.

A few minutes later, there was another knock on the door. This time, another guy stood at the doorstep. He said his name was Dave (of all names!). He was much more persuasive than the first guy, and I let him inside. That night I lost my virginity.

*   *   *

Our family friends, Linda and Fred and their three children, Donny, Sheri (who was my best friend for many years), and their much younger sister, *Margaret (she was my sister Shivey's age), lived in a duplex with the landlords (the McDonalds) living on the other side of the house. (Sheri was the girl who is two years younger than me and the friend I introduced to the man at the Hydro construction site.) One night, my mother and Dave were over visiting Linda and Fred with me, my brother, and younger siblings. Sheri suggested we go next door and play some pool with *Willy and *Jim, the landlords' sons. I had seen these boys around over the years but never really associated with them.

While we were in the neighbor's basement, waiting for Willy and Jim to come downstairs, I realized I was in great clothes for a change. I was wearing brown corduroy pants and a tan turtleneck top and seventies-style print knit vest that complimented me. It felt great to look good for what I think was my first time. When Willy walked in the basement, my heart did a flip-flop. I felt something I had never felt before, and as we played pool and flirted together, I was at the happiest stage of my life.

Willy and I became an item and started "going around together," as it was called back in the early mid-1970s. For some reason, my MN mother thought it was fine for me to hang around with boys rather than girls, and she gave me more freedom than I had ever had before. Yes, it is a total contradiction to her earlier comments about sex and abortions, but I gave up on trying figuring out my mother's thinking.

I spent numerous days and evenings at Willy's house and loved the comfort of their home. The dinners his mother served were so wonderful I took some of her cooking ideas with me, and I always mash my potatoes into whipped fluff like she did to this day (my mother was never a good cook). One day, Willy's mother asked my mother if I could accompany them on a two week camping trip. Their family had a trailer and owned a lot across the border in

Washington State. It was during that camping trip where I consider *I really lost my virginity!*

Making love with my boyfriend of several months was so wonderful I fell in deep love with him. We were allowed to sleep together (with our sleeping bags zippered up) on top of the table turned bed in the trailer. Well, those zippers didn't stay zipped up for too long, and with Willy's parents just steps away from us, sleeping in their bed, we had crazy love sex almost every night. One night, I heard Willy's mother cough loudly, and I sensed she knew what we were doing, so I stopped the activity that night.

The year I was Willy's girlfriend was the best in my life at that point. We had many friends and always had something to do. Willy got his driver's license and bought an old station wagon and about six of us were always on the road. It really was a story out of *That 70s Show*. We went to drive-ins almost every Friday night. I saw *Jaws* at the Scott Road Drive-in theatre which had just been released!

I never worried about the bullying at school after that (for a while). The kids could see I had a very good-looking boyfriend with a car and he picked me up almost every day. We skipped school on my sixteenth birthday and together just drove around and enjoyed each other's company.

When I got home, I sensed trouble. Sure enough, the school had called Mother and told her I didn't show up to classes that day. Once again, I experienced a rage putting Mother almost completely out of control. This time, she was physical with me and pushed me over and over against a wall. Later, when she calmed down, she said I would not be seeing Willy anymore, ever. I said under *no* circumstances would she stop me from seeing my boyfriend!

I was wrong. Mother had already called Willy's mother and insisted she have Willy break it off with me. I couldn't believe my ears! I phoned Willy, and he was obeying his parents in breaking up with me. He confided in me that my mother made it impossible for him to see me anymore, as she was so very worried about me getting pregnant! There it was again, MN mother projecting her sorted background on me as if I would end up pregnant like she did at age fifteen. Willy and I were smarter than my parents, and I was secretly on the pill, but I couldn't tell her that.

This all occurred on my sixteenth birthday. Mother was so angry with me for skipping classes she didn't even bother to wrap my birthday present, which was the ugliest outfit I had ever seen. It was polyester knit jacket and a slacks set designed to look like denim—right with the yellow lines sewn down the sides of the legs of the pants. I don't know if Mother bought this hideous outfit as a birthday gift before she found out I skipped class or after. It seemed like a punishment to me anyway, and I never wore it.

After talking to Willy and his breaking it off with me, I ran downstairs to my bedroom and cried like I had never cried before. I truly loved Willy, and to have my mother step in to break us apart was something I was not able to cope with. I hated her at this point.

I learned about three months later that Willy had a new girlfriend, and the pain was just as sharp as the day we broke up. I didn't think I would ever get over him.

From then on, I became everything my mother feared I would become. I stole from stores, I drank Dave's vodka and refilled it with water, I stopped trying in school completely, and my math report card said, "Cherylann has done nothing this semester."

We had a cousin from my mother's side (Beth) stay with us for a while because she couldn't get along with her Mother my Mother told me (this was my Aunt June, the same aunt who went off on me regarding the bloodied panties incident). One day, I was snooping through Beth's clothes in a dresser drawer and I found a sock filled with change! I stole about $3 from her stash. I didn't feel good about myself after that.

That night, when Beth came home from her job at a dry cleaner's, I admitted my wrongdoing and said I would pay her back. Beth was horrified, of course, and we were never close again. Not that we were close to begin with since we had a four-year age difference. I always felt bad about what I did to Beth in stealing from her and as you can see it still bothers me.

That didn't stop me from trying to hurt my mother in any way I could. I wore loud makeup; I didn't come home after school. By then, Dave finished work as a garbage truck driver at 3:00 p.m., so if I didn't show up, he would have to stay home to be there for his own two kids.

I had never tried drugs, but I was about to enter a strange world with a new friend named Isabel. Isabel loved sniffing glue, and one day, when I went over to her house after school, we both sniffed glue and I loved it! The glue became a bit of a habit. Sniffing glue, as I know it today, goes straight to the brain and people have died on the spot from doing it. These days, they call it "huffing," I believe, and I see in the news all too often about another death from this type of drug behavior.

Nonetheless, I was extremely reckless by this time, and in addition to sniffing glue, I slept around. I was spiraling down very fast. Bullying increased by a couple of older girls who found it fun to pick on me. I never stood up for myself, and looking back, I really wish I had. Maybe if I turned on to them with my own anger, they would back off. But I didn't seem to have anger; it was more of a depression.

Isabel invited me to go with her and her new boyfriend, Taylor, to Crescent Beach one day after school. I decided to risk Mother's wrath and went. I was shocked when Taylor pulled up to a very bushy area where we were hidden from the street. Isabel said Taylor had a drug called MDA which is way better than sniffing glue. Out of control me decided to go ahead and try it. My mouth dropped open when I saw Taylor putting a liquid into a needle! Isabel said it was very safe, so I went ahead and let him put it into my veins. Oh, what a beautiful high that was! We had a case of beer with us, and we three drank and talked and just enjoyed the time we had being stoned.

I believe I went back to Crescent Beach with Isabel and Taylor two or three times over the course of a few months, and unfortunately, to me, Isabel moved away and my drug use stopped for the time being.

Things were getting really bad at home with my rebellion and reaction of my MN mother's cruel abuse. She stopped at nothing to make me feel like I was worthless, and all I could do was dream about getting out of that house. I met some people and stayed with them a couple of days and didn't contact my mother. I decided I was dropping out of school. After a few days, I finally phoned my mother and told her my conditions on coming home—I was not going back to school. I was in the middle of grade 10 when I dropped out.

Joyce, my mother's friend who had witnessed on the telephone a hysterical rampage of Mother's, had a daughter named Sharon. She was just two years my senior, and she introduced me to many new experiences, good experiences that made part of my sixteenth teenaged year wonderful. Mother let me live with Joyce and Sharon because I was out of control at home. Sharon and I played on the telephone where several people would be talking on the line, and we flirted with different guys. It was much like a chat line kids get involved with now on the computer where they talk and flirt with people they do not know.

We did go out and met a couple of the guys we talked to online, and we became a foursome group (no sexual activity). One night, Sharon had a party, and I got extremely drunk. When Joyce came home, she didn't scream or berate me at all; she just woke me up and said I needed to take my jeans off to be more comfortable. The difference between Sharon's mother and mine was incredible. I felt Joyce loved me. She was a witness to my mother's hysterics after all, and maybe she just felt sorry for me. Joyce made me *want* to behave, and from then on, while I lived with her, I never caused her to worry again.

A few months later, I went back home and tried to live with my mother again. Unfortunately, my behavior became unsafe, as I was hanging out with much older people who could have been a danger to me. At this point, I cared very little for myself and drank and partied with any group I ran into. Mother could not stand me by now. Her hostile bitterness was so apparent that when I walked into a room where she was, you could cut the air with a knife. Narcissists need supply. *Supply* meaning willing participants to their abuse. I was no longer willing to give her my supply, and my guess is she gave up on me for the time.

It was around this time Mother decided my older brother and I needed to change our names to Dave Craig's name legally. Actually, his real name is Charles Dave Craig but he goes by Dave. It was too expensive for Dave to adopt us (and God forbid Mother spend any money on me or Gus), so she had my biological father sign papers giving away his rights as a parent to Gus and I. At sixteen, I became a Craig from my original last name, Groseclose.

I was sixteen and wanted to visit my father, who was in another maximum jail at that time. As it was, he was serving time at British Columbia's most notorious prison well known for guard brutality, hard labor, suicide, poor medical and living conditions, and the list goes on.

I didn't care. I wanted to see my dad to ask why he had signed over his parental rights to Dave! I called the administrative office of Oakalla Prison and learned my visit was allowed as long as I had a padre (pastor) sitting in on our visit. The following was taken from a Web site after Googling the words Oakalla Prison Farm (1912-1991):

> Burnaby's Oakalla Prison Farm was a full-service facility which opened on September 2, 1912. The first inmate was William Daley, sentenced on July 31, 1912 to serve a year of hard labor for stealing some fountain pens valued at over $10. By April 30, 1913, some 328 prisoners had passed through the jail's doors. From 1919

until the abolition of the death penalty in 1959, 44 prisoners were executed by hanging on the Oakalla site. The first execution was that of 25 year-old Alex Ignace on August 29, 1919. Leo Mantha was the last prisoner executed, on April 28, 1959. In 1936 there were several double and even one triple hanging.

Thousands of prisoners passed through the doors of Oakalla—renamed Lower Mainland Regional Correctional Centre in 1970—before it closed on June 30, 1991. Originally designed to house a maximum of 484 prisoners, Oakalla's population peaked in 1962-63 at 1,269 inmates.

I remember walking up to an extremely large door and rang a bell to be allowed access. Several guards at once opened the door and escorted me to a bleak looking room with a man (the padre) sitting at a desk. As I sat on a chair too large for me, I waited for my dad to come. Soon I could hear the noise of chains outside of the door! When my father walked in, he was not in chains, so I imagine the guards were taking them off before he entered the room to visit with me.

My psychopath father's excuse for signing over his parental rights was because he thought we would be better off without him; he cried but without tears. He said he thought Dave made a good father and didn't want to upset the apple cart anymore. (I later found out he wouldn't have to pay child support by signing away his rights, so this was more likely his real motivation.)

*   *   *

I forgave my Aunt June for her humiliation of me in front of my cousin, Beth, and her friends, and one day, she gave me a precious gift. She said she was taking me to downtown Vancouver for a complete makeover where I would enjoy a facial and learn how to put makeup on properly by a team of professionals. I was never very good at applying eye shadow or eyeliner and often wore heavy makeup that did not suit me. I once mistook eyeliner for eye shadow, and the darkness and heaviness of it made me look like a complete clown.

My aunt took me to Pacific Centre, where I was made over, and when the team completed their transformation of me, I was in awe. I actually saw myself as beautiful! Later my aunt and I enjoyed a lunch together. This was one of the best days I can remember as a sixteen-year-old, and I felt my self-esteem go up just a little bit. When I got home, my older brother's friends were over and were also shocked at my transformation. Terry, Gus's best friend looked at me a different way, and I felt like I was on top of the world. I decided that when

I had nieces, I would pay forward when they all turned sixteen. I have four nieces, and when they each turned 16 I fulfilled my promise to give them the gift of showing them how beautiful they can look with properly applied makeup. I told them my only condition was that they do the same for their own nieces!

*   *   *

If my ages from twelve to sixteen were scary, the following chapter depicts events where I was willing to risk my own life drifting from place to place and hitch hiking long distance. I did eventually become pregnant and continued drug use. Nonetheless, the freedom from my malignant narcissistic mother's house was a godsend even if I did have to sleep in a smelly hostel from time to time.

Chapter 3—Out of Control

If there is anything that we wish to change in the child, we should first examine it and see whether it is not something that could better be changed in ourselves.

—*C. G. Jung, Integration of the Personality, 1939*

My MN mother had a few laws she didn't care for and made it well known within the family: First, when she received a DUI, the police officer was completely stupid, as everyone knows that Tic Tac breath mints can change a reading to make it appear a person was drunk, and second, when seat-belt laws came into effect, she was adamant the big brother government was trying to control her and she would *not* conform. Sometimes I just had to shake my young head to make sure my own marbles stayed in place.

The family, namely, my siblings and I, would often talk about how opinionated our mother was. You could not tell her anything—she knew it all. If you did confront her with *her wrongness* in a certain situation, her eyes would bulge and black out and her rage felt like a strike across the face.

*   *   *

I took a job at a truck stop called Kanaka Bar on Highway 1 in between Boston Bar and Lytton British Columbia. When stepfather Dave found out, he flipped his lid! Never have I seen this man show so much emotion. I could not for the life of me figure what would make him so mad about me taking this job. He even said he would disown me! Ha! As if he ever owned or had a part of my love to care what he thought.

I soon enough found out why he was so adamant that I don't work in one of his territories when he worked as a truck driver for so many years. I quickly learned that the waitresses who worked and lived in isolated truck stops were hookers for the long-haul drivers! Imagine if I told Mother what was going on at these truck stops that Dave frequented for years before he became a short-haul driver! Yes, no wonder he was angry and perhaps a little bit afraid?

I did my waitress job fine but was constantly pushing away horny drivers who often looked like they hadn't bathed in a month. The nine days I lasted at the job was nightmarish and wore me out. One night I had had it. I was talking about wanting to leave, to quit—and to quit now. My problem was I had no transportation back to the Vancouver area and nowhere to go once I got there.

This particular night, a kindly looking older man offered to give me a ride as far as Abbotsford, which was as far enough away from Kanaka Bar that I needed. I had no idea where I would go after that but figured I'd meet up with some people to help me find a place. Some of the staff took me under their wing since they realized I was not a street person and knew little about the facts of life. They told me *not* to go with this man—to wait until morning and someone else would give me a ride home. But not impulsive me. When I said I wanted out of that truck stop, I meant *now*!

I packed up the few clothes I had with me and followed the old man out to his decrepit old mobile car. As we were driving, the man, whose name fails me, said he had to make a stop on the other side of the river, the Fraser River! The only way to get across that river was to take an air ferry! I wondered what business he would have over there so late at night. It was already dark outside, and I began to get nervous. Like usual I obediently agreed to go with him; he was kind enough to give me a ride to Abbotsford, wasn't he?

Once we got across the river, I saw nothing but black. The old man said no one was around for miles, and to make matters scarier, on each side of the road was a cemetery! I became petrified and told the man I wanted to go back to Kanaka Bar. He pooh-poohed me and said his business would only take a few minutes and we were almost there. I imagined all sorts of things as we drove along the road with cemeteries on both sides. I saw no lights anywhere and knew jumping out of the car would only land me in deeper trouble than I was already in.

After another hour of driving in the middle of nowhere, we finally stopped. From the headlights, I could see a tree directly in front of us with an old road sign nailed up but not meant to mean anything.

The old man then put his moves on me. He was putting his face, lips, and tongue close enough to kiss me and then moved his body over mine and jumped on top of me! Somehow, and I really can't say how, I talked my way out of his gross seduction. I don't remember what it was I said that made him move back to the driver's seat but he did and simply fell asleep. My eyes could not close as I looked around and saw nothing but black and assumed the worst was outside the car doors. I didn't know what would happen if the old man woke up through the night, so I stayed awake and just waited for morning to hurry up.

Against my will I fell asleep. When I awoke, I could not believe my eyes. Many cars and people where milling about this beautiful spot with campsites and the calm river, where families were fishing! All I had to do was open the car door, and I knew help would be there for me. The old man woke up and simply started his car and backed out of the area. Soon we were heading back on the same road toward Highway 1.

As we drove, I saw no cemetery at all. And there were many houses, which must have just had their lights out in the lateness of the evening as we drove by the night before. We were on an Indian reservation, I realized, and was furious at the old man's lies. I just wanted him to hurry to get back to the safety of Highway 1. We went back over the ferry, and within five minutes, we were at a crossroads. The old man tried to convince me to turn left with him, toward Calgary. He said his wife had cancer and he needed to go that way. I knew I had no home or place to go in my direction, but I was not going anywhere else with this pervert. I said I wanted out at Highway 1, and I would go my own way. The old man shrugged and let me out.

I am really not too sure why this man took the left turn he did, across the ferry, or why he made up stories of no houses being around and that we were driving through a cemetery in the middle of the night! I imagine it was to scare me. But what about when we stopped by that tree? Why didn't he rape and kill me? I still wonder what that was all about to this day. Looking back I now wonder if God and his angels were with me all along after all.

When he let me out of the car, I quickly put my thumb out for a ride south—toward cities and towns I was familiar with. First, an elderly man picked me up, and I told him of my hair-raising experience the night before. He seemed genuinely concerned and even stopped to buy me a sandwich, which I really appreciated. He let me off at Prest Road in Chilliwack, and once again, I put my thumb out for a ride. This time, a man with his two boys in the backseat picked me up. Once again, I told my story of the night before

(I was still shaking about it all). I think the man was a responsible man and realized I was a ninety-five-pound sixteen-year-old who should not be out on the road at all.

He first took me to his house in Chilliwack where he seemed to be wondering what to do with me. His wife was at work, and he wished she was there to help him. Finally, he decided to take me to a hotel in Haney and pay for an overnight stay. Haney was quite a way from Chilliwack, so I was a little bit confused, especially if he was going to involve his wife. He said he would come back in the morning after he and his wife decided what they could do to help me. There was a bar and a restaurant attached to the hotel, and he gave me a few dollars for food.

I wasn't going to add this since it sort of mars the kindness within the story, but this nice man with the boys and the wife also made a move on me once we were in the paid for hotel room—this time full intercourse. I was so appreciative of his help I didn't know how to say no to him.

When I went downstairs from my room to the restaurant, I could hear music playing in another room. I asked what was going on, and the waitress told me it was a cabaret with a certain band from the 1950s and 1960s! My favorite music! I finished my food and, with the dollar I had left, went into the cabaret and sat at the bar. I ordered a glass of draft beer, and the bartender didn't even flinch or understand that I was not of age to drink at sixteen.

I saw a weirdo guy flapping around in some dance move that was more comical than anything. As I watched the people dancing, I felt good and safe and right where I belonged. In a bar, drinking to music I loved. Now I know why my parents loved going out so much!

I sipped on the same beer all night, and toward the end of the evening, a couple named Bill and Betty (real names) came up to me and asked what a young girl like me was doing in a place like this. I told them my story—the whole story—and they insisted I stay with them that night, in a house in Vancouver. I worried about the man with the boys and wife and knew he would be looking at the hotel for me in the morning, but Bill and Betty said forget about him, I needed to be safe and they would help me. I knew they were right. But I didn't even know Bill and Betty! I guess having a woman in the mix made me feel safer.

A few minutes later, a guy dripping with sweat coming off of his long hair and face came over to the bar. He was the same freak dancing in no way I have ever seen before. It turns out he was with Bill and Betty! The guy's name was Mathew, and he agreed I should go with Bill and Betty—that I would be safe with them. And so after the cabaret was over I went upstairs and grabbed my few belongings and got into the car with Bill, Betty, and me and sweaty Mathew in the back.

Bill and Betty had a nice house. I had a very comfortable sleep and woke up thinking maybe things will work out for me. To my horror, Betty said that Mathew had a big house on Fourteenth Avenue, with six suites and a large master suite with three bedrooms, and they all thought it was a great idea for me to live with Mathew until I got on my feet! Oh my god, yuck! Mathew, at thirty-three, was a socially inept sort of guy, sort of like three fingers short of a high five and very ugly to my eye. What would happen if I moved over to his house? But what choice did I have? I couldn't go home, that was for sure.

That day, Mathew came over to Bill and Betty's to pick me up. I was quiet in the car, and Mathew said not to worry, I would get my own bedroom and he would let me stay until I got a job and could look after myself. I have to admit Mathew made no moves on me. After a few weeks of living with him, I was very curious about this and asked him about it. He said he preferred to masturbate! I could not believe that anyone would prefer masturbation over real sex. One night, we made an attempt at sex, but it was a very unfortunate time—for both of us. I realized why he was sexually disinterested years later—he was gay.

One day, Mathew said he had friends, a couple with a young child, who had invited us over for Thanksgiving dinner. I loved the idea and got myself dressed up (Mathew gave me some money for clothes and accessories) to meet these new people. Mathew's friends lived on a street that was in the middle of an industrial site. The place was called Mitchell Island and directly under the Knight Street Bridge in South Vancouver, British Columbia. Apparently, this was the only street still occupied by residents; all of the other homes that once existed there had been condemned and torn down to make for industrial sites. However, the house that Arthur and Roberta lived in was cozy enough, and their little girl, Kelly, was a one-year-old angel.

I had a great time visiting these people and am not ashamed to say I had a huge crush on the man of the house, Arthur. He was about five foot eleven tall, and his hair was combed back like Elvis Presley's. He had dimples on each side of his cheeks and a hole in his chin that made him so sexy it was hard not to keep my hands off of him! Arthur did most of the cooking, as

Roberta was pretty drunk. I don't remember many conversations with her but thought she was a beauty who should be in magazines!

After dinner, I think Mathew got mad at me for something and he took off. Roberta wanted more liquor and said she was going to go to the neighbor's homes to find some. That left me and Arthur alone, and we almost immediately fell on the sofa together about to make love. Unfortunately, Roberta came rushing in the door screaming at Arthur for cheating on her before anything happened.

Arthur called Mathew to come back to get me, and from then on, we were not invited over for dinner. However, Arthur often found excuses to come over to Mathew's house, and we always struck up a great conversation. Sometimes we went to the Plaza 500 for drinks in the bar.

While I was living with Mathew, I found a job as a telemarketer for the *Vancouver Sun* and the *Province* newspapers. I must say I didn't do too badly and earned enough money to keep me in cigarettes and drinks if we went out.

I began to suspect I was pregnant. The only person who I remotely slept with was Mathew, and that was only once and not a good experience. I thought of several bad things about being pregnant (besides being only sixteen years of age); if I was pregnant, Mathew was the father and to have a child by him made me cringe.

At the telemarketing job, I met a new friend named *Melissa Twist. We hit it off really well and almost every night went out for drinks to talk about me possibly being pregnant and dream about our futures. We decided it might be a good idea to go to Calgary, Alberta, where there were plenty of good-paying jobs at that time. Thinking about being pregnant could wait.

I felt terrible just leaving Mathew and didn't want him to talk me out of it, so Melissa and I made up an elaborate plan for my escape. Mathew was out front with Arthur fixing an old car. I phoned a taxi and told the dispatch to make sure he goes to the back alley to pick me up. When we saw the cab, Melissa and I made a mad dash for the car and ducked as we made our hasty exit down the alley toward the safety of the streets.

We got off at the Plaza 500 hotel and had several drinks while we decided how we were going to get to Calgary. Because of our lack of funds, hitchhiking was our only option. We downed our last drink and set off to the bus stop that would take us to Highway 1. Our rides were mostly semi-truck drivers, and we had no incident. Our last ride of the day was only going as far as Hope, British Columbia, and it was very late in the evening. Somehow, and I don't remember how, we found the Hope Hostel and spent the night snuggled up to many other travelers and homeless people. In the morning, we were fed breakfast and off we went to the highway to hitch our way to Calgary, at least another eight—to ten-hour drive.

My memory is a little clouded, but I know that along our route, we stopped at someone's house and enjoyed the effects of magic mushrooms, a hallucinate that made the panel walls move around. I didn't really care for the feeling too much and vowed to never eat them again.

The trip to Calgary was uneventful, and we found rides with truck drivers without a problem. Sometimes we smoked pot if the driver had some. I remember in one truck a song on the radio came on, "Me and Bobby McGee," and Melissa and I sang out loud in glee of our escape from our homeland and excitement toward our new life in Calgary.

Once we arrived in Calgary, we were directed to the YWCA, where a social worker sized us up and decided if we qualified to stay there or not. We did qualify and were given a shared room that looked much like a hotel. I found a job at Eaton's shopping center in downtown Calgary in the men's underwear department, which I always found to be funny. Melissa found a job at a car wash.

We settled into a semi-normal life when I decided to phone my mother to let her know I was alive and in Calgary. Big mistake. I was received with hostility and indifference, and after two or three minutes, I hung up on her. I could not stand her tone of voice for one more second! Why did I keep trying to get her to care?

Melissa and I found friends in pubs who had tabs of LSD, and we took these drugs without question. These were fun times, and we met many new druggie friends very quickly. Unfortunately, Melissa and I got separated, and I worried about her for years, until Facebook brought us together again in 2011, some thirty-five years later.

Meanwhile, I met a new friend named Doreen Sherameta. Together we had a lot of fun, including sitting on Santa's knee together in the department store I worked at. I still have that photo. Doreen and I found a house to share with two other guys (not sexual) several miles from downtown in the North East area. Because we were quite a way from downtown, I quit my Eaton's job and found a job down the road from our house at Mac's Milk. Doreen found a job closer to the city and had to take the bus. It was winter, and the weather was extremely cold. Eventually Doreen decided to live closer to her job and left the house.

The house I shared was very nice, and each night, we took turns cooking dinner. For the most part, it was an enjoyable living arrangement. I did have a problem with one of the guys, however. *George had a burn mark covering half of his face, and to me he seemed to want preferred treatment because of it. He didn't cook or clean and had *Rick and I picking up after him. I saw this kind of behavior before—in my Mother and her own *sense of entitlement.* I wasn't going to put up with this bullshit from him. We were constantly at each other's throats.

One night, I threw a full glass of water at him, and the glass broke on him and all over his clothes. He chased me around the house for a while until we both grew tired, and finally we broke out in hysterical laughter over the event. I still didn't like him, though.

I couldn't help but continue to think about being pregnant. I didn't go to the doctor, but I had all of the signs and symptoms. I had no resources to keep a baby; my job didn't pay much, and I had no idea how I would support a baby. I was petrified my drug use would have affected the baby as well. The guys in the house said there was no way they would let me stay there with a baby.

I decided to phone my psychopath Father and his wife, my stepmother, Sunny, who was so beautiful to me. I had three half-siblings Gilbert, Danny, and Shenay, who had moved to Cranbrook, British Columbia to escape my Father but eventually Sunny let him back in. I picked up the phone and Sunny answered. When I told her my situation, I was met with love, concern, and an offer for a ticket to come to Cranbrook to live with them and figure out what we could do about my pregnancy! I couldn't believe the joy I felt that people, family even, wanted me unconditionally and would be willing to help me with my pregnancy situation.

When I got off the bus in Cranbrook, Sunny and the kids, my half siblings, were all waiting for me. Sunny later said I looked like a crazed homeless person. My hair was in knots and my clothes were dirty and ripped. My face was pale, and my eyes had dark circles around them.

I soon settled into Sunny's house (it was Sunny's because my father was rarely there, and she was the only one paying the bills as an invoice clerk). But for the first few weeks, my dad was there, and he seemed so nice and I couldn't imagine why my MN mother would say such horrible things about him. To me, at this point, I found him to be very supportive and loving as any father would be. I did not see the cracks in his psychopathy yet and Sunny tried to save my feelings about his very disturbing behavior.

The first order of business was that Sunny took me to see her doctor whose name was Neidermeyer, who later became the father of two famous NHL hockey players. It was confirmed. I was approximately ten weeks pregnant, and now was the time to make the decision to abort or not. Sunny said she would support me either way. I decided I was too young to care for a baby, and my father took me to Trail, British Columbia, for the abortion. In those days, it was still very taboo to have an abortion and it was so new that few hospitals would perform the surgical procedure.

I continued to live with Sunny and my younger siblings, and occasionally my father would show up and be the man of the hour for the kids, including me. His patience wore thin easily, however, and I noticed abuse between him and Sunny and my three half siblings, which broke my heart. He was always hardest on Danny, which tore me apart. Danny sort of reminded me of me with my MN mother—the scapegoat and easiest supply for abuse. However, my father never bothered me and, for the most part, seemed very kind and understanding. I still don't know why I was spared his psychopathic rage like so many others experienced.

*　*　*

I tried to go back to high school in Cranbrook, but like before, school was just not for me. At least this time, I didn't encounter any bullies other than the odd teacher. Eventually, I dropped out of that school as well and accepted a job as a waitress at a place called the Town and Country Inn. I was still hurting over my mother's rejection of me, but I decided to buy her something really special for Christmas, which was still months away. I went to a jeweler and put a family ring on layaway for her. Every payday, I would go down to the store and put a few more dollars on the precious gift. I couldn't wait to present this to my mother, who would surely love me once she received it.

Wrong. I mailed the ring to Mother and, on Christmas Eve, asked her to open the gift while we were on the telephone. When I heard dead silence at the other end of the line, I was confused. What was wrong? She asked to speak to Sunny, my stepmother. They talked for a few moments, and Sunny hung up on my mother. She said that I was accused of stealing the ring or at least the money to purchase the ring! I didn't speak to my mother for a long time after that, my heart broken once again by her very wrong impression of me and my character. Sunny held me as I sobbed over this Christmas event gone wrong and told me something I never forgot. She said I was a very special person and would be somebody one day. I still hang onto those words of extreme kindness and empathy.

*   *   *

I heard that Arthur was separated from his wife, Roberta, and he had custody of his now two-year-old daughter. I had such a crush on this man I decided to move back to Vancouver to try and hook up with him again. We had an affair of sorts, but it was more off than on. I took a job as a waitress and lived with Arthur for a very short period of time. I came home from work one night and found him in bed with his ex-wife, Roberta!

Something inside of me snapped, and I ran out of the house and walked to the Knight Street Bridge and started to think about suicide. I was crying so hard over yet another betrayal I could not see living another day. Something pushed me all across the bridge without my jumping over, and I continued up Knight Street, wondering what I was going to do with myself. Where would I live? Who could I call? I had no one to count on other than Sunny, but she was way up in Cranbrook. Besides, I wanted her to think things were okay with me now; I didn't want her to worry.

I saw a doctor's office and walked in. I was still crying hysterically over my newest loss, unable to control myself. When the doctor saw me, he contacted some people who came to pick me up. I was taken to a house with many bedrooms and women who seemed to be as displaced as I was. I lived in this house for a few weeks when I began to suspect I was pregnant again. I told the house mistress, and she sent me to Pine Free Clinic, where it was confirmed; I was with child again!

I telephoned Arthur and gave him the news. A few hours later, he was at the house to pick me up. I thought he was going to take me home with him and we would live happily ever after, but I was wrong. Instead he dropped me off at a friend of his on Thirteenth Street East, right behind the Biltmore Hotel—a very bad part of Vancouver.

*   *   *

I was dropped off with Debbie, who was a single mother with a four-month-old baby named Jessica. In return for rooming with her, I babysat Jessica nearly every night as I waited for Arthur to come back and pick me up. After several weeks of waiting for Arthur to save me and take care of me and our baby, it dawned on me that he was not coming back. I was on my own in a stranger's house. That old sinking feeling of wanting to die came back with a vengeance, and I searched the house for something to kill myself with. I found a bottle of pills on top of the refrigerator and swallowed them like I was eating popcorn. I did not consider the baby growing in my womb, as what would a baby want with a mother like me?

After taking all of the pills, I realized nothing was happening. I began to feel a fright like no other. What if I lived and yet killed my own baby? Debbie didn't have a telephone, and so I went next door to ask the neighbors if I could borrow their phone. I dialed my mother's number, and when she picked up the line, I told her what I had done. Her words resonate within me to this day, *"You stupid, stupid bitch! Don't you ever think about anyone other than yourself?"* I hung up and went back to Debbie's, wondering what to do next.

Not long after, an ambulance pulled up the drive and took me to the closest hospital to have my stomach pumped. From there, I was taken to Shaughnessy Hospital's psychiatric ward, where I spent five weeks. I did not hurt my baby as it turns out I had only swallowed antibiotics!

Mother was summoned to have "sessions" with the psychiatrist and myself, and her lies about me and my character during these counseling sessions made me cringe over and over again. After one particularly grueling session, I ran out of the office and hid in the cafeteria. Approximately thirty minutes or so later, the doctor came to get me. I told him how frustrated I was with Mother's lies and I would never sit in on a session with her in the room again. The psychiatrist said one of the most important things anyone could have said to me at that moment. He said, "Don't you think I can see through your mother's double talk?" The hospital never contacted Mother again for a counseling session with me.

*   *   *

A very strange event happened to me while I was in that hospital. First, I met a friend named Cindy. She had a six-year-old boy, and I looked up to her since I was pregnant and she knew a lot about babies. Second, I met an old man who taught me how to play crib. He paid a lot of attention to me, but I wasn't concerned. One thing he did say to me a couple of times was that he knew me when I was young. It didn't make any sense to me at that time so I let it go. Cindy was very concerned about his attraction to me, however, and she told me to watch out for him—she said he was following me around, and he gave her the creeps.

That night I looked up from my bed and saw his face looking at me through the small window on the ward door, and I realized Cindy was right—he was searching me out! And then it hit me like a ton of bricks! This was the same Hydro security guard my old friend Debbie McCallister and I sold ourselves to when we were twelve! As I was beginning to remember, I realized this old guy's name was Randy, and the security guy's name was Randolph! I felt sick to my stomach as I was beginning to remember and hid in my ward for several hours. Soon Cindy came to my room and said that the old guy just packed up his belongings and left! I think he realized that I came into awareness of who and what he was. I never told anyone about my experience with "Randy" because at that time, I was still in deep shame over the event. It was my fault.

*   *   *

It was clear Arthur was not going to come for me and our upcoming baby. Eventually the hospital contacted Sunny and asked her if it was possible for me to come back to live with her and my half siblings, and she readily agreed. It felt good to be wanted somewhere, and I needed a safe place for me and my precious baby. This time, I was going to keep my child, and I knew Sunny would help me through all of it.

When I arrived back in Cranbrook, Sunny had already set me up with a live-in nanny job for a single father with two children. For room and board, I would take care of the children and keep the apartment he lived in clean. The next several months went by very smoothly, and I found myself at peace knowing I was soon to give birth to a healthy baby and I would finally have someone to love and to love me back unconditionally! With my small earnings, I would buy little baby outfits and kitchen gadgets because I knew I would have to live on my own once the baby was born.

Finally life was looking good. I had so much to look forward to and I was surrounded by people who really did care about me, and I cared about them.

*   *   *

My child was due to be born on June 8, 1978. I decided to visit my mother at Easter and purchased a bus ticket for the sixteen-hour drive. I learned that she and Dave had finally separated, and I was now going to tell her of his molestation way back in my days of puberty. I remember telling her about my story as clearly as if it were yesterday, sitting at her kitchen table: When I finished, I saw the most intense hatred in my mother's eyes than I had ever seen before. She called me every horrible name in the book and threw me out of her house without ceremony. Once again, I cringed as she called me a liar and instigator of trouble. It cut to my soul every time she hurled these abusive words at me, and this time was no exception.

I didn't get it! Even in her separation from him, she was willing to throw me under the bus. I still had no idea how to protect myself from my malignant narcissist mother, and once again, I did not stand up for myself. I left to return to Cranbrook to wait my own child's birth. During the bus ride home, I couldn't stop crying. People were very kind and trying to get it out of me what was wrong. I couldn't say. What if they believed my mother's side of things? What would these strangers think of me!

I felt like I was the horrible person my mother portrayed me to be, and these feelings never did leave me.

From that time on, my mother reminded me every time I visited her or every chance she got about my "biggest lie of all," and never did I argue with her. Even at eighteen years of age, she still scared the shit out of me.

*   *   *

Soon I was going to learn what it was really like to be a parent. I could hardly contain my excitement as the day drew near. I was preparing myself to live with my stepmother again for the first several months of my child's life. Sunny was going to show me how to be a good mother to my precious baby. I had no idea the change my child would make on me and where our worlds would take us.

Chapter 4—My Gift from Heaven—Motherhood

So for the mother's sake the child was dear; and dearer was the mother for the child.

—Samuel Taylor Coleridge

Trevor Thomas was born on May 27, 1978, two weeks earlier than expected. The minute I saw my bundle of joy, I fell in love. It was at this time I realized just how "off" my own mother was. How could any mother treat her own child so badly, without an ounce of love? I could not imagine neglecting or abusing my son in any way, and I believed God sent me a gift from the heavens to show me just what love really did mean. Trevor's very breath was heaven's scent for me. I could not stop holding and rocking him, as any loving mother would do.

I took my new job as mother very seriously. I immediately put my baby on a schedule. Every morning, I would change his diaper and prepare his bath on the kitchen table. I'd lay out towels and soaps and lotions and fill his plastic tub with lukewarm water. One time, I laid him in the water and he squirted a hoop of a pee directly into my coffee! I loved it and laughed out loud! While I gave him his bath, his bottles were being boiled to prepare for another day's supply of food. I could not breast-feed my son because his birth was two weeks early, and for some reason, it took that long for the milk to appear! By then we were already on a schedule of formula, and we were both happy with that arrangement.

After Trevor was all polished up, he played in his baby seat, taking in all of the sights of what was around him. After four hours of being up and playing, I fed him his lunch bottle and laid him to sleep, where he slept for another full four hours! Sometimes I would sneak into his room and hold him while he slept just to hear his heart beat next to mine.

There is no greater love than a mother and her child!

* * *

One month after Trevor was born, I called his father, Arthur, to give him the good news of our new baby. Arthur appeared to be very excited over the news and said he was coming to Cranbrook to pick us up to live on that same street on Mitchell Island in the lower mainland of Vancouver. Arthur was now the property manager of all of the remaining homes on the street where I first met him, his wife Roberta, and daughter Kelly.

I never stopped loving Arthur Fisher. He was the most handsome man I ever met, and I thought he finally came to reason and was about to take care of me and baby Trevor. Within days, Arthur arrived with a van, and I packed up all of our belongings and went off into the sunset with my two favorite people! Arthur set me and Trevor up in one of his homes but said we would not live together. I was confused by this, but I was willing to take any morsel Arthur was willing to give me.

Since I only had a grade 9 education and no money to pay for a babysitter, I went on welfare. I remember the social worker coming to my new home (such as it was), and he told me I didn't have to live like this, in a home with just a woodstove to keep me warm and to heat water and a house in grave disrepair and ready to be condemned.

I began to look for an apartment and found one in Surrey. It was a perfect fit for Trevor and I since just off the master bedroom was a large powder room that fit his crib, change table, and dresser.

I was broke all of the time and often didn't know how I would feed or diaper Trevor. Arthur rarely helped or visited for that matter. Although he never really broke up with me, he was not a helpful partner in this child-raising business.

I had a very strong attachment to Trevor, so much that I knew when he was in danger even if I was nowhere near him. Once he was not feeling well, and I asked a neighbor to babysit him while I went across the road to shop for groceries and medicine. Halfway through my shopping, I had the worst feeling a mother could have—I could sense my son was in danger, and I didn't even think twice. I left the buggy in the middle of the aisle and ran all the way home.

I barged into the apartment of the babysitter and found my son in a loose wet diaper outside on the balcony in freezing cold weather! Since the only reason I left him with a babysitter was because he had a cold, I was furious the woman lying on her sofa would be so neglectful. I *hated* neglect! I'll never forget how I somehow knew my baby was in danger and continued to wonder if angels were watching over us.

* * *

There were many times when I worried about how I was going to feed or diaper my baby. One day, I was at the very bottom financially and had no more cash for diapers or formula. I had no one to turn to at all. I swallowed my pride and called my Mother who lived only blocks away and told her how serious my situation had become. Her response was, "You made your bed. Now lay in it!" I was not too surprised, but so saddened of her lack of soul.

About an hour later, there was a knock on my door, and when I opened it, I could have fell over from shock. There stood Dave, my molester, my stepfather, in hand were a big bag of diapers and a six-pack of formula. In addition, he handed me a check for $25! He left me with my treasures, and I immediately thanked God for this gift. Of course, Mother called me for weeks afterward, telling me to hurry up and pay Dave back. I never did get caught up enough to pay him back, but then again, he never asked for it—Mother did.

* * *

A woman in her forties named Sharon lived down the hall befriended me. She had two teenage children of her own. One day, she came into my kitchen and asked if I liked nice things. I said sure, and she said she had a way of getting me some money so I could buy more things for my baby and apartment. She said I should dress up nice for Friday night and go out with her to Vancouver. I am really not sure why I agreed to go out with this older woman; maybe I still had a hard time saying no.

It turns out she took me to a place called the Penthouse. This was a stripper cabaret that had a nasty history. A few years earlier, a shooting took place that killed the owner, who was said to belong to the mob. This was way beyond my element, and I was uncomfortable from the moment we stepped inside. Soon men, old men, came to join my new friend Sharon and me at our table. It was then that Sharon told me that she had sex with men for money and she would teach me how!

I was petrified. Again, saying no was not coming from my lips, and I allowed a man to take me back to Surrey to my apartment where we began having sex. It turns out I wasn't cut out for the job because halfway into our rendezvous, I made him stop and told him he had to go. Funny enough, he left me $80 on his exit. I had to find a better way to make money.

When I was collecting my mail from the community mailboxes, I ran into a woman with an accent. She introduced herself as Helena and said she and her husband were from Egypt and they had twin girls. We became fast friends, and she hired me to watch her girls while she worked, which gave me a few extra dollars.

I must have been getting depressed around this time because my earlier enthusiasm over managing my own apartment and child was weakening. I did not keep my apartment as clean as I would have liked, and I went out with friends, leaving Trevor with babysitters too often in my mind. Once I asked my mother if she would watch Trevor while I went out. My aunties from my Father's side were visiting her, so she said no because she was going out with her company (she would have said no anyway). Surprisingly she said my younger sister (Shivey), who was eleven by then, could babysit. I drove over to my mother's house in my beat up Ford Fairlane station wagon and left Trevor in the hands of my baby sister. I must admit I had my misgivings, but I was having a selfish moment and let my intuition go.

When I returned to Mother's to retrieve Trevor, she was home and screaming her head off at my baby son for getting into her records! I quickly picked him up and ran out to the car. Mother followed me out and spat at me that even my own grandmother, the paternal Grandma I held near and dear to my heart, said it would be better if Trevor died! I cried all of the way back to the apartment and immediately phoned my grandmother to confront her on her horrible hurtful words.

Needless to say, my grandmother was shocked at my mother's accusation. Grandma told me Mother had been telling her Trevor was extremely sick all of the time (due to my neglect), and it was in this context she said no child should suffer so many illnesses. Period. She *never* said Trevor should die, and she was horrified my own mother would say such a thing. My grandmother never spoke to my mother again after that incident.

Malignant narcissists are masters at destroying relationships, and if my relationship with my paternal grandmother were not so well grounded, she very well could have ruined that relationship for me as well. I am so grateful Mother never got to my Grandma.

*　　*　　*

I rarely saw my father during these years. He did visit once and brought Trevor a black T-shirt. I was so afraid of "the darkness" of my parents I refused to allow Trevor to wear black, and he never did get to wear that shirt.

My MN mother contaminated almost everyone I knew, including my relatives on my father's side, about my character. She would fabricate and bad-mouth me in any instance she could. One wonderful day, my grandmother was in town for her eightieth birthday. We shared the same birth month, and while we were at my Aunt Eve's house to celebrate this special day, she brought me upstairs and gave me a ring for my own nineteenth birthday. This was a very special ring, Grandma said, because she received it from my Father when he was only fifteen. He had overheard my grandmother tell my grandfather that she saw a ruby ring with two small pearls at the local jewelry store. Grandfather never bought it for her, so my Father went to buy it. He chose the wrong ring, apparently, as this ring had a pearl in the center and two small rubies on each side.

Grandma asked me not to mention it to the aunts, the uncles, and the cousins who were all at the house for the birthday party. She didn't want anyone to feel left out. Unfortunately, the ring did not fit me, and I placed it in my purse. When I stood up to go out to the store or for some other errand, the ring in its box fell out of my bag without my knowing it. One of my cousins told me that after I left, two of my aunties looked in the box and saw grandma's ring. Both immediately looked at Grandma and asked if I had *stolen* this piece from her! How they would come to a conclusion like that only I would know.

Mother had tainted my reputation by telling anyone who would listen that I was just like Ivan (my psychopath father). I was a liar, cheat, and thief. Even after all of these years of proof I was building a positive life for myself and my son; even though I had *never* been involved with the law, she saw me through her own dark eyes and repeated these black images to her gossip recipients.

The shame and humiliation didn't end for me that weekend. One of my favorite cousins, *Dawn, was staying at my place since she came to Grandma's party from out of town. After grandma's birthday party, Dawn went back to her home in Alberta. I received a call from her a day or two later when she said she had left a pair of earrings at my place. I hadn't seen them but assured her I would look. I tore my place apart trying to find those damn earrings—I was petrified my best cousin would think me a thief! I even looked in the vacuum bag to no avail. The hardest thing I had to do was call that cousin and tell her the earrings were not in my home. Dawn's tone of voice and subsequent silent treatment for some ten years told me she did not believe me, and thus my old childhood trauma of being labeled a thief stayed with me and alienated me from family, family I loved so much that I cried often at being left out of events.

Since I am not, and was not a liar, cheat, or thief in any of my adult years, MN mother did her job on me well, and as I aged with this reputation, my anger was building, much like a pressure cooker.

*   *   *

The next couple of years were very difficult for me. Not having Arthur or supportive parents to help support or raise our baby left me completely in the cold, and I did not have good examples of parenting. I was getting worried that I was not a good-enough mother for my Trevor. He deserved the best, and I sure didn't feel like I was anything close to being the best parent for him. I called social services a few times for help. I did not know how to cope with a toddler and his antics, and my frustration levels were getting scary. A couple of times, I asked the ministry to take Trevor into foster care so that I could get a much-needed break. I always made sure I visited him regularly, and he was never away for more than a month or two. Still, it pains me to this day that I felt forced to give my beloved Trevor up because I couldn't cope!

I decided to move back to Cranbrook and be close to my stepmother, Sunny (by then she and my father had permanently separated). I found a nice townhouse and took a position in a bar where I made enough tips to rent and furnish a new and cherished townhome.

Still, I was indulging my son so much, and not offering any discipline, he was turning into a very bad boy indeed. He was out of control. It took me hours to get him to go to sleep, and I was often so tired I was beside myself with frustration. One night, I took out a wooden spoon and spanked his butt four or five times very hard. The next morning, I saw some little bruises on his behind, and I cried out in despair! I phoned the social services on myself and told the social worker I had hurt my child.

A very nice man came to my door to look at the situation. I don't think the ministry of social services receives many calls from the abusive parent! When

I explained that I needed Trevor to go to sleep at a decent hour and he was not going along with the plan, the social worker, Terry, gave me a tool that changed everything.

He said every night at 8:00 p.m., put a chair outside of Trevor's bedroom door and have plenty of coffee and a magazine nearby because I was about to experience two or three nights of sheer hell as we "reprogrammed" Trevor to learn bed is bed and Mother wasn't taking no for an answer anymore. The first night was hell! I did our usual bedtime ritual, reading a story, singing a song, and saying our prayers. Then I kissed him good night and left the room, closing the door behind me while holding my breath all the way.

Of course, within seconds, Trevor was at the door crying to get out. I was to calmly, without eye contact or voice, and gently put him back on the bed. No more kisses. No more attention. Simply lay him back on the bed and walk out again. The first night, Trevor got up some thirty times, and each time, I would gently pick him up and lay him back on the bed. Trevor was blue-faced, screaming by this point, and it broke my heart! But I knew I had to trust that Terry knew what he was talking about. Finally, Trevor wore himself out and fell asleep on the floor by his bed.

The next night was just as intense, but now he wore out by the tenth or eleventh lay-down. Finally, on night three we did our bedtime ritual, I walked out the door fully expecting another long night but was pleasantly surprised to find that Trevor had given up! From that moment on, I never had a bedtime problem with Trevor again. Once our rituals were done, he was ready to go to sleep. He finally realized Mom meant bedtime, and there would be no exceptions! Life got a lot easier for me after that. Thank you, Terry!

*   *   *

I continued my job, and things were settling down for a while. Suddenly the phone woke me up one night, and it was Arthur, Trevor's daddy! I was so excited for the call I had forgotten how badly it ended when I was living down in his area of the province. Arthur had left me high and dry, and it got so bad I thought my child would starve at one point! Nevertheless, I was excited to hear from him. I was just about to write my GED; I had a good job that paid the bills, and we had a nice townhouse with all of the furnishings. How could I leave all of this behind to join Arthur, which was a risk at best? But I did. Arthur had custody of his daughter now, and he said he wanted to marry me so that we could all be a family. It was my fairy tale come true!

While I didn't have time to study for the GED exams, I did take the tests and passed (barely) before my new adventure was to begin! So off we went again, taking the twelve-or-so-hour drive to Vancouver. Now Arthur was the property manager of an apartment building in North Delta, blocks from where my mother and Dave lived. I moved in with Arthur, and almost immediately, things began to turn ugly. For one thing, his ex-wife, Roberta, phoned me to say she had found an advertisement in the Gay Personals at Arthur's apartment and several sexual messages from men were circled. I thought Roberta was just being vindictive.

Another problem was that his entire family had moved from Well's British Columbia and lived in the same apartment complex. If I thought my family was dysfunctional, Arthur's family surpassed that by 100-fold. There was wife battering with his brothers and their wives, and Eleanor, Arthur's baby sister, who was nineteen at that time, was so dependently close to Kelly she hated the idea of Trevor intruding on Arthur's love child!

One night, Kelly and Trevor were downstairs at Arthur's parents' apartment when Kelly came in with Trevor in tow. She said that Eleanor had punched Trevor in the stomach! Trevor was two years old at that time, and I couldn't imagine anyone punching a baby in the stomach. When I told Arthur about it, he justified his sister's behavior and said Trevor was driving her crazy and blah blah blah . . .

I moved out. Mother had calmed quite a bit, and I was allowed to move back into her house. She was still with Dave, but he was hardly home, and I wasn't bothered. I was more bothered by my mother's continued accusations that I was a liar. What broke Arthur and I up completely was when I made a surprise visit to his apartment and found him in bed with another woman! I should have known better. Although I still loved him, I should have figured out by now that Arthur was bad news and he would never be a good father for Trevor or husband for me. I moved back to Cranbrook and went on welfare while living at my stepmother's home once again.

A new thing was being implemented by the ministry of social services where single parents could find a place to volunteer and receive an additional $100 per month on their welfare checks! I decided to do my volunteering at the Women's Center, where an entire floor was dedicated to battered women and yet not in use! My stepmother was a battered woman (by my psychopath Father), and she knew a lot about these things, so between the two of us, we scrubbed and cleaned and found donations of cribs and blankets and other items needed to open the Emergency Shelter for Battered Women.

I went to the police, the welfare offices, and even the city's MLA, Terry Segrety, to let them know that the new emergency shelter was ready for occupants and that if they heard of battered women needing a safe place to go, we now had one. It was one of the most satisfying things I have ever done. In addition, my confidence began to grow, and I decided to move back to the coast of British Columbia and attend college.

I took out a small student loan and entered an office administrative program that was full time and would teach me the skills needed to work in an office. I gained skills such as typing, bookkeeping, calculator punching, and more. As soon as I graduated six months later, I landed a low-paying job at the British Columbia Motel's Resorts and Trailer Parks Association! I didn't care that the pay was low; I was just excited to have the opportunity to gain real work experience in an office with my new set of skills.

*   *   *

Trevor and I visited Mother at Christmas in Vernon one year when he was four years old and I was 22. Mother and Dave were still together but barely. I witnessed my younger siblings hanging around the doors of the bars our parents were frequenting, waiting for Dave to come out and give them some money so they would get lost. Smart kids.

One night, we all went to bed, except for Dave, who was still at the bar. I do not remember where my sister was sleeping that night, as I was in her bedroom alone. Always on guard when it came to creepy Dave, I awoke immediately when I found him hovering over me at about two in the morning! What he was going to try I don't know, as I made such a loud fuss it brought my Mother out of her room, where she was witness to him trying to make a hasty exit from the room I was sleeping in, Shivey's. That Christmas was the last time she called me a liar with respect to my childhood molestation accusations. Oh, she still had all of her negative opinions of me, but she never called me a liar about that again. I went home satisfied that she had seen her husband attempt to molest me.

*   *   *

It was during this time I became interested in self-help organizations. One of the first events I attended was in a church on Oak Street in Vancouver. There a Dr. Tom Hopper was giving a talk about goal setting. I listened intently as Dr. Hopper surprised the audience with real facts and figures that prove people who set goals in their lives feel far more successful in their lives than their non goal-setting counterparts! In fact, over 85 percent of people who set goals say that at least 70 percent of their goals are met within one year! This was good news for me, and I decided to take the doctor's prescription for success and wrote out my goals.

My two main issues were I needed $4,000 to pay off my student loan, freeing up my monthly income and, second, finding a Father, a good Father for my son. I was told to be specific (how much money do I need and exactly what do I want in a man, for examples). Within three months of setting my goals, I had exactly what I wanted! A friendly social worker, Anita, whom I had called on often for help in raising my son, got permission from her superiors to allow me to use the Ministry of Social Services lawyer to sue Arthur Fisher for child support! I'm not talking about a free legal aid lawyer—this was the lawyer the ministry used in family court cases! Within a few months, and before we even got to court, Arthur agreed to pay me $6,000 as a child support settlement! Funny enough, he was going to pay me $4,000 up front and the remaining $2,000 at the end of the year. I never did get that other $2,000 since Arthur claimed bankruptcy and went into hiding. My point is I got exactly what I asked for in my goals—$4,000!

My second but most important goal was about to be realized as well. Finding a good man to be my husband and Trevor's Father was at the top of my list. Trevor was not an easy child to raise partly, I'm sure, due to my overindulgence and inability to say no to his big blue eyes!

Trevor and I were living in a main level basement suite when my landlords told me that four young men were going to be moving on the upper level. I was outraged! By now I had settled down and just wanted a quiet life for my son and myself, and the idea of four guys moving in upstairs both scared me and upset my lifestyle. I was working in an office during the week and at a bar on the weekends to make ends meet. Knowing that my landlords were moving out (they were my babysitters on the weekends I worked), I was crushed.

It turns out the four "men" who moved in were all twenty-one-year-olds (I was twenty-three), and this was the first time they were living away from home! Too many times I had to tell them to shut their music down or move their cars so I could get out of the carport. However, there was one man who caught my eye. His name was Gary, and somehow I just knew the moment I met him he was going to be my husband.

We started off being good friends, and my guys upstairs often took me out to play billiards in Port Roberts at the Breakers Bar. It took about four months before Gary and I started dating. I was his first real love, and I guess he was both shy and slow at wooing me! We dated for about a year before moving in together. I told him I would only live with him for six months; if at the end of that time we were not engaged, I wanted out. I did not want my son exposed to his mother living with multiple men; I wanted Gary to make an honest woman out of me!

Sure enough, six months into our common-law relationship, Gary popped the question! I was so excited I forgot how jealous and nasty my malignant narcissist mother would get at any good news coming from my end. It turns out she was in town visiting at the time of my engagement, and the fact that Gary took me to Harrison Hot Springs to a beautiful five-star hotel to ask me to get married probably threw her over the edge of envy. My mother did as she always did and created a fight with me and left my home in a huff. This was extreme stuff, even for her. She was so far over the top in anger (and for what I cannot remember!) I called her girlfriend, Joyce, to say she had left my place in terrible shape and to look out for her—I was worried about her driving.

Needless to say, Mother never budged from whatever standpoint she was on. Therefore, I had to plan my wedding myself with a few close friends. Gary and I decided we were only going to invite our closest relatives and friends who shared in our lives at that time. We had a list of about seventy people, rented a hall, hired a caterer, and ordered flowers. My mother's friend, Joyce, made my wedding dress, which was a beautifully elegant silk spaghetti strap with many sequins. A decorated white hat topped it off, and I must admit I did look beautiful even to my own eye. The year was 1984, and I was in good style, complete with a cluster diamond ring.

I only had three months to plan my wedding since we decided if we are going to be engaged and we were already living together, we may as well take the plunge now. During the entire wedding planning stage, my mother never called nor wrote to me. I sent her a wedding invitation, but she was the only parent who would be in attendance. My biological father was in prison. My stepfather, Dave, well, I don't know where he was; I think by then he and Mother finally ended their marriage, and my older brother, once again, was invisible and I did not know where he was, but he was not at my wedding. I learned later he had bear spray all over his face and wouldn't go outside. He most likely got into trouble during one of his drug problems. Thus, my younger brother, Gilbert, on my dad's side gave me away.

I telephoned my mother a few days before the wedding and told her I really wanted her to be with me the night before the wedding. Gary's family held a rehearsal dinner, and it would not be the same without me having a parent in attendance. Mother promised to be there, but I waited in vain. She never showed.

I was suppose to be married at 11:00 a.m. on December 1, 1984, at the Lutheran Church in Ladner, British Columbia. This was the church most of Gary's friends belonged to, and I felt comfortable with the reverend. In attendance were my maid of honor and two bridesmaids (Shelly, my best friend, was my maid of honor, and my bridesmaids were my two younger sisters, Shivey from my mother's side and Shenay from my dad's side, who were both around seventeen at that time). Trevor was the ring bearer, and a little girl named *Michelle was the flower girl.

At 11:30 a.m. I was late due to ice on the roads after getting my nails done. When I arrived at the church with my ladies I learned my mother still had not arrived. We waited in a small room as the guests were seated and waiting. The organist played beautiful love songs, and the groom, best man, and two groomsmen were all in place, waiting for this wedding to take place. But no mother of the bride!

Finally, forty-five minutes late, I made the decision to walk down the aisle without my mother. Halfway to Gary, my mother made a hasty, loud entrance and ran up the aisle toward me. I stopped the procession and gave her a hug and pointed her to a seat at the front. Mother looked terrible! She was without makeup, her permed hair was a ratty mess, and she was wearing what looked like a second-hand rabbit fur jacket! Her face and eyes told me she was hung over.

I ignored the obvious embarrassment and married Gary. It was a beautiful wedding in spite of the drama my mother created. After the wedding, we had photos taken and set off for the Odd Fellows Hall, where an afternoon reception was being held. We hired a disco band, and since friends and family decorated the hall beautifully, we all danced in celebration of our marriage.

Out of the corner of my eye, I watched Mother. Sure enough, she was making a scene going from one guest to the other, crying and telling them about how selfish I was for not inviting Aunt Mildred, an aunt I hadn't seen in over fifteen years! If Mother wanted specific people invited, she would have told me; instead she chose to bad-mouth me on my wedding day to the guests I did invite.

When the reception ended at 6:00 p.m., Gary and I drove in his yellow 280ZX car to Whistler, British Columbia, for a four-day skiing honeymoon. I was on top of my world, and nothing was going to ruin my day, especially not my mother.

I learned from my sister-in-law later that Mother cried all the way back to Vernon. She called me after my honeymoon and said I almost caused her a heart attack on her drive home. She blasted me for the way I organized my wedding and whom I did invite and whom I did not invite. We did not speak for a couple of years after that fiasco.

*   *   *

Before I married Gary, I took a higher-paying position as an accounts receivable clerk at Reandex Home International and stayed there for over two years. Meanwhile, I became addicted to school. After successfully passing my office administration certificate program, I went to a real college and studied Human Resource Management and then changed my focus to Criminology. I was fascinated with the criminal mind and supposed that had a lot to do with my own father being a habitual criminal. Unfortunately, my last credits were to be held as an internship at Willington Youth Detention Center, where things did not fare well for me.

I did not mind the young residents and enjoyed taking them to their court hearings and on big-boy prison tours. However, I knew as a career, I could not work with the guards! I would guess many of these men went into the job to enjoy power over others—for what I witnessed as far as the treatment of the residents was no less than disgusting! Boys as young as twelve were being physically and verbally abused on a regular basis by the guards. I often wondered how these kids were going to come out of detention after all of the abuses and injustices they received by the adults put in their charge. I feared for them. I feared for all of us.

I completed the Criminology program nonetheless, and I joined a lay counseling workshop that lasted some two years, six months of theory and two years of counseling within the community. This gave me the experience I needed to be placed in a helping role for a career.

I was lucky. I obtained a six-month assignment with a business school. The school had a contract with the government in an effort to put forty women back in the workplace with both office administrative skills and professional and personal development (PPD). My job was to teach the PPD portion, and I was a very happy instructor, working with women to help them integrate back in the workforce, much like myself just a few years before.

I later accepted a Job Club Instructor position with one of the largest government-sponsored career centers in Vancouver. I must have done something right because within three months, I was promoted to Program Manager of the downtown Vancouver branch. Now I was gaining experience hiring instructors and support staff, as well as training new instructors on the program curriculum, which I tailored to suit people on income assistance.

I continued to go to school in the evenings and on weekends. I returned to my Human Resource Management studies at the British Columbia Institute of Technology. This is one of the most recognized schools in British Columbia, and my husband had graduated from the Electronics and Technology program in 1982, the same year I met him. I didn't have to complete the program before I was hired at one of the largest five-star hotels in Vancouver. My job was Employment Manager, and looking back, I would have to say this was one of my most satisfying career roles.

*   *   *

During my entire career, I involved myself in many business and political organizations. I look back today and regret not being home more often for my son and husband. I was very fortunate to have a supportive husband, who took over many of the parenting responsibilities for Trevor. Gary was Trevor's soccer coach, Beavers, Cubs and Boy Scouts leader, baseball coach, and more.

Trevor was tested and found to be gifted in his intelligence level. However, he was always a year or two behind in emotional intelligence. I blame myself for this since I indulged him with not only my love but things as well. Trevor had every gadget a child could wish for. Gary was in the information technology field and taught my son advanced computer maintenance and operations. In the late 1980s, Trevor was already a bulletin operator, a form of early e-mail, and had a nice system set up at home. He was one of the only kids who had his own computer, and many primary teachers at his elementary school who had no idea how this new technology worked asked for Trevor to show the younger children the fundamentals of computers.

Socially, however, Trevor failed miserably. He could not get along with most of his teachers or other kids at school. I often wonder if this wasn't because he was an only child and had surpassed educational expectations to the point of appearing arrogant. Yes, he was cheeky. One time, the school principal called and said he was teaching Trevor's class that day and all Trevor wanted to do was read while the lecture was going on. This infuriated the principal to no end, but he had to admit that when he called upon Trevor to answer a question about the lecture, Trevor looked up from his book and gave the correct answer. Yes, I can see how the teachers would be annoyed with a boy like Trevor.

This negative attention was a constant in Trevor's educational history. It did not help him make friends, at least the right friends. Gary and I were constantly at the school, fighting for our son. A strange thing about Trevor: he never learned how to handwrite. He would always print his assignments. In grade 5, he came home with work to be redone over and over again. This time to the teacher's liking.

I saw my son become increasingly frustrated and was worried that such a small thing was ruining his grade 5 experience. I decided to pay the teacher a visit and told her I wanted no more handwriting for Trevor. He was smart. He could pass a test with flying colors on any subject. But for the handwriting and bad attitude, he should have been skipping grades. Trevor was typing at a very high speed by now, and he was much more comfortable with keyboarding than writing. If he was asked to handwrite a story, we might see one small paragraph. Tell him to type it, and we saw a four-page essay!

I really didn't like the school system myself, having had a very hard time of it in my own experience. I knew that not every child fits into the rigid mold public schools set. I didn't do Trevor any favors by constantly sticking up for him, however. What Trevor was witnessing was my bailing him out, and as a result, he began to seriously oppose authority (at home, we had very few problems). I set my son up for trouble in the years to come.

Trevor's advanced reading was a problem for me. I once found books by Stephen King and other horror story writers and felt Trevor was not emotionally strong enough to read these violent books. I went out and purchased several "self-help" books by Og Mandino, who wrote life skill lessons in the form of stories. Trevor loved these stories, but there were not enough books for him to read since he usually read one to two books a week. For the sake of my son's emotional well-being, I also purchased positive thinking, subliminal messaging, and self-help tapes by Doctor Wayne Dyer for Trevor to fall asleep to. I was trying my best to offset his bad experiences at school by filling his head with the positive messages I wanted his mind to be filled with.

*   *   *

The on-again, off-again dance I had with my mother continued. She was drinking very heavily at this stage and would call late into the evening, slurring her words and spewing her resentments to me. I have to admit my counselor's training gave me a good ear, and people often appreciated my ability to just listen. Sometimes, however, I would blow up in a raging fury at Mother—usually by mail (and by e-mail when that became a popular form of communication). I asked my mother once why she would call me when she was drunk—I was the daughter, and it was hard on me to listen to her drone on and on about her personal issues in her slurry voice. Her reply was to say that alcohol was her tranquilizer and she needed it since her life was so horrible because of my Father. I cannot articulate how hostile Mother's tone was—constantly. It was worse than listening to nails on a chalkboard to me.

In spite of my educational and career accomplishments, I never did gain the love and support of my mother. In fact, it seemed the harder I tried to be a success, the more she resented me. What mother does this? What mother is jealous of her own child? I could never imagine not wanting the most and best for my son. I knew my mother was very sick, and there was nothing that was going to change her ways. To try was to risk her wrath, which I was still very, very afraid of. None of her children were close to her once they moved away. She called us all ungrateful brats many times. I was still the worst child she had, so she said, but this did not mess with the fact that I would be her listening ear when she needed it. I couldn't figure her out, and I didn't bother trying to guess until much later.

*   *   *

Having my own child to love and raise the way I thought a child should be raised was my biggest success, looking back. I will never understand parents who use their children as pawns or slaves or who deliberately fill their little heads with negative images of their other parent. I am not saying I was a perfect parent. I did the best I could with what little information and income I had. But I tried. And when I knew I was slipping up, I reached out for help for the sake of my child. The results were to have raised a baby to a man who both loved and respected his own mother, me! Trevor was truly a gift sent from the heavens to me. Trevor taught me what love really was.

*   *   *

Little did I know that years down the road, my gift would be returned to God, and once again, I would be left alone in this world without the true love I had grown accustomed to.

Chapter 5—Sociopathy Inherited

The consequences of your denial will be with you for a lifetime—and will be passed down to the next generations. Break your silence on abuse!

—Author unknown

Shivey came to live with Gary, Trevor, and I when she was about seventeen years old, soon after my wedding. She was having problems with our MN mother (so it wasn't just me!). Right away, we had problems with Shivey, who was refusing to finish high school, yet demanding a job with a salary higher than $25,000 in 1986, which was an outrageous wage for a young person with no skills! She eventually met her soon-to-be husband, *Darren, who was several years her senior but just as immature. I never did like Darren. In fact you could say I was afraid of him—he was so angry all of the time, a lot like my MN mother.

Shivey got pregnant almost immediately and moved out to live with Darren and his friends. When I visited, I was afraid for my sister since many people in their apartment building smoked pot—even when pregnant. My sister insisted she was not smoking but her best friends were. I didn't believe her at all and worried about my soon-to-come first nephew's well-being.

Shivey and Darren married when she was about five months along in her pregnancy. Within weeks, however, trouble was brewing. Darren was spending his evenings drinking with his buddies while my sister was stuck without a car in a remote area. After their child, Darren Jr., was born, things just got worse. I had to bring food and diapers to my sister; meanwhile, I tried very hard to get her to leave this man who was clearly not ready for parenting.

Eventually, she allowed me to sign an apartment lease for her and Darren Jr., and she was on her own. I gave her some furniture, and we picked up a few other items at thrift shops. Darren Sr. rarely visited, and my sister was essentially doing the single parenthood alone, not unlike myself several years before. She went on welfare and made a few friends in the apartment complex she lived in. She appeared very unhappy.

*   *   *

On May 9, 1986, a Saturday morning, I was on my way to a weekend job as a respite worker for a foster family when the phone rang. It was my sister telling me that Darren Jr. was dead! I couldn't get any details out of her at that time other than that he died in his sleep. I dropped the phone in grief and almost vomited.

I telephoned Gus and asked him to check up on Shivey. I had to go to my job. (At this point, I was too concerned for my employers, and instead of just driving out to comfort my sister, I went to work!) Gus called me later and said he, Shivey, and Darren were at the bar and Mother and Dave were on their way from Vernon. By the time I got off work, it was nearing 6:00 p.m. and Gary, Trevor, and I went to Gus's basement suite to see the family. Everyone was there. The first thing my sister said to me was to stop crying or I would make her cry! I couldn't help it. The day was a flood of tears and sobbing for me at the loss of such a beautiful baby boy. To see my sister sweetly smiling and telling me not to cry was disturbing to me.

I helped my sister and her husband make funeral arrangements in a fog, and on the day of the funeral, my heart broke for my sister and baby nephew. Against the funeral director's orders, she picked baby Darren up and held him. He was a shell of a child, and I knew when I saw him that his soul had already transcended to the heavens.

*   *   *

Apparently, Darren Sr. came over the night of baby Darren's death, and they hired a babysitter and went out drinking. Darren Jr. was just four months old, and he had a slight illness, which is still unknown to me. Shivey told me that when she and Darren Sr. came back to her apartment (he was going to stay the night), they put the crib mattress in a tiny storage area away from the bedroom.

At 8:00 a.m. the next morning, Shivey told me that they were curious as to why the baby was not crying for his breakfast. Darren Sr. went into the storage area and pulled on the baby's legs toward him (the room was very narrow). Darren said that he picked the baby up and instantly knew he was dead and dropped him to the floor! An autopsy was performed, and the coroner listed the death a sudden infant death syndrome (SIDS) case.

What really angered me about my sister at this time was that the night of the funeral, Shivey insisted on going out to dance with Darren and his friends. She didn't hold a wake as most people do. She wanted nothing to do with the family she wanted to go dancing with her friends! My sister went dancing the night of her child's funeral! What mother does this? I learned the hard way many years later that this is an extremely odd behavior of a mother who just lost her child. Yes we all grieve differently. This wasn't just different. This was bizarre to me.

* * *

For about a year, two of our male cousins on my P Father's side were staying at Gus and *Sandy's house with their two beautiful daughters, aged three and under one year (I believe). The fear for me was that the older cousin, *Kevin, was earlier convicted of sexually molesting his stepdaughter; and the younger cousin, *Richard, had raped his nine-year-old sister when he was fifteen years old! I couldn't stand that my brother had such poor judgment as to allow these men to live in the same house as their baby girls! However, I had to trust that my brother and his wife would protect their daughters.

With the exception of my youngest brother, Dylan, all of us had children. We often compared notes when talking about our MN mother, about her strange dramatic behaviors and hypercritical nature. We spent a lot of time visiting each other's homes to exchange dinner parties. Trevor was the oldest cousin, and he was proud in his role as babysitter while we played card games.

One evening, Shivey, Sandy (my sister-in-law), and I were sitting around the table at Shivey's apartment when Sandy told us a story that bowled us all over. Sandy's affect or demeanor made me believe her story was going to be quite funny. Sandy said that the second cousin, Richard, had dropped over a few days ago and their eldest daughter, *Cathy, ran into her bedroom and brought out a nude Barbie doll and handed it to Richard and said, "You can sleep with this baby okay?"

Stunned silence.

Shivey and I looked at each other, and I knew we were both thinking the same thing. Later on, in a telephone conversation, Shivey told me that when changing Cathy's diapers when she was babysitting the year before, she saw rawness or sores of some sort around Cathy's vagina! That was enough for me. First, I telephoned Sandy and asked her if she didn't think it was strange for a child to bring out a nude doll and offer it to a known rapist to sleep with. Sandy became furious with me for suggesting such a thing. Of course, all of the tapes my mother planted in my head (and everyone else's) rushed through me—what if I was wrong? What if I am just causing trouble?

But the story wouldn't leave me. After several discussions with my sister, Shivey, who had more access to Gus's kids as a babysitter, I became convinced I must call the Ministry of Social Services to at least ask their opinion on the story. I was afraid of "causing trouble," so I did not give out any names other than a slip about Cathy's first name and age, her being premature, and born at Grace Hospital. That was all the ministry needed to find Gus and Sandy and their girls! I did not give the address or phone number of my brother or his wife; I was afraid I was wrong and I would lose my siblings forever and be called a liar.

A social worker found and visited Gus and Sandy's house and interviewed both of them and Cathy, who was barely four at that time. Gus called me later and said whoever called on the welfare people would pay dearly for it (which is kind of weird since neither he nor Sandy were ever the source of the sexual abuse accusation/inquiry). Gus also called Shivey. This is the sister who danced on her son's funeral day; the sister who also fed me the whole sore vagina stories about our niece, Cathy; and the sister who encouraged me to call the ministry. In any event, in one sentence, my half sister ruined my relationship with Gus and my two precious nieces for over ten years! When Gus telephoned Shivey to tell her that the welfare had investigated a sexual abuse allegation against cousin Richard regarding his daughter Cathy, Shivey said, "Oh my god! It must have been Cherylann . . . She was talking about phoning the welfare!"

One of those things that make you go "hmmmm." Is my younger sister a malignant narcissist herself? She caused so much trouble between my brother and I we never really recovered our relationship.

*   *   *

Once again, I'm the bad guy, and in one fell swoop, I lost all of the family, including Shivey, after I confronted her about telling Gus I called the ministry.

I was the family scapegoat once more. I still believe to this day that my niece was molested by one or both of these cousins. Kill me for saying it out loud if you must.

*   *   *

My young son, Trevor, was the one who endured the most pain over the family's typical silent treatment punishments toward me. He loved his little cousins and didn't understand why our weekends or Thanksgiving and Christmas holidays with family was suddenly stopped. It broke my heart to see my son suffer, and I could never understand how my siblings could not miss Trevor as much as I missed my baby nieces and nephews. I'm too sensitive, they say.

*   *   *

Gary and I tried to have our own children, but we learned I suffered from endometriosis, a disease causing infertility. The doctor said I was lucky I had Trevor at a young age because this disease is a progressive one that can only be fixed by microsurgery, and even then, there was only a slim chance I could bring a child to term. I had several of these microsurgeries to open my tubes to allow a pregnancy.

Twice I became pregnant, and Gary and I allowed ourselves to become excited. Unfortunately, both pregnancies were ectopic (caught in the tube) and had to be aborted. The second surgery to remove our baby from my tubes was a disaster even though we had the best of the best doctors according to everyone else.

I was in a lot of pain even four weeks after the surgery, but my younger brother on my dad's side (Gilbert) was getting married. He lived in Cranbrook, some ten to twelve hours away, and we were planning to drive. I called the fertility specialist and told him my pain continued and if I should come in for a checkup before going on this trip. The specialist at Shaughnessy Hospital pooh-poohed my pain and said I had nothing to worry about. Wrong.

The day after my brother's wedding, I was squirming around on the bathroom floor in severe pain. Gary was getting upset with me. (Marriage to Gary was not a bed of roses as he had some narcissist traits in him, meaning he was low on the "feelings for others" scale.) I knew there was no way I could make the trip back home without seeing a doctor. I insisted we stop at Cranbrook General Hospital, and after one look at me the nurses put me in a bed to await an ultrasound technician. I was found to be bleeding internally; even my lungs had blood pools, the doctor said! I was flown back to Vancouver by air ambulance. Gary and Trevor made the drive.

Apparently, the doctor had left a portion of my fetus in the tube, and it continued to grow until it exploded within me, risking my life by a thread. If I were the suing kind, I'd be a wealthy woman today. I was beginning to have a problem trusting doctors at this point and never went back for more microsurgeries to attempt to have a baby. Now that the decision was made, Gary and I were happy to just be the parents of one son, Trevor.

* * *

Shivey was on and off with me. I never saw her directly hurt anyone, but I recognized her as a relationship destroyer, such as my MN mother was. She spoke evil of a lot of people, and I knew if she was talking trash about them, she'd be talking trash about me. However, I took any speck of family I could, and as long as she never hurt my son, I welcomed her into my life whenever she wanted in. One summer, she took Trevor with her and her children to Vernon to visit mother and some of her childhood friends (my sister's senior years were spent in Vernon when Mother and Dave moved there).

The story according to my sister was that while at Mother's apartment, Trevor was leaning on the back of her sofa. Suddenly and without warning, our MN mother went into a shocking rage directed at my eleven-year-old son! When I asked my sister what sparked the explosion, she said Mother was saying things to him like *"Stay the hell off my sofa! You have no respect for other people's things. I'm not rich like your parents!"* First of all, Gary and I were not rich. We were working-class people who happened to have decent careers and own a house (with a full mortgage) and two cars. You could not get inside of my malignant narcissist mother's head to imagine what she was thinking. However, I see now after researching the patterns of malignant narcissists that they are extremely jealous people. A psychopath has the same nasty trait.

Beat the shit out of me with your verbal abuse, but by God, you start abusing my son and I would have shaken the shit out of that woman had I been witness to this outburst on my son. My sister, thankfully, took my son out of the apartment, and it was the last time he saw my mother with the exception of the odd Christmas dinner with me standing big beside my son to protect his emotional well-being. Mother was no closer to her grandchildren than she ever was with her own children. She wasn't a "kid" person.

* * *

I really enjoyed our family visits with my sister's family when Shivey was speaking to me. It was always fun to share in making roast beef or turkey dinners and play cards later. On many of these occasions, I had too much to drink. I seemed to drink more when I was around family than at other times. One night, I drank so much you could say I was "falling down drunk."

Little did I know at this time that my sister was videotaping me. I asked her why the next day, and she said she thought it was funny. I didn't. First, I don't like to be drunk and out of control, and second, I was worried that the video would get into the wrong hands, namely, my son Trevor. Whenever we held a party, I always made sure he was in bed; and I made sure all of the beer and wine bottle mess was cleaned up before he got up. I did not want him to know his mother in a bad condition; I wanted to be a good example, even though sometimes I wasn't.

My intuition was right to be concerned about Shivey keeping that videotape. Trevor was twelve years old when he visited my sister's family for the weekend a few months later. Trevor was shocked when his aunt showed him the tape that she made of me in a horribly drunken state! He asked me about it the minute he came in the door, and I was furious with my sister for showing a young impressionable child this tape! This is yet another example of malignant narcissism—inappropriate communication with a child. She was trying to ruin my relationship with my own child! If she wasn't "trying," she sure as hell was reckless about it. I knew the signs all too well. I just didn't know what this weird behavior was called at that time.

*   *   *

When Trevor was thirteen years old, I came home from work early. Usually Gary and I made the return trip into Vancouver together to our respective jobs, but this day I was not feeling well and took the transit home. As I lay on my bed, the house was very quiet. Just as I was about to fall asleep, my eyes popped open to the voice of a very strong male in my inner ear. The voice said, "Trevor is in trouble." I jumped up and looked around. There was no one there! I searched the house and found no one. That voice was a man's voice, so not my own, and I was disturbed by this mysticism to say the least.

I didn't make that much of a deal about it, but I did ask my son if everything was all right, and he assured me it was. I mean, everything seemed okay, so the only thing I could do was to file that voice's message to retrieve later if needed.

Trevor's problems in school were reaching new heights, however. In grade 8, he graduated to junior secondary level, where he now had eight teachers and classes to deal with. The school was insistent that Trevor go on a medication for ADHD (attention-deficit hyperactivity disorder). We had tried this route way back in grade 2, and I couldn't stand what the medication did to my son's personality. I also heard that kids put on Ritalin often turned to street drugs as teenagers. On Ritalin, it was like the light left his beautiful bright eyes, and he became like a zombie to me. So when the junior high school social worker insisted Trevor would need medication now (we were told this before he even started school that year—before they could even assess him at the new school!), we took him to see a psychiatrist for their opinion. The psychiatrist put Trevor on a mild antidepressant that she said tended to help ADHD children.

One day, we got a call from the school to pick Trevor up. He was expelled! Gary and I rushed to the school to find out what went so wrong. Apparently, he was in the social disability class and acting up, so the social worker put him in an empty room, except a desk and a chair. There was nothing on the walls, no stimuli but for a small window on the door. It was a jail. After a couple of hours of this seclusion cruelty, Trevor's anger boiled over. He picked up the chair and threw it at the window, which broke, and he was expelled from school for this behavior!

First of all, if a child really has ADHD, you must have *stimuli*! They lack it in regular school settings as it is, let alone when completely isolated. The lack of common sense on the part of school systems baffles me to this day, and our children suffer for its stupidity.

We took Trevor completely out of the school, and I spent many days lying on my bed, crying for my son, who had so many difficulties in large groups and with authority. I prayed. I got angry. I phoned the newspapers to report the school for putting my child in a jail-like setting for hours. A reporter and his cameraman came to our house for an interview, and we obtained a two-page spread about the school abuse the next Sunday edition of the *Vancouver Province*.

My prayers about what we were going to do with our thirteen-year-old child were answered when a woman who had seen the newspaper article called me to say there was a special school designed especially for ADD and ADHD children, and it was only about a ten-minute drive from our home. Unfortunately, the school was expensive and we had only a small amount of money to offer. The school was somewhat lenient with us and allowed Trevor to enroll at $600 per month instead of the usual $1,000 per month.

The formula for dealing with gifted ADHD children was simple. Once the child has mastered an educational requirement, stop forcing them to repeat the work over and over again, causing boredom and subsequent class disruption. For example, in math within the public school system, they would have hundreds of questions covering the same thing, such as long division. At the new private school, they would give Trevor five questions, and if he mastered these, he was considered complete at long division or whatever other subject they were to study. Trevor excelled at Glen Eden Private School, and we finally had three years of peace without a school constantly telling us to fix from home whatever the problem was at school.

* * *

Life returned to normal at our house; we ate dinners and Sunday breakfasts together and played board games on Sunday nights with Trevor. Gary took Trevor on camping vacations, and we went to Disneyland twice—Trevor's happiest place on earth! Trevor made some friends, and he was settling in very well to his new school.

By the time Trevor was old enough to work, at aged fifteen, I was the Employment Manager at a large hotel in Vancouver. I hired Trevor as a dishwasher and banquets employee. Trevor was making more money than he could keep up with, a mistake we would all pay for dearly in later years.

* * *

Gary and I decided to have a house built for ourselves in Abbotsford, British Columbia, which is some eighty kilometers from Ladner, where we lived for most of Trevor's life. The move meant I would have to quit my favored job, but Trevor purchased himself a car and wanted to continue to work at the hotel after school and on weekends. The move, more importantly, meant Trevor could no longer attend the private school that was doing so well for him, and he would have to return to public school.

We were not worried, however. How many parents can boost a gifted child who wanted to work? Maybe he had matured enough to go to senior school! Besides, I was going to work from home as a Recruitment Consultant and would be more available to Trevor should he need my guidance. It turned out we were wrong. Putting Trevor back into the public school system turned him and our family upside down, and the long-term consequences were about to present themselves.

*　　*　　*

Negative upbringings have a way of catching up with you no matter what your age. Some call this phenomenon Post Traumatic Stress Disorder. My coping skills were mostly fine during the first sixteen years of Trevor's life, but my own background and continued narcissist family verbal and silent treatment abuse toward me would soon cause my life to take a downward spiral I wouldn't wish on my worst enemy.

Chapter 6—You Think Being Grounded Is Bad? Try Prison

A child seldom needs a good talking to as a good listening to.

—*Robert Brault*

Trevor was my sweet boy who always showed the deepest respect for me. We had a bond nobody could break since the day he was born. Drugs were a different breed altogether. When Trevor began his grade 11 classes, he was working and had too much money on his hands to manage. He met people who had access to drugs and thus came the crash of Trevor's and the rest of our families' happy life.

We saw the signs almost immediately. Suddenly Trevor lost all interest in his beloved computer and spent most of his time skipping classes. When Gary and I put our foot down and made him give up his job, anger and resentment set in. Within a few weeks, Trevor sold his computer! Now I knew something terrible was going on in my son's life, but I felt powerless to stop the dive downward.

* * *

As my recruitment business was starting, I took on a six-month assignment teaching twenty unemployable women life skills. One day, I was looking at my intake sheet on the group who would be potential students of mine. One name popped out at me, Debbie McAllister! Debbie was the twelve-year-old girl on the street who introduced me to Randolph, or Randy, whatever his name, and the disgusting things we allowed him to do to our virgin bodies.

When Debbie met with me for an intake session, I barely recognized her. Her face was full of acne potholes, and she looked worn out and beaten. I took her to my office and reintroduced myself to her. Shock came to her face as she stared at me. I had not been involved in drugs since the early 1970s, and the difference in our physical dispositions was glaring.

I had one question for her: I knew why I allowed that man to take advantage of me, but what on earth would possess her to allow this man to molest her? She told me since she was eight years old that her older brothers routinely molested and raped her. She said by the time she was twelve, she couldn't care less about her body or self-esteem. I recognized the feeling. After talking for a few minutes, it was clear she wasn't a good candidate for my program; she would have to get clean first. I told her as soon as she recovered to come see me and I would help her find a career she would be happy with. I never heard from her again.

Meanwhile, Trevor moved out of home and flopped on various friends' sofas. I was beside myself with worry. Trevor continued to phone me, and I made sure I did not express hostility as my own mother did to me so many years before. I wanted him to keep in touch with me, as much as it hurt to know he was suffering on the streets.

* * *

One day, I received a phone call from a stepfather of a young girl who said they were inviting Trevor to move in with them. He had been dating their fourteen-year-old daughter, who was out of control, punching walls and exhibiting complete oppositional defiance to rules and regulations of the household. Trevor was eighteen at this time, and I was worried sick that this girl would not be good for him. *Hank, the stepfather, told me that Trevor had a certain way of calming *Angelina down, and they thought it would be a good idea for Trevor to move into the household so they could get a much-needed rest from Angelina's outbursts.

My heart sunk. I knew they were wrong, that the only thing that would come of this union was more bad news for my son—and very likely a baby. Trevor, I knew, was not prepared for fatherhood, and surely to God, a fourteen-year-old girl who had psychiatric issues would not be!

I visited Angelina's home often to visit Trevor and was soon told that Angelina was pregnant. Around this same time, Trevor and Angelina were caught shoplifting in a grocery store. They were hungry and stole chocolate milk and steak. For some reason, Angelina was never charged, but Trevor was. He had previously stolen a radio from a car and was charged and convicted to community service. With my criminology background and remembering people who steal or conduct some other crime usually have done so many times before getting caught. I doubted this was the first time Trevor had stolen. The money Trevor gained from stealing all went to drugs for himself and Angelina.

Trevor received a harsh sentence for stealing the milk and the steak. He was remanded for four months, where we would have to visit him behind glass walls. Meanwhile, I brought Angelina with me to many of our visits. This gave me the opportunity to try to talk her into other pregnancy options, such as abortion or adoption. I told her the risks of birth defects due to her drug intake, and the enormous responsibly having a child would bring to her and Trevor. I talked about my own difficulties and said if I had to do it all over again, I would wait until I was in a secure relationship and no drugs.

All of my talking was to no avail. Trevor came out of jail, and they gave birth to a beautiful baby boy they named *Tyler. I received many calls from Angelina's mother, who was at her wits end with the three of them. She was doing most of the parenting, and Trevor and Angelina were still engaged in drug use.

Soon the Ministry of Social Services got involved and told the kids they would have to take parenting lessons or risk losing their son. Trevor and Angelina thought her mother, *Cindy, was the culprit in phoning the ministry. (They were wrong, it was Angelina's grandmother who called. She never liked Trevor, and every time they were in the same room, fireworks sparked.)

Trevor thought love was enough to raise a baby. It is not, of course. A child needs food, good sleeps, clean diapers, structure, and loving care. Angelina and Trevor decided to move out of Sandy's house and rented an apartment. Meanwhile, I had a friend who was the comptroller of a very large processing plant, and she agreed to hire Trevor at a good wage. Unfortunately, fights began to break out between Angelina and Trevor, and he was concerned Angelina would do Tyler harm if he left them alone. Trevor rarely showed up to work, even though I offered to pick him up and drive him. At that time, I didn't understand why Trevor would give up a good job that would feed and house the family while Angelina stayed at home with Tyler. I was baffled because I knew Trevor was a good worker from his days at the hotel.

I found out years later that Trevor was afraid Angelina would hurt the baby in some way. She had been threatening to kill Tyler if Trevor left her. One day, she attacked Trevor, and he called me saying she poked his eye out—it was bleeding! I rushed to their apartment and saw Angelina in action—she was completely out of control and certainly not capable of being a mother to Tyler.

I worked with the social workers, but for some reason, they saw Trevor as more of the problem than the mother of the child! I later learned they were getting all of their information from Angelina's grandmother, *Marie. Tyler went into the care of Angelina's grandmother, the grandmother who hated Trevor! Trevor had supervised visits, and I was the supervisor. One day, when I went to pick Tyler up to take to Trevor's new apartment, she was particularly mean to me.

As she was dressing eighteen-month-old Tyler, she told him he was going to see his uncle, Mark! I asked her why she would say that to Tyler, and she replied that if Tyler knew he was going to see Trevor, he would cry! I knew that Trevor and Tyler had a loving relationship and Trevor would never deliberately hurt Tyler or take drugs while with him. I also knew Tyler would not cry at the sight of his father; they were very close.

I took Tyler to visit Trevor, who had a new girlfriend, *Sylvia. She was also eighteen, sweet and much more mature than Angelina. She loved Tyler, and together Trevor and his new partner asked me if they could take Tyler on a walk in his stroller. I had to think about this, as it would have been against the ministry rules of supervision. However, knowing the calmness of the two of them and their obvious clear heads, I let them go, telling Trevor to be back in one hour.

When the kids returned, they had bad news. Angelina saw the two of them walking out of the A&W fast-food restaurant and started a fight. Sylvia and Trevor hightailed it home to avoid a confrontation, but I knew the damage was done. Angelina would tell her grandmother of this new reunion, and the fact that the two of them were out alone with Tyler when they were supposed to be supervised by me would ruin my supervision arrangement. I would no longer be trusted!

That Monday, I got a call from a ministry social worker, Kim (I think this was her real name), who was as cold as ice on the telephone with me. She would not listen to my story and simply stated I was no longer able to supervise Trevor with Tyler, and not only that, I could not see Tyler until a court said I could! My heart burst as I tried to reason with this woman, but she would hear none of it. She also said that Angelina's grandmother had another complaint—that Gary and I did not feed Tyler on this visit, did not change his diaper, and left him a filthy mess! All of this was completely untrue and just showed me how far this great-grandmother of Tyler's would go to keep Tyler away from us.

It is true that we did not use the jar of newborn-level mashed peas (Tyler was way too old for this food at eighteen months old!) or diapers that Maria had packed for Tyler. We had our own diaper bag complete with everything Tyler would need. Tyler ate both fries from A&W, with Trevor and his girlfriend, and after Trevor's visit, my husband and I took Tyler to Boston Pizza, where he ate rib bones and macaroni and cheese like there was no tomorrow. He was perfectly content to eat safe big-people food and had a blast at the same time. Not only that, just before we left the restaurant, I completely changed Tyler into fresh diapers and outfit. He went back to Maria's spotless and full.

The social worker either did not believe me or preferred to not listen to reason. She essentially called me a liar and told me if I wanted to see Tyler again, to get a lawyer. My background of being called a liar came flooding back to me. Bad thoughts were entering my head, thoughts of wanting to run, run out of this world.

Not only that, Trevor had done nothing wrong while taking his child out for a short walk, and I felt utterly helpless to help him. I could see Trevor's frustration levels rising, and I knew he did not take well to having authority tell him he was a bad father and needed to be supervised. Meanwhile, Angelina, the girl who threatened to kill Tyler, the girl who beat on my son's face and eyes, was able to see Tyler without difficulty. She had her grandmother on her side and that was good enough for the social worker.

*   *   *

Trevor fell back on his drug intake with a vengeance. He was now taking crack cocaine and ecstasy in addition to pot. He once again turned to stealing to get the money he needed to support his habit. Try as Gary and I did to turn our son around, it was an impossible feat. Once drugs become a crutch emotions, mostly anger, seep out and ruin the druggies' relationships very quickly. That nice girl he was seeing left him, and most of his friends were dealers or drug takers themselves. Trevor could not hold down a job at all by this point, and money had to come from somewhere.

I received a call one day from Trevor, saying he had just been convicted of stealing from Sears Department Store. He and Angelina were together and putting things in Tyler's stroller. Once again, it was not Angelina getting punished, but Trevor was tried and convicted and sent to a camp in Chilliwack, British Columbia, blocks from where Angelina lived with her mother and siblings. Tyler was still living under the full-time guardianship of Maria, the great-grandmother.

I made the thirty-kilometer drive to the camp to visit Trevor and went through humiliating searches by dogs and guards. Once Trevor and I were seated outside on a picnic table, Trevor told me something that tore my heart out. In the camp as a prisoner was no other than my own Father, Trevor's grandfather! My psychopath father was getting on in his years and, after a failed bank robbery attempt, was sent to this camp with little bars or guards, usually reserved for men without escape histories. I didn't want Trevor anywhere near my Father, as I knew some of the things my dad would say to him would only make Trevor a more advanced criminal than he had already become. He would talk inappropriate talk to Trevor, giving him bad advice that could only make Trevor worse in his anger toward authority.

I searched out my Father, and he was shocked to see me there to visit him. I told my Dad that I was trying to help Trevor become free of drugs so that he could live a normal life. One thing my father never did get into was street drugs. He was hooked on Tylenol 3s and Xanax, but he stayed away from pot, crack, or meth. I asked my dad to talk to Trevor about drugs and the damage they could do to him and his family. I don't know if he ever did or not.

At that time of my father and son in the same prison camp, I was losing control at home and with my business. My emotions were way out of whack, and I wanted to die. I thought my life would never have peace in it, and my shame was like a knife slowly tearing my body in half. Of course, knowing how my Mother felt about me and Trevor, both of us having these "evil eyes" just like Ivan would now make her right; with the exception of me, I never did have a problem with the law and was, by all accounts, a law-abiding citizen and loving parent. That didn't matter in my mind. Trevor's failures were my failures, and nothing could remove these misguided feelings.

I felt like a piece of meat between two slices of bread; I was being consumed with a criminal family, and my worst nightmare of Trevor becoming like my habitual criminal Father was too much. My feelings were exaggerated, and I overreacted to anything and everything by this time. I wanted out. I wanted to die. I remember writing a letter to Joey Thompson, a columnist with the *Vancouver Province* newspaper. In my letter, I said I felt like leaving this world without opening the garage door. Interestingly, Joey wrote my letter in its entirety and added a cartoon figure of a woman with a drink of wine in her hand. Joey did not know this at that time but her cartoon figure looked exactly like me!

I received a call from my sister, who lived only a few blocks from me. We were on better terms at this stage (she seemed to enjoy it when I was in trouble with my family). Shivey said that Mother phoned her after seeing the article and said she knew it was me who wrote it! All of my family knew my style of writing, and Mother recognized me immediately. Instead of phoning me to ask about my suicide hint—about not opening the garage door when I left—she called Shivey, and they both had a wonderful bitch session about what a lost cause I was.

Did my MN mother call *me* in concern? Of course not. A Malignant narcissist is cold and empty when it comes to providing love and care toward their own children. It broke my heart that I was caught with such a negative and scary letter for the world and my family to see. Shame on me again.

*　　*　　*

Dealing with the law courts, the ministry of social services, Trevor and P Father in jail, and a business that seemed to grow in leaps in bounds in spite of all of my personal issues, things became too much for me. My first course of action was to run away. Gary and I were fighting constantly, and one weekend, I was supposed to go on a business trip with him to Penticton. I decided I was going to run away that weekend instead. I arranged for my staff to take over for the ten days I planned to be away.

Years earlier, my Father gave me a *National Geographic* magazine that had an antique map of West Virginia (so I thought; it turned out to be an old map of Virginia before the state split into two separate states). The significance of this map was there was a very small town called Groseclose on it! Groseclose was my maiden name before my father gave up his rights to me and my mother changed my name to Craig, my molester stepfather's name. The newer maps did not show Groseclose, so I would have to find the town without a current map.

When I landed in West Virginia after a long train ride, I rented a car and stopped in a restaurant to ask some questions about my map and the whereabouts of a small town called Groseclose. I asked two postman patrons if they would take a look at the map and help me determine where this namesake Groseclose town was. They both thought the map looked pre-civil war and it must be in Virginia, as they had never heard of a town called Groseclose in West Virginia.

I got back into my rental car and had the most wonderful drive I had ever experienced! Rolling hills backed with old Southern mansions were in abundance. I felt like I was at home! I kept driving south to find Groseclose, Virginia. I was on one particular lonely road when I saw a large barn with music from a band filtering out. I decided to stop and ask the band members if they had ever heard of Groseclose. I don't know who this band was, but they were rich. The barn was better-looking than any house I had ever lived in, and the band members were dressed in leathers and metal far beyond a garage band starting out.

Two of the band players looked carefully at my ancient map. They seemed genuinely interested in my search, and both thought Groseclose would be farther south, perhaps along Highway 81. They gave me one piece of advice in their Southern accents before I left in, "Sweetie, if you are going to drive around, you need to put some clothes on back here in the South!" I looked down at myself and saw I was wearing a pair of shorts with a tank top. I got back into the car and kept driving. I decided to sleep in the car that night, and as luck would have it, I found a twenty-four-hour Wal-Mart, where I could purchase some real "Virginia-style" clothes. I bought a long cotton dress and floppy hat, as well as a pillow and blanket to sleep comfortably in the car with.

When I woke up in the early morning hours, I was amazed at the beautiful sights around me. Creeks and trees along with those stunning mansions mesmerized me. I put some lipstick on and started the car. Within a couple of hours, I found myself on Highway 81. I passed a town called Marion and kept going. Within a few minutes, I saw a sight for my sore eyes! A sign saying Groseclose 5 Miles! I found my namesake town!

I pulled into the one gas station and brought my map into the store. The young clerk really didn't seem too interested in my good find, but he pointed me out to a couple of historians in the area. This town was no bigger than a gas station, teahouse, and some very old homes and buildings. I went into a store that looked like a part-thrift and part-antique store. An old man came down the rickety stairs, and I told him my story, about how I was a Groseclose by birth on my Dad's side and I came all the way from Vancouver, British Columbia, to find this tiny town. The old man was very helpful and even gave me the names of some Grosecloses's who were still living there. He said the town was named after the first Groseclose, back in 1750, named Peter. He told me I'd find a whole bunch of Grosecloses's at the local cemetery, which thrilled me to pieces.

I had done so much driving by this time I knew my time was running out. The train was leaving West Virginia the very next day, and that left just over a day of exploring.

I made sure I saw the old schoolhouse, the churches, and the cemetery that was filled with my ancestors. I was shocked at how many babies and women in their twenties were buried. The cemetery was very run-down, but the strangeness of seeing my family name on so many ancient tombstones was thrilling. I didn't have time to search out any live Grosecloses's but made a note that I would look them up when I returned home.

After my visit to Groseclose, Virginia, I made the several-hour drive back to West Virginia to catch my train on time to get home within my ten-day limit. I felt at peace and was able to let go of the problems I faced at home if only for a short time. Later, in 2000, I returned to West Virginia for our Groseclose family's 250th reunion of being in the United States. It turns out that Peter Senior was from Germany originally. He married a Swiss girl, and together they made the boat trip to Pennsylvania and then to Virginia, where they built a large family and a town was named for them. Peter and his wife had several children, and I have many, many cousins as a result of it, which makes me very proud.

A couple of years later, I took two of my aunties and my uncle to the next reunion, and they were thrilled to have finally found their history as well (my Father could not come since he had a criminal record and could not cross the border). We all bought a large *Groseclose* book filled with our family tree and stories about the old South living, which was written by Clarke Groseclose.

*   *   *

I came home to the same problems I left with. Trevor was put on a work camp duty across the street from where Angelina lived, and he could see her waving from the front yard! My son was always very impulsive and didn't often think of future consequences. When he saw Angelina he realized he was missing out on his baby and could no longer tolerate being in the work camp. He escaped! Mind you, escaping from this camp was a simple matter of walking across the street, but to the law, it was just as bad as making an escape from a medium or even maximum prison.

Trevor and Angelina hid out at a dealer's house for several days before Trevor finally turned himself in. Both of the kids continued their drug use, and when Trevor came forward, he was sent back to the Surrey Pretrial center, where it is about as maximum as you can get, for short periods of time. He shared a prison with Clifford Olsen, who was a notorious child killer visiting the prison from his usual Saskatchewan maximum prison while he tried to get an early release in the city where the crimes took place. Olsen killed at least eleven children, and he had no hope of an early release, but he was infamous for trying anything he could to stay in the newspapers. This is who my child was in prison with!

I began to drink heavily. I was getting more and more depressed. I was also entering peri-menopause and went to the doctor for blood work to confirm this. Interestingly, I had a hysterectomy several years earlier and was told by my ob-gyn that I would go into early menopause since I only had one scarred-up ovary left. However, the blood work showed no signs of menopause, and thus the doctor simply put me on Paxil, an antidepressant.

I deteriorated on this drug. I drank more; I was finding it harder and harder to get up to go to work. I put my personnel agency up for sale, and it sold for a fraction of what it was worth, but I was unable to hold down the business and deal with Trevor's issues—of course, the business would go before I'd let my son go.

One night, I had several glasses of wine. I went to the hospital completely distraught and out of my head with worry and inner pain. I wanted to kill myself so badly at this point, but I thought maybe I could get some help instead. I did not want to kill myself for the sake of Trevor and my grandson, Tyler.

*　　*　　*

I was found passed out in my car by a nurse who called for a stretcher. I was sent to the psychiatric ward, where I was introduced to Dr. *Peter S. Within five minutes of meeting Dr. Peter (author's nickname for the doctor), he diagnosed me with bipolar disorder! I was shocked and curious as to how he would come up to this drastic conclusion. After doing a lot of research, I realized that he was judging me because I was a successful business owner, newspaper and magazine columnist, and now crashed to the ground. Dr. Peter did not seem to care that I had situations, circumstances, and a background from hell that made me drink like I did and want to die.

I learned doctors like to give out labels so that they could issue pharmaceuticals and feel like heroes for saving souls such as mine. But neither the doctors nor the drugs ever did save me. I went on a cocktail of extremely strong "brain drugs"—drugs for epilepsy even though I never had a seizure in my life, more antidepressants, and I don't know what else. I became a foggy walking zombie. When I went back to the doctor to complain about these strange electrical buzzes in my head, he said it couldn't be; it was part of my "illness."

*　*　*

My P Father was now released from prison, and it looked like he was actually going to live a crime-free life. He got a job in Vancouver with the BC Housing Authority, where he was a property manager in an apartment building made up mostly of down-and-outers: drug addicts, ex-criminals, disabled people, etc. My Father was doing very well with his job and decorated his own apartment with things he found at garage sales. I also suspected he stole things from the apartments of people who passed away before their families could claim their things. Once a psychopath, always a psychopath, but at least he had toned down his criminal activity and hovered around the edges of just plain drunkenness and sexual prowess.

He did have one girlfriend named *Reena, who was about twenty years his junior and very beautiful. She was a wild gal, but I liked her, and she and my Dad made a good couple. Reena too had some run-ins with the law but mostly concerning drinking and driving. She was also into crack, something my Father never did get into. I remember many fights between the two of them, but they always came back together as a couple.

My Father was addicted to the prescription drugs, Xanax and Tylenol 3s. My stress levels were often off the charts being so high, but doctors refused to give me any of the good drugs that would calm my nerves, so I often purchased Xanax from my father.

My Dad and I took his brother, Hilliard, back to North Vancouver to the Army and Navy Club to relive their youthful days when they were the men about town. I really enjoyed these pub-hopping outings, where I could forget about my own problems at home. As I said in earlier chapters, I always did get along with my Father, and I believe it is because he never judged nor put me down as my Mother and other family members did. And he never went into a rage with me, unlike he did with so many other family members.

*　*　*

Stress and painful experiences were about to put me in a world of doctors, prescription drugs, and an endless stream of discrimination as a result of the diagnoses the good doctors were handing out. It was not until much later I realized that my pain was situational due to an extremely painful childhood and an inability to cope with tough realities within my own family. I also learned that doctors were not always right and to get second and third opinions if necessary. My new mantra is "If it doesn't make sense, it isn't true." This, to me, goes for psychopaths and doctors. We need to take more responsibility for our intuition (sixth sense) and body.

Chapter 7—It's a Mental Mental-Health World!

Diseases of the soul are more dangerous and more numerous than those of the body.

—Cicero

The following (real) experiences are not in complete order of my life. Later chapters will show my need for continued psychiatric care due to unbearable situations I was faced with as time went on. For now, I am writing only about the mental health system as a chapter by itself before the worst was to come.

*   *   *

Malignant narcissists and psychopaths breed children with mental health issues. Unfortunately, for our mental health systems in North America, psychiatrists tend to ignore the real problem and instead feed beaten down people with drugs or warehousing them in psychiatric wards. It has taken me years to figure out most, if not all, of my "craziness" is a direct result of the abuses by my parents and siblings, who are without love, empathy, or compassion. It may seem to the reader that an almost entire family cannot be MN or Ps, but in my experience, yes, they can. I have never felt more empowered once I realized I was allowing myself to fall victim to the psychopaths and the malignant narcissists within my family.

*   *   *

The Tsunami of Depression. Really?

> In 1999, 11 million prescriptions were filled for anti-depressants in Canada.
>
> Four years later, that number nearly doubled to 20 million.
>
> In 2003, 1.5 billion dollars was spent on medications for mental or emotional problems
>
> Two years later, that number doubled to 3 billion dollars.
>
> Source IMS Health

After accepting the colossal amount of drugs dished out to me by my first psychiatrist as an adult, my physical and mental health deteriorated to the point of complete nonfunctional ability and deepened desire to kill myself. I became bedridden and completely isolated from work, family, and friends. I refused to answer the phone. I refused to go out. The electrical buzzing going on in my head (due to the heavy doses of drugs prescribed to me) was worsening and yet I was ignored by the doctor who prescribed the litany of psychiatric medications. "It's all in your head, Cherylann. Do you see now how sick you are?"

The bipolar or manic depressive diagnosis just didn't make any sense to me. I know bipolar people, and I didn't feel like I related to them. At the very least, I would have liked some of that euphoric part of the disorder, but that was never in my disposition. I remember my Aunt June, the same aunt who humiliated me so many years ago regarding my bloody underwear, the same aunt who took me to Vancouver for a facial and makeover, was diagnosed as being bipolar. She was extremely loud, inappropriate, nervously energetic, and fast-moving and talking, followed by bouts of severe depression.

As I mentioned in an earlier chapter, this aunt (by marriage) later jumped out of a seven-story window and ended her pain then and there. In this case, as in so many other suicide cases, the prescription drugs did nothing to cure my aunt's diagnosed mental illness. I remember she attended my fortieth birthday party, and she was carrying around an armful of large blister packages filled with medications. She made a point of showing me how many pharmaceuticals she was ingesting. After she died, I had to ask myself what was the point in the so-called state-of-the-art pharmaceutical treatment she was given?

I was told by two doctors that most people like to get a diagnosis that gives them an answer for their inner demons. Rarely, if ever, will we find a psychiatrist willing to take an hour to listen to the patient who may just need to let out the pain deep within their souls simply by talking and getting some simple objective and competent feedback. Perhaps a little validation?

After being diagnosed with bipolar, I had several encounters with the medical community that proved to me that ignorance is rampant when it comes to dealing with diagnosed mental patients. Here are just a few of my experiences with family doctors once I got my condition and medications branded into my medical files by psychiatrists:

Refusal of Health Treatment due to Mental Illness

I was sick. I was coughing so bad it was difficult to catch a breath. My ears ached. I felt like I was run over by a truck. My condition got so serious late one night my husband took me to the Chilliwack General Hospital, not far from where we lived. In the waiting room, the nurses quickly put me in the rooms with beds to await a doctor. I saw the worried look in their eyes as I gasped for breath in between hysterical wheezing coughs.

I remember filling out a form, and one of the questions was what medications I was taking. I was honest, of course, and named all of the psychiatric medications Dr. Peter had prescribed for me. Big mistake. The hospital doctor came to my bed and carefully read over my form. In one minute, he decided my condition had little to do with a physical ailment and more like a drama queen who was depressed and likely acting out for attention! This young doctor, whose name fails me, did not listen to my chest, did not check my ears, and did nothing for my symptoms.

My husband and I left the hospital bewildered. The next morning, I went to a walk-in medical clinic and was found to be suffering from asthmatic bronchitis and a double ear infection! He prescribed a heavy dose of antibiotics and a steroid puffer, and within a few days, I began to breathe and feel well again.

Why did that doctor at the hospital not check my chest? I was coughing up a lung and yet he didn't even use a stethoscope on me! Why did he not check my ears when I said they were screaming with pain? Negligence, stupidity, and most of all discrimination of mental health patients come to my mind. If I were the suing type, I would have had his doctor's license!

Mental Health Counselor Malpractice

In the sick room, ten cents' worth of human understanding equals ten dollars' worth of medical science.

—Martin H. Fischer

I decided I needed someone to talk to. I looked up the local mental health society, and a case worker was assigned to me. The woman was extremely obese and often talked about her own problems during my hour of time. I'm not sure why I continued to see her for several visits because she was certainly not a counselor on my side. At this stage, I was still naive and too trusting of people in authority. I could sense her fear of my "diagnosis" of bipolar. When I would talk about some of the problems I was having with my husband, she constantly took Gary's side, even though she had never even met him! I felt worse every time I left her office.

I was a trained lay counselor myself, and I had never heard of her type of counseling. To me, a counselor is one who listens objectively and who empowers his or her client by helping them to feel better about themselves! Several times during our meetings, she would ask me about my "bipolar" symptoms. "Are you suicidal today?" she would ask with bulging eyes, showing her fear. Once she even called my doctor to let him know she had everything under control—she was now ensuring I didn't do anything stupid like commit suicide! She had a lot of gull and high opinion of herself. I never felt good with this counselor, and by the time I fired her, I was a complete basket case, my self-esteem in ruins. I lost my trust in talking to counselors at this stage.

Sexual Abuse in the Hospital Emergency Room

A doctor is just a person with a responsibility to his or her patients to do no harm. Some just don't get that part of their exam.

Cherylann

One evening, I felt the left side of my body go limp. I stood up to try and shake off the feeling, but it would not go away. It was not until years later that I realized the symptoms were a result of taking so many "brain drug" pharmaceuticals.

My husband took me to the hospital, where we waited in the emergency room for several hours. Finally, I was put in a bed, and the curtains were closed. I was told a neurologist was not in the building but an intern doctor (a specialist of everything, I was told) would see me. It so happened that I had earlier spent time in this hospital's psychiatric ward, with the diagnosis of bipolar after a suicide attempt. It was right there in my files.

After several hours of waiting, I told my husband, Gary, to go home and I'd call him after I was seen by a doctor. It was after midnight, so Gary left, which was one of my biggest regrets I later said to him.

A young good-looking doctor finally came to my bed, and one of the first things that came out of his mouth was "I know you have been here before for psychiatric reasons, including a suicide attempt." I knew what was coming. He was going to ignore my symptoms and blame it on an imagined dramatic event I was trying to pull, much like the doctor at Chilliwack General Hospital.

But he did want to do an examination. He had me stand up and put my left foot up and then my right foot. I kept falling over and using the bed as a railing to stop myself. Suddenly, I felt the doctor's hands holding both of my breasts to balance me! I didn't know what to think. He was a professional; I was a mere patient with a psychiatric history. He held his hands on my breasts for far too long for comfort. He then had me lie down on the bed and opened up my top. He used his stethoscope, pushing hard on my upper chest and then going down and down farther. He was using that scope almost so low he would have been on top of my nipples if I didn't push him away and stop him. I felt molested. The doctor then said there was nothing wrong with me and quickly left my bed area.

I got up, called Gary, and went home. I told him what had happened, but Gary had very few emotions and so didn't say much. He was never one to stand up for me when it came to confronting other people's bad behavior toward me.

The next day, the sensation of my limp left side left me. I was angry, however. How dare that doctor first talk about my history of poor mental health and then proceed to molest my breasts! I decided to phone the College of Physicians and Surgeons. An investigator from the CPS who used to be with the Royal Canadian Mounted Police (RCMP) made an appointment with me and came to my home to hear my story. I got the feeling the investigator was sympathetic and concerned about my experience. After I had finished my story, showing her exactly what the doctor had done, she said their office would do an investigation and get back to me. I heard nothing for months.

Finally, I received a phone call from the investigator who informed me that after a thorough examination of both parties, the CPS put a restriction on the doctor—he could no longer see female patients without a nurse present! I could hardly believe my ears; finally, someone was listening to me—and believed me! I have a feeling this was not the first time the doctor had a similar complaint made against him. I was satisfied with the result and was pleased with the system finally going right!

Different Psychiatrists, Different Diagnoses

After about a year of listening to Dr. Peter and his analysis of my having bipolar, I was suicidal again. My desire to die was now becoming a bad habit, and my coping skills were lessening to the point of seeing no way out other than to die.

I saw no less than six different psychiatrists over the years. I am not exaggerating when I say that each one provided me with the shortest amounts of time. And yet every time I received new diagnoses and newly prescribed medications to try, all to no avail.

It was not until years later that I learned my mother was a malignant narcissist and had a whole bunch to do with my poor mental health; even as an adult she knew how to push my low self-esteem buttons.

Anti-depressants never worked for me, and believe me, I tried them all in hopes of feeling better. One doctor diagnosed me with attention-deficit/ hyperactivity disorder (ADHD) and gave me the powerful drug Adderal! Another said I suffered with borderline personality disorder (BPD) after exactly seven minutes of talking to me. He wanted to send me to a behavior class with borderline people and give me medication. I walked out of his office, disgusted with the lack of time or questioning before his brilliant revelation of what was wrong with me in such a short time.

I later looked BPD up on the Internet and found not one borderline personality disorder symptom matched my situation! I did know some borderline people, however. The ones I knew were loud, interruptive during group meetings, had poor relationships with their families due to their own bad behavior, and the list goes on. The television film "Obsessed" was about a woman with BPD . . . a stalker who went so far as to boil the family rabbit to get her man! I had none of these indicators. I think this psychiatrist glommed onto the part of my short story where my family abused me and decided my family could not all be the culprits of my distress—it must be me! I took his prescription and threw it in the garbage.

I knew his report to my family doctor would be negative. Until then I always had a good relationship with my family doctor—he is the one who sent me to the psychiatrist because of my extreme anxiety. After that report of my "oppositional defiance" due to not taking his treatment for "borderline personality," my relationship with my family doctor was never the same again. I could sense his tiptoeing around me, and I saw the fear in his eyes of his now dealing with a mental case.

I had to find a new family doctor and my new one, Dr. Adam, has been my doctor ever since. I do not like changing doctors and feel it is important to let at least one doctor know me inside and out. Now I have a respectful, honest, and caring doctor-patient relationship for which I am so grateful. Thank you, Dr. Adam!

*   *   *

One psychiatrist did have a diagnosis that made sense to me, Post Traumatic Stress Disorder (PTSD). The extreme abuse I took as a child and teenager made life very difficult for me to cope with situations later in my life. I have flashbacks of excessively painful memories that never leave me. I've been anxious and isolated increasingly as I grew older. PTSD is reserved for those who experienced or witnessed brutal life battles. I was one of those who experienced relentless abuse and painful situations throughout my life that seemed to never stop. Two or three chapters down the road will show you just how mental the mental health system really operates in the way I was treated after more traumatic events.

Most psychiatrists, with the exception of the one diagnosing me with PTSD, ignored my family history of abuse and other situational troubles. My abusive experiences should have been red flags for the doctors; instead, most doctors enhanced my feelings of shame and humiliation and choose to label me with all sorts of mental health ailments and fill my body with heavy-duty medications to relieve my symptoms. I still put too much trust in doctors at this point, and it wasn't until 2006 that I threw away all of my medications, deciding they were doing me more harm than good.

*   *   *

While I continued to battle my emotional breakdown demons, my son, Trevor, became clean from drugs, and his life was looking brighter. He and Angelina's great aunt were fighting it out in the court systems so that Trevor could have access or even custody of his beloved son. Angelina's great aunt was unable to have children of her own, and she wanted to raise Tyler herself. It was a long and costly battle, and Gary and I stood by our son as any loving parents would do. We knew Trevor had improved his life drastically and was ready to parent his child with a little help from us. We had no idea what was to come that would shake my world to the ground.

Chapter 8—From Ecstasy to Hell and Back

Experience is the best teacher.

—Author unknown

I was so proud of my son, who finally decided to say *no* to drugs. He was in a pickle, however, since he had no job or money to offer his son a good home. Trevor had made it all the way to the Supreme Court of Canada, where he received a wonderful commendation from the Lordship overseeing the hearing for his evidence and obvious changes in his lifestyle. Trevor had just one more trip to Provincial Court for a technicality, and we had full confidence he would finally have custody of his precious son, Tyler.

*   *   *

Mike was Trevor's primary drug dealer in the past and saw my son sitting by himself, drinking a beer at a local pub, pondering how he could improve his employment status. His self-esteem was at the bottom, and all he could think about was getting access to his son again. To date, his work history was nothing to be proud of. That fateful day, Mike approached Trevor and offered him a job. Dealers love ex-users because they can be trusted for not stealing drugs, and they make for great mules. A mule is a person who transports drugs for the dealer. Mike offered Trevor $2,000 to take a twelve-hour drive to Fort St. John in British Columbia. Mike would accompany him, and Trevor did not have to deliver any of the drugs to users. His only job was to be the driver of Mike's van, where 2.5 kilograms of cocaine was screwed into the panels of the dealer's SUV.

Trevor was not a street-smart drug user, and he was impulsive and he was poor. He was happy to come into some money but did not realize that by telling others that he had this (illegal) job and someone might contact the police who would put Trevor and Mike on surveillance, which is exactly what happened.

I later learned that the police followed Trevor and Mike all the way to Fort St. John and watched Trevor get out of the SUV and go into a bar where he promptly picked up a girl for the evening, while Mike did his business delivering the drugs. I don't know where Mike was picked up, but Trevor was picked up at the motel he was staying at with the gal as he came out of the room.

Trevor was twenty at that time, and Mike was in his thirties and with a family. He was a native Indian man with a long record for drug dealing and trafficking. He knew the ropes, and when they met up at the courthouse, he threatened Trevor to keep his mouth shut or he would be killed! While Trevor had shoplifting and an escape record from a jail camp, he did not have a drug record of any kind—he was a user not a dealer or trafficker—until this moment in time. (Trafficking is transporting drugs and worthy of a lengthly jail sentence.)

When Trevor phoned me to tell me he was in jail for drug trafficking, I immediately made the long drive to Fort St. John to find out what was going on. None of this made sense to me! Trevor and Mike were about to be remanded in court, and I wanted to be there.

I sat directly behind my son, and Mike sat beside him as a codefendant. I was furious that this Mike guy kept putting his arm around Trevor, as if they were the best buddies in the world. I knew this would not look good to the judge. I also sensed Trevor was uncomfortable but did not know how to push the much larger Mike away from him.

Two police officers, both no older than twenty-two or twenty-three, were overly official in their commentaries during the hearing. They did not separate the differences in guilt between Mike and Trevor during this hearing, and I was curious as to how they could not see that Trevor was hardly involved save for the drive to the small town of Fort St. John. It was Mike who had the "scorecards," cards that showed the users to be given the drugs. It was Mike's handwriting. It was Mike's SUV. It was Mike's drugs. It was Mike's deal.

Trevor and Mike were held without bail, and I went home alone, crying all the way. How could this happen? We were so close to having our son back, and now he was held in a prison several hours away from home, and for how long we had no idea. I told my son he could call me three times a week while they awaited their trial, and I would look for a lawyer for him in Vancouver. I wanted to make sure I kept in contact with Trevor because to me, he was still my baby and I knew if he was found guilty, he would be looking at a three—to five-year sentence! My coping skills were very poor during this time, and I spent most of my days in bed.

In addition, once again, I would have to tell my whacko family about Trevor's situation, and for sure my mother would have things to pick on and say about my son. I never felt so helpless in my life. Kill me, but please don't hurt my son!

Mike and Trevor were held for a full year before a trial was set. I'm really not sure what went on with the prosecutions office during this time, but by the end of that year, Trevor was let loose with no record at all. All of *his* charges were dismissed!

Meanwhile, I am proud to say that Trevor took that year in remand to do some real soul searching. He spoke with a life skills coach in the prison often, a fellow who seemed to take a liking to Trevor. Together they made plans for when Trevor would be released. Trevor registered with a college on Vancouver Island to study heavy-duty mechanics. When he was released, he came straight home, barely going out for fear of running into his old "friends."

Trevor was released in August 2000 and started school that September. He took out a student loan and gave it all to me so that he wouldn't be tempted to spend it. He rented a dorm on the site of the school and came home every weekend to study. I spoke to Trevor often while he was at school to make sure he didn't feel alone or abandoned. We loved our son and were concerned he would run into the wrong people. Every Friday we went to the ferries to pick Trevor up, and every Sunday, we drove him back to Horseshoe Bay to take the ferry back to the Island.

One day, I asked him if he met any girls at the school. He said there was a "Mexican" girl who was so beautiful he was afraid to approach her. Trevor himself was a very handsome guy, and I had a mother's intuition this gal and Trevor would soon get together. It turns out that Ximi (Hee Mee) Maza was an international student from Guatemala, studying tourism management at the same college. She was in the same dorm as Trevor, and once they hooked up, they were inseparable. After a few weeks, Trevor brought her home to meet us, and we couldn't have been prouder.

Ximi was as beautiful as Trevor said, and her personality was equally delightful. She spoke three languages fluently, without so much as an accent in English, Spanish, and French. Her family in Guatemala was very wealthy, owning a chain of gourmet delis and liquor stores. But Ximi was very down to earth and clearly in love with our son. They both continued with their studies and spent their weekends together at our home. Sometimes the college kids would have bonfires and hang out together on Friday nights. We were no longer worried about Trevor since he gave drugs up long ago now, and we were just happy he was finally living a happy youthful life doing normal college kid activities with the girl he loved.

*   *   *

I rarely heard from my mother or siblings during this time. They were punishing me again for some imagined infraction or another. That was the way of my family—the silent treatment that sometimes lasted for years. If anyone has ever experienced this kind of cruelty, they know what I mean when I say it is the most painful torture one can endure within a family. It is indifference to you, to your life, and to your sense of belonging. The silent treatment within families keeps you from extended members such as nieces and nephews as well, and this is the part that ate at my heart all too often. What bothered me most was it just didn't make any sense! Regular communication did not seem to occur to my family. If they were mad at me, talk to me about it for Christ's sake. But this would not satisfy their lust for cruel blood and they never did.

*   *   *

After Trevor graduated from the heavy-duty mechanics program, the kids decided to live together in the lower mainland of British Columbia, and Ximi would find another college to finish her studies so that she could be with her man, Trevor. I loved Ximi. She was like the daughter I never had. We had long talks, and she knew all about Trevor's past but saw through his troublesome teen years and fell in love with his respect for me and her, his sense of humor, intelligence, and loving nature, especially his love for his son, Tyler.

We were at the courthouse in Chilliwack one day in December of 2002 to push forward Trevor's application for custody of Tyler. On the way home from this hearing, Trevor asked me to pull over; he wanted to go into a government building for a few minutes. Ximi followed him in, while Gary and I sat in the car, wondering what was going on. What seemed like hours later, Trevor and Ximi came back out to the car, and Trevor passed me a piece of paper—it was a marriage license! It was then that he told me he and Ximi would be getting married and as soon as possible! They set the date for January 18, 2003, and decided to have a civil wedding in our house with a justice of the peace and then have the larger wedding in Guatemala that summer.

Gary and I were thrilled to pieces and were so pleased that Trevor's life was looking up. He had his career ready to go and a girl he loved and wanted to marry, and he was very close to gaining custody of Tyler.

Trevor and Ximi went to Guatemala to ask her father for her hand in marriage. Trevor insisted he gain the support from her parents, who gave it to them with their love. Trevor had never been out of the country before, and the entire trip was thrilling for him. They brought home photos, and the glow in the faces of these two lovebirds was enough to make me cry.

I tried very hard to reach my sister, Shivey, to let her know of the upcoming nuptials, but she would not answer her phone or return my messages. I don't know why; I rarely knew why the silent treatment was inflicted upon me and my family. Jealousy? Who knows? Needless to say, she did not come to Trevor's wedding. I didn't bother to call my mother to invite her, as she never did like Trevor and she certainly never showed me any love. She would turn this wonderful event into a drama that no one would be able to stand. Besides, my father would be there and Mother would make a drama scene about that, which I wanted to avoid for my son.

I didn't know where my older brother was, and either my younger brother said he could not make the trip down or he too did not answer my calls. My memory is sketchy on this issue because I just cannot imagine why my younger brother would ignore me. We always had a close relationship.

*   *   *

My psychopath Father attended the wedding. I felt lucky to have someone from my family be present for my only child's wedding, and he never caused a scene other than being a little drunk from time to time and a bit of a pathological liar which I learned to ignore. Also in attendance were two of Ximi and Trevor's best friends from college who were a wonderful couple and another friend (whose name fails me) who was living with Trevor and Ximi.

One of the best days of my life was to go with Ximi to shop for a wedding gown. Since her parents were in Guatemala, I filled that role for her and admired her stunning beauty as she modeled a variety of beautiful wedding dresses in a small boutique near our home. Ximi decided she would wear the same dress at her wedding in the late summer in Guatemala. She looked like a goddess to me in her beautiful wedding dress.

The Canadian wedding was small but very charming. After the ceremony at our home, we all went to White Rock Beach and had a wonderful dinner together in a restaurant overlooking the sea. I was bursting at the seams with pride. I was hurting, however, that Trevor did not have any of his extended family or his son at his important day. He never talked to me about the strangeness of it all, but I knew he was questioning within his own mind. Now that I think about it, he was probably blaming himself for his indiscretions with the law.

* * *

Trevor and Ximi had a small basement apartment during this time and both worked for a call center until Ximi could re-attend school and Trevor could find a heavy-duty mechanics job. Jobs were very hard to come by in British Columbia during this time, and I felt so bad for Trevor that he couldn't just jump into his newfound career. I didn't want Trevor to lose hope. I was always trying to make life better for my son, and it hurt me to see Trevor struggle so hard to find the dream job he was after. Trevor always loved to work on cars; Gary taught him much about the mechanics of an engine when he was a young teenager, and semi-trailer trucks and other heavy equipment was just bigger and better machinery to work on. It would also pull in a pretty good income to support his family!

* * *

In February, one month after the wedding, I could tell something was up with Trevor and Ximi, although I couldn't imagine what. Trevor seemed more stressed than usual, and Ximi avoided talking to me about it, preferring to let Trevor tell me. Finally, at Easter time of 2003, I learned their secret. A girl named *Mary found Trevor and told him he was the father of her two-and a-half-year-old daughter! Before worrying me about it, they had DNA tests done that confirmed Trevor was indeed the father of a little girl, *Amanda Margaret.

The story goes that just before Trevor did his drive to Fort St. John, he had a one-night stand with a gal he met in a pub. I guess it was a little more than a one-night stand, as they dated for a week or so. I remember Trevor bringing Mary to our home, and I caught her red-handed stealing dimes from my change-saving container! She looked like a hood, wearing all black, and her eyes were like steel. I didn't like this girl from the beginning. And I guess Trevor didn't either because he soon dumped her, and his problems with the drug trafficking charge came soon after. Trevor had no idea that he had impregnated Mary.

I immediately welcomed this precious child into our home, and we had an Easter egg hunt with her. She was pale and far too thin for her age, and her clothes were dirty. Trevor was very upset that the mother of his child was Mary, as he disliked her immensely. I gave Trevor the lecture on loving the child more than hating the mother, and he agreed and provided child support and took her to his and Ximi's home on weekends. Ximi told me Trevor was like a big kid with Amanda, jumping on the bed and playing on the floor with her little toys.

Mary was living with a fellow named Jeff, and Trevor could hardly stand him. In addition, once Mary caught up with Trevor, she phoned him several times a day. Finally, Trevor stopped answering her calls other than to pay child support or pick her up for their weekend visits.

Mary called me one day to complain that Trevor was not answering her calls. I didn't know her that well and had no idea at that time that she was leaving some twenty to thirty calls on his answering machine, driving Trevor and Ximi crazy with frustration. Nonetheless, Trevor treated Amanda with the love she deserved, but he tried very hard not to run into Mary. Trevor was just married after all, and this was a setback that would shake the steadiest of marriages.

After a few months of knowing Amanda, I was in love and had her come help me with my garden while babysitting for Mary, who was attending a small business school on student loans. After she had completed that program, she did not find a job and took out yet another student loan to study, working with the elderly in nursing homes. I was troubled that Mary moved so often and always in homes with several people living in it. The sickly look of Amanda and her numerous bruises and black eyes also had me concerned. When she visited, she always only asked for water and was thrilled when I offered her juice, milk, or chocolate milk—her favorite! I made sure she ate nutritious lunches or dinners and bought her new clothes to suit her beautiful face.

*   *   *

Meanwhile, Trevor was continuing his quest to gain custody of Tyler. Time moves so slow in the family law courts, and we were all very frustrated that Trevor did not have Tyler in his loving arms yet. We knew it was coming, but *when* was the $64,000 question.

*   *   *

Mother's Day of 2003 was the best day of my life. I will never forget that Gary's parents, his sister and her husband, Gary, myself, Trevor, and Ximi went to the Sheraton Inn for a fancy Mother's Day brunch. Trevor walked in with a bouquet of flowers for all of the women and sat down beside me. He said he loved me and was so grateful I never gave up on him. How could I? He was my one true love in life, and each passing year was just getting better and better for him. When Trevor was happy, I was happy.

After our brunch, we all went out to the sidewalk and talked for about an hour about nothing. I just felt so much love at that moment I can never forget the time. Gary and I realized we were now talking to a man, no longer a boy who needed us to bail him out of situations. He was a wonderful person who would give the shirt off his back to a person in need. I raised a beautiful young man, I thought to myself that day.

*   *   *

Ximi's parents gave Trevor and Ximi money to purchase a BMW car and for newer furniture. Trevor was in love with the BMW, and he often came over to our garage to work on it, with Ximi sitting in the front seat, listening to music as she watched her loving man. Trevor still had not been able to find a heavy-duty mechanics position, and they began to think about moving out of the province to Alberta, where jobs were in abundance.

Trevor and Ximi took a trip with their friends to Edmonton, Alberta, and almost immediately Trevor was offered a job as a heavy-duty mechanic with a trucking company! He was to start in two weeks to give the kids enough time to clear up loose ends and move their furniture. They found an apartment to live in and were ready to go. I was both sad and ecstatic for my son. He was about to embark on his own life with his new wife—and Tyler would surely be with them soon—as well as have full access to Amanda whenever he wanted. Theirs was a ready-made family, and Ximi was as excited as Trevor. Her goal was to return to school in Edmonton and open a club after she completed her studies.

The day Trevor packed up the car with Ximi in the passenger seat, I waved them good-bye. I was so proud of my son, who had overcome so many difficulties in his child and teenage years. I was ready to cut the apron strings and let him manage his new life, even if he was moving a long way from home.

*   *   *

For some reason, call it the empty-nest syndrome if you like, I became severely depressed after Trevor and Ximi left. I was bedridden and couldn't even answer the telephone. I talked to Trevor and Ximi a few times that first week he was gone, but the second week, I didn't even listen to my voice messages; I was so sickly in bed.

Finally, the second Friday they were gone, I listened to my messages and learned Trevor had called three times! I felt awful that I didn't answer the phone. I immediately called, and Ximi answered the phone. She said Trevor was downstairs, working on the car. We talked for about an hour; she was so excited that Trevor was to start his new job on Monday and she was going to go back to school. Ximi said that later that night, she and Trevor, along with some new friends they had met, were going to the West Edmonton Mall, to a club, to celebrate their new life. Trevor was to be the designated driver, and Ximi and her girlfriend were happy to "just let loose"! Ximi asked me if I wanted her to go down to get Trevor for me, but I said, "No. Just tell him I called and that I love him."

*   *   *

I could never have imagined how fast my life would change that weekend. I learned a very important lesson: cherish every moment you have and every moment you have with your child. You never know what can happen.

Chapter 9—Stolen Love

Rage, rage against the dying of the light!

—Dylan Thomas

On June 28, 2003, the Saturday morning after I talked to Ximi, I felt much better. I was excited for my son, who was to start his new job that Monday. I was thrilled that Trevor's new life was just beginning and on such a positive note. Ximi's excited voice and promise of a good future rubbed off on me, and I finally got out of bed that day.

* * *

I was designing a wall plaque with polymer clay in our living room while watching some television. I was going to make a pretty wall ornament for my new granddaughter, and Gary said he was going to take the recyclables to the market. As I watched my program, I let my fingers push and pull at the polymer clay on a board when I suddenly heard a commotion at the front door. I heard Gary say, "Wait!" but there in front of me in my living room were two police officers. Gary pushed past them, and I stood up in my tattered nightie to find out what was going on.

I looked inquisitively at the officers and knew instantly my son was dead. Their eyes told me, and when they confirmed he had been in a serious car accident and passed away, my heart shattered into a million little pieces. I grabbed Gary and held him as I looked into his eyes, begging him to tell me it wasn't true. His tears told me my Trevor, my love, my only one, was taken away from me forever.

I ran around the living room like a mad woman. I grabbed all of the photos of Ximi and Trevor's wedding off the fireplace mantle and held them close to me and rocked my body as I continued a silent screaming, which I could not hear but knew the neighbors would. Abruptly I stopped in front of the glass doors to our yard and stood for what seemed like hours staring at nothing. My mind left me completely for several minutes.

Gary was asking the police officers for details, and I grabbed the phone and the first person I phoned was my MN mother. Why, oh why did I keep trying to find love within her cold heart? The first thing she asked was "Was Trevor drinking?" Her voice had the usual sharp coldness. She said she could see the news on an Edmonton Channel, and they were reporting that Trevor burned in the accident. I threw the phone at Gary and went to the officers to ask about Ximi, Trevor's wife. Was she okay? They said they were unable to report that to me, and we would have to get in touch with the police in Edmonton to get more details.

I never thought I could feel so despondent and lost as I was that day and for many, many days thereafter. I went into shock and crawled around the kitchen floor, begging God to bring Trevor back to me. On May 27, almost exactly one month before we celebrated Trevor's twenty-fifth birthday. He was just starting his beautiful new life! How could he be just . . . gone! My screams made me think I was going to die from heartbreak. Why couldn't I just die and let this all be over? Maybe this was just a nightmare. But it wasn't. It was all too real that the boy I gave birth to and loved with all of my heart was dead, and nothing or nobody was going to help bring him back to me.

After Gary hung up from talking to my mother, I dialed my best friend, *Veronica Reedwell's number. Together we cried like babies at the loss of such a beautiful young man. I hoped Veronica would bring him back, but she had no words that could comfort me other than her mutual love of Trevor and her understanding of the pain I was suffering. When I cried, she cried, and when she cried, I cried louder, and then we both whimpered quietly, saying nothing.

Gary phoned the police in Edmonton, and we learned Ximi was alive at an Edmonton hospital, with severe injuries, although we had no idea how serious. We had to get to Edmonton! I didn't even know how to reach Ximi's parents in Guatemala to let them know of our children's wreckage. The police finally left, and Gary booked the next flight to Edmonton.

I couldn't stop crying on the one-hour flight to Edmonton. I know people were looking at us, but I didn't care—my son was dead, and the tears and sobbing just wouldn't stop.

When we arrived, we immediately booked a rental car and headed to the hospital Ximi was at. We found her in intensive care, and my knees buckled at the sight of her beautiful face. She was awake, and she whispered her parent's phone number for me to call. Ximi's father did not speak English and passed the phone to her mother who could understand what I was saying: "There was a car accident. Ximi is alive but in critical condition. Trevor . . . is . . . dead. Please come." Gary took the phone, and they made arrangements for her to call him back with the time and flight number so he could pick her up from the airport.

Meanwhile, I went back into Ximi's room and asked her if she was in pain. She nodded yes, and I told the nurse who was at a desk just two feet from her to get her some medication *now*! I was beside myself with fear for the well-being of Ximi, and no one had yet told her that the love of her life had died in the car accident. I held her hand and told her gently that Trevor did not survive the accident. Tears rolled down my dear daughter-in-law's face, and together we cried over the anguish of loss we were both suffering.

*   *   *

I asked where Trevor was, and they said he was sent to the Edmonton Burn Hospital. I shuddered to think about what kind of burns my baby suffered but did not yet have the nerve to ask. I didn't want to know. I wanted to remember the Trevor who squeezed me tight and then waved good-bye to me with his big toothy grin as the kids left in their beloved car for their Edmonton dreams.

Gary found a hotel for us to stay at and left me in the room to cry in the bed by myself while he picked up Ximi's mother from the airport and took her to the hospital to check on Ximi's progress. Ximi's prognosis was improving by the hour.

*   *   *

Shivey, my sister, showed up several hours later with my niece. She was camping at the time of the accident, and my younger brother went in search for their campsite to let her know the news of Trevor. Shivey wanted to come to Edmonton right away, as she remembered a conversation we had several years before at her kitchen table when I told her that if anything ever happened to Trevor, I would kill myself. I could not imagine a life without my son.

Back at the hotel, I had some medication with me and swallowed it all. Dying was my coping method by this point and not being able to be successful was frustrating beyond words. The pills I took weren't enough to kill me. When Gary found me, he called the paramedics, and they took me to the hospital. I was released after an examination. I walked out of the hospital, and my niece and I sat on a curb waiting for Gary and my sister to come out. I didn't know where they were. I don't even remember if this was the same hospital Ximi was in. Everything at this point was a complete blur, and I remember very little of the first few days in Edmonton. I just remember my niece being with me, sitting outside on the street after I swallowed those useless pills.

*   *   *

The next day, I remember two of Trevor and Ximi's new friends surrounding us with love. Landon moved to Edmonton with Trevor and Ximi to try and gain a new start in life as well, and he soon met Ondrea and the four of them became fast friends. Gary and I were supposed to go to Trevor and Ximi's apartment and collect as many belongings as we could. I was unable to go into the apartment, however. My pain wouldn't let me. Today, I wish I had searched out things that I could keep in memory of my son, but I wasn't thinking about such things at that time. Fortunately, Landon and Ondrea grabbed things they thought we would want, and I still have these precious belongings of my son. I plan to give them to his beloved children when they are old enough.

We learned that an autopsy was required but could not be performed until Monday. The wait was excruciating. I knew we were going to have to have Trevor cremated in Edmonton to bring him home to Surrey for his funeral. I never believed in cremation, as the whole thought of burning my boy to ashes made me cringe with the ghastliness of it all.

Immediately after the autopsy, Trevor was sent to a crematorium, where we were to identify his body. This was another part of the death process I could not do. I wanted to remember my son as he was when he was alive. Also I knew by overhearing conversations that his injuries were outrageously horrible, and I didn't want to look at such a spectacle of my beloved beautiful boy.

After Gary identified Trevor, he came outside and told me he was burned up to little puff of a beard on his chin, which was the style for young men at that time. Gary said that Trevor's face was not harmed and his wretched body was covered by a sheet. I sat in the car with both of my legs remaining outside of the car door. I covered my face with my hands, as I knew within moments after the identification that my son was going to be cremated, burned to ashes.

*   *   *

Back at the hotel, my sister was working on a technically advanced cell phone with her best friend, *Ellen, who was arranging the obituary and other things that needed to be done as soon as possible. They tried to involve me in the funeral process details, and all I could do was read what they wrote together and approve it. I didn't care what was written until much later. My son was dead, and in those first few weeks, I cared about nothing. Another thing my sister and Ellen were working on was a musical slide show presentation for the funeral. This I very much appreciated. I was a hopeless case, and to have people take care of these details was a godsend for me.

*   *   *

Ximi was in the hospital for less than a week. She had lacerations covering her face and eyes from the broken windshield glass, a broken arm that would require a foot-long rod to be inserted, a bruise on her brain, and some other minor injuries. Both Trevor and Ximi were wearing their seatbelts, and Ximi had a deep scrape across her chest caused by the seatbelt.

When she was released, Gary and her mother took her to the mangled car to retrieve some of their belongings. A watch that Ximi purchased for Trevor was recovered from the glove box. Apparently, the watch was too loose, and he didn't want to risk losing it in the club, so he left it in the car. Ximi later went to the apartment and chose things to take with her back to our home. Ximi and her mother were going to rent a van filled with Ximi's things and take the long drive home to our place, and Gary and I flew home with our few precious items.

*   *   *

Gary and I did not know this at that time, but Ximi was having some serious problems staying in our country! In fact, she had been given orders to be out of Canada by July 1! This was just a few days after the accident, and I was furious with our government for insisting she leave! I couldn't imagine the stress Trevor and Ximi must have been under when they moved to Edmonton and dealing with cold-faced immigration officials.

Apparently, since Ximi was no longer at school, her student visa ran out and she had no right to be in Canada. I learned that the reason Trevor wanted to marry Ximi as soon as possible was in hopes that it would help her case to stay in Canada. The rule is she would have to return to Guatemala to apply to reside in Canada, and this process could take a year or more! Neither Trevor nor Ximi could stand the idea of being apart for so long, so Trevor was considering going back to Guatemala with Ximi to wait out the bureaucracy. I knew none of this and felt terrible the kids did not turn to us for help.

Ximi did hire a lawyer, but most of the immigration lawyers in Edmonton knew the laws for India and China but not Guatemala. Because of drug cartels and other political and social difficulties within Guatemala, not too many countries wanted their citizens to immigrate to our country. What really pissed me off was that Canada had zero population growth in two years! Our country is so big I just could not understand the reasoning of our government.

No amount of money Ximi's parents had could help. We managed to get a lousy three-week reprieve for Ximi so she could attend her husband's funeral, but that was it. Ximi would be deported if she did not leave on her own accord! Ximi and her mother stayed with us during this time, and between the death of Trevor, the funeral, and issues that went on with my family (namely my malignant narcissist mother), the stress was beyond bearable.

Because Ximi's lungs were in jeopardy, she had to hire a doctor to fly with her to Guatemala after the funeral. She was able to get a couple of extra weeks for rest before she left us. She was still so ill I will forever hold anger for Canada's indifference to our deceased son and loving daughter-in-law's plight. We e-mailed MLAs and other officials for help, all to no avail. We just lost our son and now we were going to lose our precious Ximi as well. The stress when we returned home to get ready for Trevor's funeral was far too much for all of us to bear.

*   *   *

My mother came down from her home in Vernon; she said she was going to stay with me for two weeks after the funeral. I didn't know how to process that information based on the past trouble-making performances of hers. However, I needed my, or at least "a" mother. People, friends, and other family members have told me for years to give up on trying to gain my mother's love, but I must be slow or something because I thought this stay just might work out considering the horrible circumstances surrounding the death of my son and my need for as much love around me as possible.

It didn't work out.

The day before Trevor's funeral, celebration of life, or whatever else you want to call it, my mother decided now was the time to put my son down, especially for the bad boy he was during his "druggie days" and the time he showed her no respect by leaning on the back of her sofa. She wouldn't stop. In front of Ximi and her mother, my mother went on a rampage of words that cut me to the core and made me bleed from my soul. My son had just died and my mother chose this time to make sure everyone in the room "knew" what a bad boy he was!

I cracked. I have never been a violent person but this day I literally picked this lady up and threw her out of my house. Shivey was with us, and she took Mother back to her place. I hated my mother so much at that point; her cruelty was beyond what most people could imagine. It was one thing for my mother to hate and assassinate me with her cruel words, but when she started in about my deceased son, I had had reached my boiling point.

The day of the funeral was surreal. There I was sitting with my husband and Ximi and her mother on the left side of the room and my own mother and Shivey on the other side of the pews! Shivey had set up the PowerPoint presentation, and for the strangeness of our fractured family, it was a very moving tribute for my son.

We went back to our home after the funeral, and my favorite cousins I grew up with, my best friends, and others who cared about me and Gary were all there. I saw my mother sitting with some people I somehow recognized but couldn't quite place them. Then I realized it was Linda and Fred, Mother's long-standing friends who loved to hear all about my *bad* antics as a child. Neither Linda nor Fred approached me, hugged me, or said so much as an "I'm so sorry for your loss." No, they were there to support my mother in case I beat the shit out of her.

Now, of course, I would never do such a thing, but what Mother told these people regarding my kicking her out of my home is anyone's guess. This is what I dealt with all of my life when it came to Mother. She would bad-mouth me to anyone who would listen, and I would be left standing there, wondering what I did wrong to deserve the silent treatment from people I did not know since childhood.

I remember reaching out to Fred; I had questions about his days from World War II, to which I remembered he lost his entire family. I couldn't figure out how he lost his family when I always thought the war in Germany was about the Holocaust of the Jewish population. Other than that, there were no words of kindness spoken to me by these people. If there was an outreach to me, I don't recall, but I do remember the disapproving look in Linda's eyes.

*   *   *

Gary and I received the autopsy report about a week after the funeral. From what we could see, he had some alcohol in his system as well as marijuana! I was stunned. Years later, the accident was deemed to be the fault of the other driver, who turned left into Trevor's speeding car in an intersection, but our son did bear some responsibility for his speeding, according to the police report.

The Tragic Ending of Trevor's Life

Ximi told us the story of the night Trevor died. Trevor, Ximi, Ondrea, and Landon were going to go clubbing at the West Edmonton Mall. I knew that I had spoken to Ximi earlier that Friday night, and she said she was excited to get out and let off some steam. She said that Trevor was going to be the designated driver, but I guess he slipped and had a few anyway. There was another young man, who was just eighteen years old, who met up with the foursome and asked Trevor if he could invite some girls to sit at their table. Trevor asked Ximi, since he was only asking so that the young man would have some female company as well. Ximi was intoxicated but agreed.

The next thing I was told was that the foursome went to Humpty Dumpty's Restaurant for an early breakfast. It was about 2:00 a.m. Ximi was very intoxicated by this point, and at about 3:30 a.m., Trevor told Landon and Ondrea he was going to take her home. Landon and Ondrea stayed back, and the last words Trevor said to Landon were "I'll leave the door unlocked for you." Ximi told me later, about a year later, that she was very drunk and screaming at Trevor as they passed through that intersection, and Trevor "put the pedal to the meddle" in hopes of getting her home as soon as possible. She said it bothered her that all those girls had joined their table, even though Trevor asked her if it was okay. Ximi remembers nothing after the car was hit.

The police told us that Trevor's speed limit was approximately ninety-five miles per hour or 130 KMs. The other driver and his passenger had few injuries, but the car hit Trevor's door, and the car swirled around and around until it finally rested against a light post.

An off-duty police officer and two teenage kids witnessed the accident and ran up to the scene. They were able to pull Ximi out of her window, but a fire broke out on Trevor's side. The engine was resting on his knees when it burst into flames. The paramedics and the fire trucks were called, and the fire was put out, but they could not get my son out with the engine firmly entrenched on his knees. The Jaws of Life were dispatched, but even that could not release Trevor. Trevor was still alive at this point but unconscious, from what I hear. The policy goes that if a person is alive and trapped in a vehicle and the Jaws of Life could not get him out, they had to take his legs off! This is an unbearable thing to imagine as his mother.

Trevor was transported to the Edmonton Burn Hospital where he was found to have 80 percent of his body covered in third-degree burns. In addition, he had three skull fractures and a ruptured spleen. All of this in addition to his amputated legs. My strong spirited Trevor still lived on for two and a half hours!

When I heard the details of the accident, I knew I would never recover from the details of my son's atrocious injuries. Was he conscious during this time? How much pain was he in? Did he know he was dying?

My world fell apart, and I had no idea how I would carry on. Nothing in my lifetime of pain and hurt could compare to what God had in store for me now. I lost my only true love, the unconditional kind, in a split second. How was I going to carry on? Oh, God, please take me!

Chapter 10—Dead Mom Walking

If tears could build a stairway,
And memories a lane,
I'd walk right up to Heaven
And bring you home again.

—Author unknown

I felt myself die inside the moment my son, Trevor, passed away so cruelly. It was only a matter of time before I would take my own life, I knew. I was raised by a mother who made it her mission to make my life as miserable as hell, even as an adult, and I knew I had no other support to carry me through the unthinkable—losing my child to death. My husband was not able to be there for me, although I think he tried at first.

Ximi and her mother left, Gary went back to work, and the house was an empty cold shell of a place I called hell, much like my heart. I did not like being in my own skin. Why would God do this to me? Little did I know more pain was yet to come my way.

*   *   *

We had to see our grandson, Tyler! Gary and I went to the Chilliwack Court House and applied for visitation access to our beloved grandson. This turned out to be a very messy process, and my memory of events is very poor. There are certain things I do remember well, however. When we got to the hearing, we were told that Angelina wanted her great aunt, *Marlene, to adopt Tyler. That suited Gary and I fine because we were in no shape to raise another child. However, we did want access to Tyler for visits and special occasions. For some reason, this was not acceptable to the maternal side of Tyler's family! They were going to fight tooth and nail to keep us away from our grandson!

Could God take anything else away from me? I was beside myself with anxiety and depression. First, I lost my beloved son Trevor, and then Ximi was sent packing back to Guatemala by our government. To lose Tyler would be the kick off the cliff for me. Mary, our granddaughter's mother, was very open to us seeing Amanda at any time we wanted. In fact, Mary became a pesky pain in the ass to Gary and me, phoning constantly. (Sometimes thirty times in a day, she would leave messages if we didn't pick up the phone!) It is not that we didn't want Amanda, but that we didn't know her as much as we knew Tyler and Mary was pushing her daughter on us at a time I was incapable of giving love to a child I barely knew. That would change later, as Amanda and I are very close today, but for that period in time, our focus was on gaining access to Tyler.

* * *

At one of our hearings, Marlene's lawyer showed up to say that Marlene had a brain tumor and would be unavailable for at least six months! They asked Gary and I if we would wait until six months passed before continuing with our application for visitation with Tyler. While this really didn't make a lot of sense to us, we felt sick for Marlene! We did not wish such a serious illness on anyone, not even the lady who was stopping us from seeing Tyler. Without thinking, we readily agreed to the six-month wait. Our bad.

When the six months was up, we were back in court and Marlene's lawyer announced that during the time we were waiting patiently to see Tyler, Angelina had signed the adoption papers for Marlene to adopt Tyler and the adoption was now complete and we now had no rights for access or any other kind of visitations! I got physically sick at the thought of never seeing our precious grandson again. How could anyone be so cruel? Was the brain tumor just a ruse to stop us from interfering with the adoption? Gary and I were so beside ourselves we didn't even think to ask our lawyer if we could fight to get access even if Tyler was adopted. We gave up.

Gary and I drove home in silence, and my tears flowed like a waterfall that wouldn't stop. I had now officially lost everything. I was falling out of love with Gary at this time and wondered if he ever did love me. He was emotionally unavailable for me and was unable to give me the kind of love I needed. My nickname for him, however mean, was *emotional zombie* because that is what he reminded me of during times of crisis. Gary was not raised in a particularly loving family, and so I knew where he got his lack of sensitivity from.

I found an online group for grieving parents, and I did find some solace in being able to talk about my loss without judgment from the other 300 members of the group. But still, I wanted to join Trevor. I had to leave this cold awful world and be with my son, wherever he was. I took my opportunity when Gary, just weeks after Trevor died, went camping with my sister, Shivey, and her family.

By then, I was excited to join Trevor in heaven, and I now had my opportunity. I went to my doctor and asked for prescriptions to help me sleep and reduce my anxiety. I was given high doses of medications that I knew would let me fall into blissful sleep, forever. There would be no mistakes this time.

I laid out the newspapers that so brilliantly described the horrid accident and death of my precious son. I put Trevor's ashes on the coffee table along with his favorite visor cap that he wore constantly. I took out a Coke from the fridge and gathered all of the medications I was going to swallow within minutes. I said a prayer to God, telling him I was so sorry I was too weak to carry on and had nothing left to offer this world. I then began popping the pills. Slowly at first and then by the handful. I was on our sofa, staring at the French doors that led out to our backyard, when I heard a commotion, then glass breaking, and a SWAT team of police officers breaking in with their batons flying high in the air as they all stumbled in!

I watched the spectacle in slow motion, as I was already beginning to fall into my blissful sleep. I remember nothing else except waking up in a baron hospital room by myself. Soon a nurse came in and asked how I was feeling. Stupid fucking question. I was alive, wasn't I? I felt like shit! How on earth did those police officers know I was killing myself that night? What the hell went so very wrong?

*   *   *

It turns out that my online support group of grieving parents were watching my e-mails to the group very carefully. These moms were pros who also lost children to death by accident, murder, and suicide. Some of them had experience with suicide as their own child had taken their lives and were particularly watchful of the signs. One woman named Sue saw something in my last e-mail that made the hair on her head stand up straight, and she contacted the moderator of our group to ask her opinion. They spoke on the phone to a few members and decided I was in trouble, now!

Most of the members of this group are in the United States. They did not know where in Canada I lived. They knew nothing about me other than my e-mail address, which did not indicate my whereabouts. The moderator must have known my last name from when I filed the application to join the group. Sue knew a Royal Canadian Mounted Police (RCMP) officer in Ottawa, our nation's capital, and gave him a call. From there, I don't know how they located me on the other side of the continent without an address or phone number but they did, and I lived. Were my angels still watching out for me in a surreal divine way?

*   *   *

I was in the hospital for about a month. Gary came to see me and said a doctor told him my situation was very grave, terminal even. He told Gary I would one day be successful at ending my own life. When Gary was telling me this, he had tears in his eyes, something I didn't see very often. I felt so bad for Gary, but how could I go on living when I had nothing left to live for? I wanted to care and love my granddaughter Amanda enough to keep myself alive, but my need to die exceeded my ability to use Amanda as reason to live at this point. Trevor, Ximi, and Tyler were all gone from my life now, and I felt the life suck right out of me like a vacuum.

While I was being warehoused at the hospital, I was blessed to have so many people throughout North America, my friends on the Grieving Support Group, send me letters and phone calls of love and concern. Even one of the police officers who found me came to visit me to see how I was doing. It was very, very touching and wholly unexpected. In my experience, people who try to take their own lives are looked down upon, stomped on even, for their stupidity, cowardice, and lack of empathy for others who would be left behind. Living after a failed suicide attempt can often cause the tormented soul to try again and again—like a drug.

In fact, I see suicide as a coping method much like drugs or alcohol. The only difference I believe is that suicide is the fastest way out. I have heard about people who cut themselves, starve themselves, drink themselves into oblivion, inject dirty needles into their arms, and on and on to hurt themselves. The end result often leads to death, and it is my opinion they just want to avoid the stigma of suicide and die slower and less obviously. Other less evident methods of suicide are drinking and driving, speed, or engaging in other reckless behavior that could be life-threatening. Suicide comes in many colors.

People who kick down a living or dead suicide with nasty remarks have their own internal problems to deal with. Unjustified judgment against their fellow friend or family member is the most self-centered act known to man. No one can get inside another's head and understand why people do what they do to themselves. Those who judge someone negatively because they attempted or succeeded a suicide are the most coldhearted people I can think of. People who are happy and satisfied with their lives as a whole may never ever even consider killing themselves and have no idea of the torment others feel so deeply, deeply enough to want to leave this world.

Some people, however, do commit or attempt suicide as a means to hurt or manipulate others. These creatures are the psychopaths and malignant narcissists I speak so often about in this memoir. However, it is extremely rare for a malignant narcissist or a psychopath to seriously attempt to kill themselves and even rarer for them to be successful since their attempts are so feeble. Their attempts are more about manipulating others to get what they want from them.

*   *   *

There may be another reason some people who constantly try to kill themselves but never succeed: divine intervention. Since my first attempt at seventeen years of age, I have probably tried to end my life over ten times. Each attempt more serious than the last. One of the worst feelings for a true suicide is to wake up in a hospital having to face people who you know very well is judging you harshly. Trust me, only divine intervention can be the reason for me living to write about my experiences.

My last attempt (long after Gary and I separated) was nothing other than the universe or God interfering in my plans. I laid my plan out so well I had twenty-four hours before anyone could find me dead. I swallowed a full bottle of sleeping pills, a full bottle of gravel, and a full bottle of Benadryl. This was at 10:00 p.m. I was bound and determined not to let out any indication to anyone that I was going to die that night. I lived alone at this point and was free to do as I wished, even die.

The next afternoon, I heard the phone ringing in the distance. I tried to get up but couldn't. I fell back into my coma. Later the phone was ringing again, and nothing made sense. I continued to lie on my bed, drifting in and out of sleep. The phone rang again; I fell out of my bed and crawled to the telephone and picked it up. It was my best friend, Veronica, and she told me later I was talking gibberish and then hung up on her.

Veronica told me later she was trying to reach me all day. She lived several hours from me so couldn't just drop over. She had no idea what I had done, but for some reason, she wouldn't give up calling on that day, waking me for brief moments of time, which I am sure kept me alive.

Suddenly I heard someone banging on my door. It was so loud I was afraid. I knew it was Frank, a fellow (whom I'll talk about more later in the book) who I had set up a date with to go play bingo with that next night after my suicide. I felt he would be the best person to find me. Frank was another one of those friends who just never gave up on me. Frank knew my history of suicide, and when he didn't get a response at the lobby door, he had someone else let him in and began banging on my condo door and screaming at me to open the door up.

I crawled; I tried to stand up and kept falling over. I felt like Gumby, the rubber toy of my childhood days. It seemed like it took me forever just to get to the door, and I was banging my body up unmercifully all the way. When I finally reached the door, my fingers wouldn't let me turn the knob to open the door, and I told Frank this. He kept pushing me to try and between standing on my knees and pulling on the door knob, I kept falling over. Frank kept screaming at me, which I believe kept me awake as much as the telephone ringing earlier did. Finally, the door flew open and Frank picked me up off the floor. I was dead weight, but he carried me to my bed and called the paramedics from my bedroom.

When I woke up in the hospital, I was beside myself with grief. Here I had done it again, hurt two people I loved so much, my best friends, and lived to see the pain in their eyes and voices. It was too much to bear—waking up.

There is no logical reason for me to have lived that attempt. I took far too many pills and was alone for almost twenty hours with the poisons in my system. Why did Veronica choose that day to telephone me over and over again? How did I get to the door to let Frank in? I was in true awe at the strangeness of being alive after such a serious attempt.

Since that suicide didn't work, I decided that there is a plan for each and every one of us, and if it is not your time to die, you will not no matter how hard you try. If it *is* your time to die, you will. My point is this: leave people who are successful at suicide alone. Do not judge them, do not call them names, and do not kick them while they are down. It was their time to die, and nothing could have stopped the death.

Too many people think that if a loved one dies to suicide, it is about them, the survivor. It is not, and if I can get one point across in this chapter about suicide, it is that it was meant to be and everything in the universe is working as it is supposed to.

My sister-in-law, Sandy, happened to work at the hospital I was sent to, and she told my brother, Gus, I was in the hospital. He called me, and when I told him what I had done, he screamed and swore at me so loud I had to move the phone away from my ear. This brother spent most of his life as a crack drug addict and alcoholic and yet he was the loudest of them all in beating me further to the ground for trying to end my life. Cold.

*　*　*

I do not believe in secrets and would like to tell my story in its entirety, truthfully and fully. However, I have decided to not go into the details of my many other attempts after the ones described in this memoir to date. I stop for the sake of my grandchildren. I am already wretchedly sorry they are going to read such scary behavior by their Nana.

Today I love these children so much it hurts me to have to admit my suicide weaknesses here in this book. I want them to know that if I had known them the way I know them today, I would never ever deliberately put them through this kind of loss. They already lost their daddy to a dreadful car accident, and to lose a grandmother to suicide would only harm them even more emotionally—something I am not willing to do when in my right mind. I pray I remain suicide attempt free for the rest of my days. If something happens and I am successful down the road, it will not be because I do not love my grandbabies; it will be because my soul once again became so tormented I went to the point of no return.

*　*　*

Suicide is a secret affair. Many suicides are covered up by the police or the families by stating the dead had an accident or were murdered. Suicide can be so hush-hush that to even talk about it can get you into trouble because it generates so much fear in people. I even belonged to a team of survivors of psychopaths and narcissists where a moderator of the online group kicked me out of the forum for just talking about my painfully unsuccessfully suicide attempts! This was supposed to be a therapy group for survivors of extremely abusive partners, mothers, fathers, and siblings!

I imagine I will get into some trouble for even writing about some of my experiences in my own memoir, but I'm done with secrets, and if you have something negative to say to me about my suicide attempt history, keep it to yourself. You don't know anything about it because if you did, your heart would reach out to me with love not judgment, hate, or indifference.

* * *

Everyone has problems. Some suffer horrific lives worse than others, and some people are poor in spirit, yet we do not know it. Masking family and love problems serves no one. If you look across the street and watch the Smiths seemingly living the good life, nice husband, attentive wife, beautiful and well-behaved children, and nice house and car, you know the people I'm talking about—they have it all. Or do they? Some people are so afraid to speak out about their problems they let it fester and boil within their cocooned worlds they never recover. Rest assured their pain will seep out eventually, if not in their generation, in the ones to follow.

I've watched many situation comedies that seem to bear witness to family dysfunction to the point of being hysterically funny. Thanks to television, we can get a glimpse at how other families live, or so we think. The TV people sarcastically appear to hate each other or are so obviously narcissistic they are laughable. But the next week, all is well again, and nobody ever gets hurt in the end. This is not real. Not even Roseanne's mother (her character name fails me), Evelyn, Charlie, and Allan's mother on *Two and a Half Men*, or Christine on her show *The New Adventures of Old Christine*, are as painful as real life for so many of us. These narcissistic characters are downright funny because they suit so many families of today, and it is fun to laugh at ourselves from time to time. It only gets ugly when the "malignant" part sets in—and we don't see those on situation comedies!

* * *

The next chapter is as controversial as you can get but I cannot write this memoir without including my experiences in the months and years following my son's death. The spiritual events that happened after Trevor died was as real as the page I am typing on. You be the judge.

Chapter 11—Hello from Heaven!

We are not human beings having a spiritual experience. We are spiritual beings having a human experience.

—Dr. Wayne W. Dyer

Sociopaths rarely believe in anything bigger than themselves, but this chapter is an insert to my experiences after the death of my son, which outlines some bizarre news I want to share. I believe all of my experiences are true and can be backed up by over half the population who had after-death experiences.

* * *

Three months after Trevor died, I was in bed in the wee hours of the morning when I *felt* the impression of someone sitting down at the bottom of my bed. I jumped up and looked but saw nothing. I have never been exposed to ghosts or spirits and never really gave it a thought, but this instance gave me a moment of pause. Then I went back to sleep.

The very next morning, the same thing happened. Something or someone *was* sitting on the bottom of my bed! I jumped up and intuitively knew it was the energy of Trevor. I called out his name and felt the bed go back up as if he left. I was shaking so hard I couldn't wait to tell my grieving parents group of my strange experience. I learned I was not alone. About 10 percent of my support group also had experiences of their loved ones coming back in one form or another. The message they felt aware of from their child was always the same, "I am okay."

One gal in my group suggested I purchase the book *Hello from Heaven*, by Bill Guggenheim and Judy Guggenheim. This paperback is a detailed study of over two thousand people who claim to have had afterlife experiences where they saw, heard, or felt their loved ones after they died! What amazed me by the time I bought and read this book is that I shared almost all of the same identical experiences as the people in the study. The most common types of afterlife communication are sitting-on-the-bed sensations and electrical nuisances in addition to other direct and indirect signs.

My most common experience was the electricity within our home suddenly acting up. In my depression after returning home from the hospital, I did a lot of reading in my bed; beside me was my lamp, which constantly flickered on and off to the point of total annoyance. I had Gary check out the wires and light bulb, which he changed. However, the same flickering occurred over and over again.

One night, I was so agitated by the off-and-on light I changed rooms to read. The lamp beside the guest room bed began flickering off and on! At that point, I knew it was Trevor playing games with me. I couldn't ignore my new reality anymore.

Trevor's wife, Ximi, told me her alarm systems at home were constantly going off for no explainable reason. She walked into her bedroom one night and her room became illuminated with a pale blue light, and she felt a sensation of complete and pure love. This sign lasted for over five minutes!

In a later chapter, I will talk about my visit to Guatemala in 2004 to visit Trevor's wife, Ximi. For the purpose of this chapter, I will tell of my many experiences in her home. One night, I was just drifting off to sleep when I felt beyond a doubt someone tucking in the blankets all around my bed. I thought it might be Ximi's maid. (She comes from a wealthy home and so it didn't seem too far-fetched that a maid would tuck me in, I guess.) Anyway, I sat up and saw no one! No one was tucking me in, yet I will swear that was the sensation as I was about to go to sleep.

More mysterious events continued to occur. Ximi and I were watching some DVDs on her computer in her bedroom when suddenly, the television turned on by itself! The remote was far away from both of us and so it could not have been either of us sitting on it to make the TV turn on. Ximi and I stared at each other for a moment when the air conditioner made a noise and turned off! (It turned right back on minutes later.)

I do not have enough space in this chapter to go on, but needless to say, when I was with Trevor's wife at her home, we were bombarded with signs from whom we knew to be Trevor's spirit.

Meanwhile, back at home, I continued to experience supernatural events. My telephone would ring, and I could hear white noise and a faint male voice but nothing else! One night, I was tucking in my granddaughter, who was staying with us (she was three years old at that time), and she asked who the man in the mirror was. I looked behind me where my dresser and mirror were and saw nothing. But Amanda saw something that made her ask me about it!

Amanda received a lot of subtle messages, especially feathers. She would bring me feathers every day that she found outside. I never saw one feather in all the years we lived there and was shocked at the numbers she was bringing in. One day, we were visiting my aunt Eve's, and all of us were sitting out on her patio and Amanda was standing nearby. For no particular reason, I looked over at her and saw, in slow motion, a large feather drifting down in a semicircular fashion and land right on her head! All of us at the table witnessed this and thought it was a very strange event, the way it floated down and landed on Amanda's head. That was the last feather Amanda ever brought to me.

*　　*　　*

My best friend, Veronica, told me that her husband's mother was coming to visit from England. It turns out she is a popular medium in Britain and Canada! She asked me if I wanted a reading from her, and since I already had some afterlife experiences, I agreed. Veronica was skeptical of the whole thing and said she would tell her mother-in-law nothing about Trevor (except that I had a son who was in a car accident) so that she could see for herself if there was anything to what I was experiencing, the afterlife.

I met Barbara at Veronica's home. She had asked me to bring an item owned by any deceased person I wished to get a reading from. I brought Trevor's favorite hat and a doily my grandmother crocheted for me years before she died.

I was not very open to having a person who did not know my son or grandmother give me a psychic/medium reading because I was still uncertain of my own encounters. In addition, I tried one of those online mediums, and she was so far off base with everything it really turned me off of mediums.

I gave Barbara my items and sat beside her on Veronica's sofa. Barbara said there was an elderly lady with her. She was telling Barbara that my son was with her and was doing fine. Barbara said a young man peered over the older lady and had a wide grin on his face (Trevor was always smiling). He was asking me something about a vacuum cleaner. I just about fell over on the floor when I heard that: just the day before, I was vacuuming my stairs when I had a sudden frustrating moment and kicked the vacuum all the way down the stairs! No one knew about this incident, and I began to listen to Barbara much more closely after she told me about that.

She said a lady was in a car with Trevor and he had an accident. Barbara paused for some time and then asked, "Was there a fire?" As mentioned in an earlier chapter, Trevor's car did catch fire, and he was very badly burned. She said it looks like it was a "posh" car (Trevor was driving his BMW). She said it was white, with two long doors. True.

Barbara said Trevor was asking about a watch and a glove box. Again, earlier in this book, I mentioned that Ximi retrieved Trevor's watch from the glove box after the accident—there was no way for Barbara to know this either! She said Trevor was very concerned about the lady in the car. He was floating above and had no fear but was watching everything going on below him. He was attached to a silver string while hovering above. She said Trevor saw the medics put a neck brace on him, and he wondered why. Trevor's next comment concerned being at the hospital and overhearing a nurse asking the doctor if she should put a "wrap" on him. I didn't know what a wrap meant until I talked to friends later who said when someone is badly burned, they put a burn wrap on the body.

The reading I received from Barbara was nothing short of shocking for me. She said many more accurate things about my son and grandmother, but I'll leave those observations for another book.

* * *

By this time, I was used to getting many types of "signs and messages" from Trevor and became a true believer that we are eternal and we can come back to our loved ones. I got a lot of flak from some of my Christian friends who said I was "playing with the Devil" by encouraging this sort of activity. We are trained from our respective churches that once we are dead, we head straight up to heaven or downward to hell. We certainly don't hang around our *alive* loved ones! I now believe this type of teaching is wrong and closes off our ability to really understand the universe and souls and how they function.

Symbols

Another strange newness since Trevor died is symbols I am seeing over and over again. My symbols are usually the number 111, 1111, 1117, or 911

(911 happens to also be my birthday). I will see these numbers several times in one day and often for several days in a row, day and night. For no good reason, I will glance at a digital clock and it will be 1:11, 11:11, 11:17, or 9:11. I will suddenly notice these numbers on a license plate or outdoor sign as well.

One very eerie night, I was in Florida visiting a friend who lost her twelve-year-old son, Justin, to an ATV accident. We had just returned from Pavo, Georgia, where many of us from our online support group met up for a retreat. I decided to extend my visit to the southeastern part of North America. Lorna lived in Orlando, and we arrived very late. I went to sleep on Lorna's sofa for the night.

At precisely 1:11 a.m., I woke up and my eyes diverted directly to a digital clock (I did not know where her clocks were, but as soon as my eyes opened, they were looking at the 1:11 on a clock). I watched in wonder for a few moments when I suddenly heard chimes coming from her backyard. It sounded like someone had an instrument and was banging on these chimes so loud, as if to get someone's attention. *Bang, bang, bang . . .* the noise would not stop. It was far louder than the usual twinkle of chimes, even in a storm, and there wasn't even a slight wind that night.

When the noise would not let up, I decided to take a peek out her back door and looked into the complete blackness and saw nothing. I stared hard in the direction of what I assumed to be the tree with chimes on it; freakishly, in my mind's eye, I saw a young boy banging the chimes with great strength. I was so spooked I ran back inside and locked the door behind me.

The next morning, I asked Lorna if she had a tree with chimes on it and if she didn't hear the banging going on the night before. She hadn't. I could have been pushed over with a feather when she said she had *over fifty orange trees out back and every single one of them had chimes on them!* No, no, *no*! It was one tree and one set of chimes that I heard and saw in my mind's eye. If one set of chimes could make such a racket, then all of them should have been hammering!

To this day, I see my symbols. Sometimes I will see the 1:11 and 11:11 morning and night for an entire week. Something spiritual is going on because these sightings of the exact same numbers are a complete scientific impossibly in my opinion.

Orbs

Google the term *orb* and you may find the same essential definition as what I am going to share. It took me a long time to understand what an orb is or why they appeared in photos from time to time without rhyme or reason. As the months and years continued and as I interpreted the many types of "afterlife" terms, I now believe I have a good handle on describing what an orb is.

I was at a grieving parents retreat in Chilliwack, British Columbia, when the host came out of her home and said that the photos taken that night are now loaded on the computer, and she said I should come in because I may want to identify one of the orbs. Huh? Not knowing what she was talking about, I decided to follow her and others into the house. There, on Shari's computer, I saw numerous photos of the garden outside, and each picture revealed a party of orbs (round translucent balls of varying sizes and colors).

Shari's garden is special. This woman, amazingly, lost three of her precious children at different times to accident, murder, and suicide. One of Shari's ways to cope was to build a "Garden of Tears" at her home in Chilliwack, where people who have lost close relatives can come, share, put memorials up, and gather for retreats. The home is situated next to a river, and Shari proudly grows many flowers and plants, angelic figurines, etc., in her special yard garden.

When I looked at the photos of Shari's garden, my mouth dropped open in awe. In every single picture, taken by different cameras by different people, I saw a mass of orbs (balls) that seemed to have faces in them! Since this was the first time I heard of an orb, I was very skeptical and a little put off that the girls would have me look inside some of these balls (by zooming in) to see if I can see Trevor's face! How absurd!

I was wrong. I now completely believe and understand that what I witnessed (and continue to see) are spirit orbs. In my research (and finding the occasional orb or orbs in my own photos), I now believe that as spirits, we are free to roam earth and often (but not always) have a protective bubble surrounding our new form. Some continue to house a visible face of what they looked like before their earthly death.

I read a book not long ago that also confirms my new knowledge: this book was about a man who had a near-death experience (NDE), and he felt himself floating toward the ceiling. He wrote in his book that he had the distinct feeling he was in a bubble. I cannot remember the name of the book or I would cite it here.

When Orbs Came Alive for Me

Until recently, I always saw orbs as "still" figures. This is because I was viewing them in "still" shots, I soon learned. All of that changed when that same friend from Orlando sent me a video that was set up in her friend's home by paranormal investigators. That house was experiencing a lot of so-called haunted activity, and the owners wanted to capture the goings on with a video shot. They got what they asked for: clearly and without question, as the camera was focused in the laundry and kitchen in the middle of the night, I saw the motion detectors go off and two orbs speedily dashed around the rooms! A voice was audible that sounded like "I'm sorry, I'm sorry." It was the voice of a child, whether boy or girl, it could not be determined.

Friends who knew I was still researching the afterlife sent me photos to ask if I thought they were orbs, and I am grateful to have many on file. Orbs come in many sizes and colors but are always the same shape: round. The most common ones are clear white; some are pale pink, green, or blue, and a few (very few) are brilliant purple or blue. It does not matter what camera is used, film, digital, video, etc., and two or more people often capture the same orb(s).

My granddaughter's barn is full of orbs, all of the time—it does not matter when or who takes the photo. At first, I thought Trevor came with a bunch of his spirit friends to celebrate Amanda's first horse show: now I just wonder about the history of the farmland and what the hell went on there to cause so many to remain behind.

Do Spirits Always Come in an Orb or Bubble?

My short answer is no. I have seen spirits in a few common forms. The first time was when I thought my husband had come upstairs to check on me and turn around and go back down the stairs. I went downstairs to ask my husband why he would do that—come all the way up, turn around, and go back down. He didn't. He had not left the sofa. Well, I know what I saw, and I saw a spirit in almost completely human form. It was not Trevor's full body, in reflection, but I know the top of a body when I see one, especially when it is staring at me in my doorway.

Another experience with a spirit was when I was staying with a friend in Nakusp, British Columbia. I couldn't sleep, so I got up to watch some television, which was on the left of my view. Suddenly, I had the strangest sensation that someone was standing beside me, to my right. I slowly looked over (with the hair standing at the back of my neck), and three feet above ground was a six-foot mass of what looked like cloud. It had an unrecognizable bodily form in its mist.

I have grown to know in my experiences and research that spirits visit us in many shapes: in orbs (in a bubble), in human form, or in spirit mass. As a person who has bought and sold many homes over the years, I will not even look at a home I am considering purchasing when I see orbs in the listing photos. To me, those homes have unfinished business hanging around that has nothing to do with me. I have enough of my own dead relatives and spirits to manage, thank you!

*   *   *

I have now read over two hundred books on the subject of the afterlife and am now a true believer of eternity for all souls. I find it hard to believe that so many credible people could be wrong or lying about their paranormal encounters! In my view, we fail to evolve when we stick to one type of teaching without investigation. Many people dismiss such mysticism without so much as opening up a book about it. Interestingly, the Bible itself is full of supernatural events and yet if the good news comes from the people of today, we are told we are simply imagining things due to our grief.

I remember the loud male voice I heard in my inner ear way back when Trevor was thirteen years old. The voice was clear in saying, "Trevor is in trouble." I was not in grief at that time, and so it defies the logic of imagined messages from beyond.

Three years after my events started happening, I became worried about Trevor and whether or not he was hanging around me because he was worried. I took a long time to relax in my grief, and since Trevor and I did have a very close bond, I did not want him to worry about me anymore. One night, three years after he died, the light was doing the usual flickering and I decided to talk out loud to Trevor to tell him I was fine and that if he saw a bright light around him, I wanted him to walk into that light. I said I would be okay, and it was time for him to move on in his destiny. I also told him I would always remember and love him—and I would see him again. After that hour-long talk, my lamp never flickered again, and I stopped getting messages and signs of his presence.

When I tell people about how my experiences started and stopped, they say I must have imagined things and when I was ready to let go of Trevor, the imagined events stopped. I say Trevor was the one who finally became ready to move on to the light. I cannot be told my experiences never happened; it was too real. People who have never had such encounters would have a difficult time believing these events; I understand that.

* * *

The Dream

I never believed in the afterlife before my own personal experiences, and I sure as hell never believed in reincarnation! However, I was introduced to an international bestseller called *Many Lives, Many Masters*, by Dr. Brian Weiss. Dr. Weiss was graduated Phi Beta Kappa, magna cum laude, from Columbia University in New York in 1966. He then went to the Yale University School of Medicine and received his MD degree in 1970. Following an internship at the New York University-Bellevue Medical Center, he returned to Yale to complete his residency in psychiatry. Upon completion, he accepted a faculty position of the University of Miami, heading the psychopharmacology division. There he achieved national recognition in the fields of biological psychiatry and substance abuse. After four years at the university, he was promoted to the rank of associate professor of psychiatry at the medical school and was appointed chief of psychiatry at a large university-affiliated hospital in Miami. By that time, he had already published thirty-seven scientific papers and book chapters in his field.

Years of disciplined study had trained his mind to think as a scientist and physician, molding him along the narrow paths of conservatism in his profession. Dr. Weiss distrusted anything that could not be proven by traditional scientific methods. He was aware of some of the studies in parapsychology that were being conducted at major universities across the country, but they did not hold his attention. Like me, it all seemed too farfetched for him.

Then he met a patient named Catherine who changed everything. For almost two years, he used traditional methods of therapy to help her overcome her phobia symptoms. When nothing seemed to work, Dr. Weiss tried hypnosis. In a series of trance states, Catherine recalled "past life" memories that proved to be the causative factors of her symptoms. According to Dr. Weiss, she also was able to act as a conduit for information from highly evolved "spirit entities," and through them, she revealed many of the secrets of life and of death. In just a few months, her symptoms disappeared and she resumed her life, happier and more at peace than ever before!

Nothing in Dr. Weiss's background prepared him for this. He himself was absolutely amazed when these events unfolded. You'll have to get the book to see what Catherine revealed during her sessions with the doctor, but these experiences were just too real to dismiss. After approximately five years of the regression therapy, Dr. Weiss finally came clean with his fellow scientists, risking his entire career. To Dr. Weiss's amazement many psychiatrists also involved in regression hypnotherapy also came forward with similar stories. Dr. Weiss had started a revelation in the psychiatric community by coming forward and today doctors are documenting stories of past life experiences their patients discuss while in a hypnotic trance.

Dr. Weiss says his book, *Many Lives, Many Masters*, is a small contribution to the ongoing research in the field of parapsychology, especially the branch dealing with our experiences before birth and after death. In his book, he claims nothing was added and nothing was deleted, save for repetitious parts of Catherine's hypnotic states.

* * *

I heard that Dr. Weiss was going to be giving a lecture with James van Praagh, a medium, in Seattle, Washington, which is not too far from where I lived in British Columbia. I decided to attend and was surprised to learn that as part of the conference, Dr. Weiss was going to conduct a mass "past-life regression hypnosis session" for all attendees.

I've never been one to go under hypnosis and doubted I would experience any past lives, often called past-life regression therapy. True to form, while I very much enjoyed the conference, I did not get hypnotized. After the seminar, I had my book autographed by Dr. Weiss and told him I could not "go under." His response was that later on I may experience a past-life experience or something similar during a dream or dream state.

It was about a month later when my dream came. My dream is as clear today as it was when I woke up from a this bizarre experience in 2005.

I was following a little girl who appeared to be approximately ten years old. She was wearing a red coat with fake black fur trim on the sleeves and hood.

I felt like I was invisible and floating in the air about three feet from the ground, following this child down a tree-lined street with wartime houses on each side of the narrow street. The street reminded me of North Vancouver, where both my parents and I were born and raised. The little girl ran into her home and was speaking to her Mother and an old man who was sitting in a big easy chair. I recognized the lady as being my mother's mother, although I was only nine months old when she died. I recognized the old man as being my Great-Grandfather, Thomas. I think I must remember these people from photos because I never did know them as a child since they had died when I was very young. From my dream, their faces are very clear and real to me, however. It was like I knew them.

I recognized the furniture as being from the 1940s, and the dress of the Mother seemed to be of the same era. The living room was neat and tidy, and there was a six-inch step up to a landing just outside of the master bedroom. On the wall just outside of the bedroom was a hook where the lady kept her purse.

That part of my dream ended, and I suddenly found myself in a blue shadowish area. I saw four beings varying in size from largest, which I instinctively knew as being my older brother, Gus; then me; then my younger sister, Shivey; and finally the smallest being Dylan, my young brother. I don't know how I knew who was who but I just did. The forms were faceless but shaped like humans. The beings were translucent blue, darker blue than the air around me. The forms had yellow grids on them.

Suddenly I heard a loud male voice who asked, "Who will bear the brunt of that little girl's anger?" I knew the voice was talking about that ten-year-old girl. I saw myself, from behind, raise my hand. I was in a pre-life state, agreeing to come to earth to be this woman's daughter and bear the brunt of her anger! My mother was born in 1940, and everything just seemed to make sense and come together for me as for why we had such a turbulent relationship.

This dream was so real, and it made so much sense I felt like I should take action of some sort. Like reconcile my life with hers (my mother) because this was in the cards according to my pre-life dream.

I read more books on the subject of souls, near-death experiences (NDE), reincarnation, the afterlife, and more. I was glued to the subject from the moment I had this dream. I now know, not just believe, that our lives are planned out, and we come to earth in soul groups to learn lessons or to teach others lessons. Coming to earth, to this life, is an exciting thing for souls since we learn so much more, and faster, when we are incarnated. We know the beings in our soul group intimately and often interchange roles throughout our reincarnations. My malignantly narcissistic mother may have been my child in another life or my husband. We are souls. We are spirits having a human experience, as Dr. Wayne Dyer says, not humans having a spiritual experience.

*   *   *

Setting the ghosts aside life had settled for me somewhat and I was preparing to go to Guatemala to meet up with my daughter-in-law to see how she was doing, and to find out if I could help in any way get her back into Canada through the Canadian Embassy in Guatemala. Ximi and I had spent many days on the internet talking about our mutual love, Trevor, and I was excited to be with her once again. Little did I know how this trip would cause me to lose Ximi forever by yet another relationship destroyer in my family, my sister.

Ivan and Eleanor's wedding in 1956

Cherylann's psychopath father in his early years

Cherylann's mother, Eleanor Groseclose aged 20

Cherylann's Aunt June (by marriage to Chester Bentson).
She died jumping from a 7th floor window while on a colossal amount
of pharmaceuticals while in her 70s.

Arthur Nolan Fisher, Trevor's Biological father

Cherylann's last year of school, faking a smile for the camera

Proud Mom & Trevor
at Baby Shower

Cherylann proudly displays her newborn at a baby shower
put on by Stepmother, Sunny.

18 Year old Cherylann showing off baby Trevor.

Grandma with her children: From left to right:
Pearl, *Thelma, Hilliard, Cherylann's father, Ivan, and *Eve

Cherylann's grandma holding baby Trevor with mother looking on.

Cherylann and *Gus with *Dylan and *Shivey

Cherylann's paternal grandparents, Gilbert and Margaret Groseclose

A rare photo of Cherylann and her mother with Gus to the left of the photo

Cherylann's mother said Trevor Thomas also had 'evil eyes' as a child

Cherylann on her marriage day in 1984

Gary and Cherylann enter the hall after their wedding ceremony

Gary with Trevor and flower girl, *Michelle

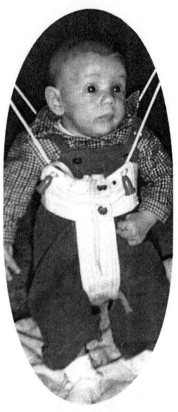

I loved looking after all of my little cousins!

Shivey's Baby Darren Jr.
(01/86 - 05/86)

Trevor loved to look after
all of his cousins!

Trevor with all of his beloved cousins!

Cherylann leaving to find her namesake town, Groseclose, VA

Cherylann with Groseclose Town Historian

Groseclose Town Cemetary

Cherylann takes her Aunts and Uncle to Groseclose in 2000

Groseclose 250 Year Family Reunion where we met over 350 "Cousins"

Cherylann with her beloved paternal Grandmother, Margaret Groseclose

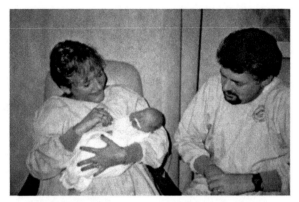

Cherylann and Gary with newly born, *Tyler.

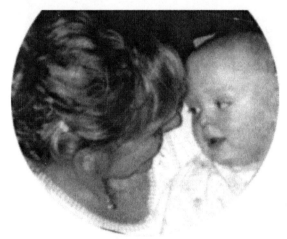

Cherylann having a loving discussion with baby Tyler.

Cherylann's mother in the only photo of her holding her great-grandson, Tyler.

Cherylann and Gary in Mexico (1999)

Trevor holding his son, Tyler at a Craig family camping reunion.

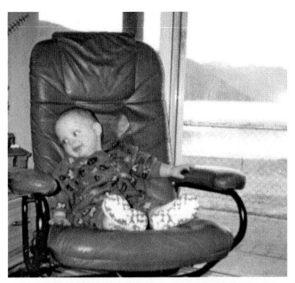

Tyler enjoying the sights around him at Nana's townhome in 1999.

Trevor having a supervised visit at the park with his son, Tyler.

Trevor and Ximi's civil marriage on January 18th, 2003

Ximi and Trevor after a reception dinner at White Rock Beach.

Ximi and Trevor showing off their wedding rings.

Ximi and Trevor in love

*Amanda wanting to do some gardening at Nana's in the rain!

Cherylann with granddaughter, Amanda, on one of their many vacations.

Amanda having a break while walking a family friend's dog

Amanda with her own dog, *Lady.

Amanda with one of her beloved horses

Amanda during one of her horse competitions. Age 8

Amanda *horse swimming!*

Amanda win's many awards for her horse riding efforts!

Tyler and Amanda finally united.

Tyler loves his music: drums and piano.

Trapped in flames

Police couldn't pull driver from burning BMW after 4 a.m. crash

By PAUL COWAN
Staff Writer

A man died yesterday morning after being trapped in a blazing BMW, while passing police officers managed to pull the other passenger to safety.

Police made the rescue from a white BMW 325i after a two-vehicle collision at the junction of Stony Plain Road and 142 Street shortly before 4 a.m.

The officers were there within about 30 seconds and managed to pull the woman from the passenger side," said traffic investigator Sgt. Glenn Slack.

"But when they went to get the driver, his car burst into flames."

Fire Officers arrived to find the car engulfed.

They eventually cut the driver from the car and he was rushed to the University Hospital with serious burns to 80% of his body. He died in hospital.

His passenger was taken to the Royal Alexandra Hospital where she was being treated for a head injury.

The car burst into flames after slamming into a silver-coloured Nissan Pathfinder SUV that was turning off Stony Plain Road onto 142 Street.

The two vehicles met in the intersection and both suffered major damage," said Slack.

The eastbound BMW appeared to be speeding according to a witness, he said.

The female driver of the SUV suffered a broken leg. Her passenger also suffered lower leg injuries.

The fire is believed to have started in the BMW's engine compartment and spread quickly.

Slack said the driver was pinned in the wreckage and even if the police officers had gotten his door open, it is highly possible that they would not have been able to pull him out.

The force of the impact pushed the westbound SUV back onto Stony Plain Road.

Debris from the BMW was thrown in front that, in arcing from the vehicle, which

TOP: The mangled wreckage of a BMW 325i, suspected of speeding at the time of a collision, lies near the intersection of 142 Street and Stony Plain Road yesterday morning while city police investigators take measurements.

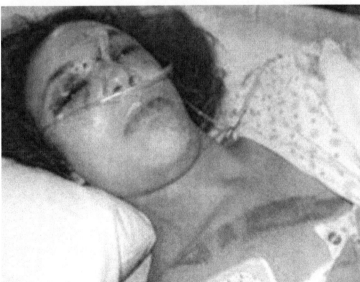

Ximi the day after the crash that killed Trevor. The other driver was found at fault.

Tyler and Amanda visit their Dad's graveside.

From left to right Shivey, Gus, and my niece at mother's condo in Vernon, BC

Cherylann with her half-brother, Dylan, before all hell broke loose

Gus and Dad liked to hang out together.

Dad and Uncle Hilliard still trying to be the 'men about town.'

Cherylann in Havanna, Cuba (2006)

Gilbert, Sunny, Shenay, and Gilbert's daughter Danni.

Ivan with Great-granddaughter, Amanda

Uncle Hilliard at the Army and Navy Club. He is 75 in this photo.

Cherylann and Uncle Hilliard while father is in palliative care.

Frank DeSmet

Cherylann in Egypt dancing with an African tribe group of musicians
(spring of 2007)

Cherylann enjoying a moment on a Mediterranean cruise (2005)

Trevor

Cherylann now loves to ride her scooter around town!

Cherylann enjoys her sister dogs, Callie and Sadie

Cherylann is finally reunited with Tyler and Amanda together.

Chapter 12—Guatemala

You'd have to be inhuman not to be flattered. But it was so obsessive, so quick, that some part of me didn't trust it.

—Robert Redford

A very strange event happened in 2004 when I decided to fly to Guatemala to visit my daughter-in-law. It had been a year since Trevor died, and Ximi and I were on e-mail almost daily, providing each other comfort since he passed away. We knew that Trevor's two loves were his wife and me, and we loved to talk about Trevor all of the time. It was our way of grieving together.

What was strange was that when I told my sister that I was taking this three-week trip to Guatemala, she told me she was coming as well. Shivey barely knew Ximi, and I found it odd she would want to spend that much money on a trip to visit someone she didn't know. The other part of the strangeness was Shivey didn't ask; *she told me as if she had some sort of entitlement.* I was taken aback by her insistence that she accompany me and shook my head in wonderment of her nerve. She was not invited!

I would be staying at Ximi's home, and there was no offer for my sister, the one who did not even show up at Trevor's wedding, to stay with Ximi's family at all. Shivey was so pushy about the topic I was very concerned that Ximi or her family would think our family was strange (which it is) and would reflect badly on me.

Finally, I told my sister I had already booked my flight (alone) and made arrangements to stay with Ximi for the entire three weeks. There was no room for her to be in attendance. I was very stern with her and said there was no place for her in Guatemala at this time.

Imagine my shock when Shivey phoned me days later stating that she had also booked a flight and would be staying at a hotel in Guatemala while I was there! What the hell? She would be unwelcome because I wanted to share Trevor with Ximi, not my neglectful, selfish sister!

However, I didn't have a backbone, so I just went along with her plan (what choice did I have?) and included her with Ximi and my activities while we were there. I just couldn't leave Shivey at her hotel alone. And so we went to clubs and on tours and even took a flight to Belize to stay at one of the islands on the Keys, San Pedro. There were moments we had very good times, but other times, I noticed Shivey taking Ximi away from me to talk to her privately. Knowing my sister was artful at making up lies about me (very much like my mother), I was constantly concerned she would ruin my relationship with my precious daughter-in-law. What could she say that would turn Ximi away from me? I didn't know and I still don't know.

I don't think like Shivey, and it just never occurred to me that after that visit, I would never hear from my daughter-in-law again. She would not respond to my e-mails or telephone calls. To me, this is the danger of the sociopath. Watch your back as the invisible swords are very sharp and can ruin even the best of relationships. Sociopaths are a jealous people, and I know that Shivey said something that caused my daughter-in-law to avoid me like the plague after my visit with her. There can be no other explanation, especially with Shivey's strange behavior in booking the flight to Guatemala after I told her no.

*   *   *

I had to set aside the odd happenings in Guatemala and my loss of Ximi; because things were about to change for Gary and myself. We were about to become the full time guardians of Amanda!

Chapter 13—My Awakening

If you are going through hell, keep going!

—Winston Churchill

Gary and I were noticing some very disturbing things about Mary and Amanda, our granddaughter. Her mother was either unable or unwilling to provide a safe home for her. In the first year we knew Mary and Amanda after Trevor died, they had moved eleven times in one year! Mary always lived with different men or families on welfare, with her boyfriend of the month. I gave up my career after Trevor died because I felt the life had been sucked out of me and my self-esteem was almost nonexistent. However, I offered to babysit Amanda on a daily basis so that Mary could go to school and obtain a job to support her daughter.

During this time, I noticed Amanda did not have a bedtime and was often cranky tired when she came to our home. I did everything I could to make Amanda's days fun. We grew a garden. I had parties and playdates for her. I gave her three nutritious meals a day, and I saw her blossom into a beautiful healthy little girl from the pale skinny girl I first met. I was getting very concerned when I would pick her up in filthy homes, often with unexplained bruises, and dropping her off always left me with a sense of dread. Mary often complained to me that she had no food in the house, and on weekends I would bring over bags of groceries, which were shared by whomever she was living with at that time.

One day, Mary said all of her windows were shot out by an unknown assailant. Amanda was sleeping in one of the bedrooms at that time. The next day, in the early evening, I went over to pick up our granddaughter and the broken glass from the gunfire was still all over the floor! Bags of garbage were torn apart by animals inside and outside of the home. At this time, she was living in an old and decrepit basement suite with a guy named Jeff. I am not sure but I think this was the same Jeff Trevor hated so much when he would go pick Amanda up for a weekend visit.

There is much more to this story, but I must leave it out to protect my granddaughter. However, I did tell Mary that if she did not hand over Amanda to Gary and me until she sorted her life out, I would call the Ministry of Social Services and she would most certainly lose her daughter due to severe neglect. Without so much of a blink, she agreed, which I think is the most loving thing she ever did for her daughter. Or, it was her plan all along so that she could carry on with her partying lifestyle.

We went to court to make the guardianship legal and to the Ministry of Social Services to file the change of residence and guardianship of Amanda. I did not tell them all I knew about this mother who was at the very least negligent toward her only child. Mary reminded me of my mother. She was selfish beyond words and had no maternal instincts that I could see; I was not going to allow my granddaughter to live in a hellish environment.

At first, Amanda was very unhappy about the situation because she loved her mother in spite of her neglectful ways. Amanda didn't know any better of a life. It broke my heart to see my granddaughter so unhappy and missing her mother; I encouraged Mary to visit as often as possible and invited her over for all holidays.

*   *   *

One of the greatest diseases is to be nobody to anybody.

—Mother Teresa

Even though I had Amanda to care for, my heart was shattered over the loss of my only son, and my own emotional well-being was rapidly declining. My self-confidence and career were gone, I was losing friends because they could not face the tears of a grieving mother, and I decided I needed to leave Gary, my husband, in December 2004. On April 1, 2005, I finally left our family home and purchased a two-bedroom condo in the Okanagan of British Columbia. I brought Amanda with me and enrolled her in kindergarten. It was just the two of us now, and I prayed to God that I could raise Amanda with the love and nurturing she deserved.

*   *   *

It was on my twentieth wedding anniversary in 2004 that I decided I had had enough. I wanted a divorce. Trevor was gone, and life was too short to waste on someone who did not or could not love me.

The events leading up to the separation were many. Simply put, I was unhappy in my marriage for many years. Gary's nasty comments and lack of sensitivity for my feelings was wearing me down more than I could take. Don't get me wrong, we still had our good times together, but our marriage became more like a brother-and-sister relationship.

We were on a vacation in Mexico for our twentieth anniversary when I finally realized Gary did not love me, not in the way a wife or husband needs to be loved. We went on a sunset dinner cruise, and I brought out my gift of a watch and anniversary card for him that fateful Wednesday. I looked closely at my husband, waiting for him to show me his gift. He offered up nothing. My eyes teared up, and I wondered if this was the end for us. Did Gary fall out of love with me? Did he ever love me? Was he trying to make a statement to me? Every anniversary, especially the milestone ones, we exchanged gifts and cards and went on an exotic vacation. I was usually the one who organized our day, but at least Gary always gave me a card!

Another disturbing incident during that vacation was I had an accident on a scooter. I drove over an unmarked speed bump and tumbled off the bike and fell flat on my back. I was unconscious for a few minutes when I felt Gary slapping my face screaming at me to wake up and that he wasn't going to pay for a Mexican hospital! Within seconds, I saw a very large man run up to Gary, and he picked him up and threw him away from me, telling Gary not to touch me and wait for the ambulance to come. It was that second I realized a stranger loved me more than my own husband. Words cannot describe my pain, and not just the pain riveting through my body. I have no idea why Gary would be so upset about money for medical attention since we were well insured.

Also leading up to the end of my twenty-year marriage to Gary was being fed up with his behavior when we were with my siblings. I noticed that when we would visit my brothers or sisters, they would "tease" me in hurtful ways. I was always the family scapegoat, but having my own husband treat me in the same disrespectful way was now unbearable. Gary seemed to really enjoy my family and always went along with the masked insults toward me. We had many arguments on the way home from family functions because I was often hurt that Gary did not stand up for me.

I believe that when we are born to psychopaths or malignant narcissists we tend to attract people who are unable to show their love, even to the point of being empty nasty souls themselves. I didn't know what Gary's problem was, but I do know he was unable or unwilling to stand by my side as a good husband would do. Like in high school, if teasing is funny to everyone else except the target, it is bullying, and bullying is abuse.

And so I had had enough and was ready to move on with my life. I moved to the same small city (Vernon) my mother lived to hopefully renew our relationship. I always loved the Okanagan and much of my family lived there for years, starting with my paternal grandmother so many years before. The Okanagan Valley is followed by several small cities and towns, following ninety miles of Lake (Okanagan Lake to be exact!), which was a perfect prescription for my love of sun baking by the water!

The Okanagan Valley is a region located in the province of British Columbia, defined by the basin of Okanagan Lake. The region's population is approximately 350,927. The primary city is Kelowna, where I currently live. The Okanagan is known for its dry, sunny climate, rolling mountains, sagebrush hills and vineyards, and lakeshore communities. The economy is retirement and commercial-recreation based, with outdoor activities such as boating and water sports, snow skiing, and hiking. Agriculture has been focused primarily on fruit orchards, with a recent shift in focus to vineyards and wine.

This heavenly place was an opportunity to start my life over with my beautiful granddaughter.

* * *

The construction of my condo would not be complete for several weeks after I left Gary. Using the extra time and the money left over from my separation, I decided to take six weeks and travel. I contacted Amanda's maternal grandparents and asked them if they would keep our granddaughter while I was abroad. I was free for the first time since Trevor was born and excited to travel to exotic places, such as England, Ireland, and Greece.

A highlight of my trip was taking a Mediterranean cruise carrying me to Turkey (Istanbul, Europe), Turkey (Asia or Turkey Minor), Santorini, Mykonos, and Patmos. Learning more about John the Apostle and his place of exile in Patmos, where he wrote Revelations, and Turkey Minor, where apparently the book of John was written and where Mother Mary lived and died, helped me understand the age of Christ much better. In addition, I was thrilled to visit

Ephesus! The following information comes from *Wikipedia* about the history of Ephesus, and you can see why I would be so excited to see this wonder of the world!

> **Ephesus** was an ancient Greek city, and later a major Roman city, on the west coast of Asia Minor, near present-day Selçuk, Izmir Province, Turkey. It was one of the twelve cities of the *Ionian League* during the Classical Greek era. In the Roman period, it was for many years the second largest city of the Roman Empire; ranking behind Rome, the empire's capital. Ephesus had a population of more than 250,000 in the 1st century BC, which also made it the second largest city in the world. The city was famed for the Temple of Artemis (completed around 550 BC), one of the Seven Wonders of the Ancient World. The temple was destroyed in 401 AD by a mob led by St. John Chrysostom. Emperor Constantine I rebuilt much of the city and erected new public baths.
>
> The town was again partially destroyed by an earthquake in 614 AD. The city's importance as a commercial center declined as the harbor was slowly silted up by the *Cayster River (Küçük Menderes)*. Ephesus was one of the *seven churches of Asia* that are cited in the *Book of Revelation*. The *Gospel of John* may have been written here. The city was the site of several 5th century Christian Councils (see *Council of Ephesus)*. It is also the site of a large *gladiators'* graveyard. Today's archaeological site lies three kilometers southwest of the town of *Selçuk*, in the Selçuk district of İzmir *Province, Turkey.* The ruins of Ephesus are a favorite international and local tourist attraction, partly owing to their easy access from Adnan Menderes Airport and via the port of *Kuşadası.*

I stayed in Santorini for four days and nights, renting a suite built within the mountain. The homes were chalk white, and I loved walking the cobblestone steps circling the residential areas. Mykonos was another favorite island that simple beauty cannot describe enough. Istanbul was full of history, but I was shaken by the fundamentalist Muslims and their behavior toward Western tourists. I witnessed a group of children all dressed in black from head to toe and their mother's slapping their heads for just looking at us in the bus! I did visit a palace that had a history so enthralling I could have spent all day there. Alas, my ship was about to depart, and I had to hurry back.

One of the reasons I wanted to visit Ireland was to find Limerick, the city where Pulitzer Prize winner Frank McCourt described so brilliantly in his book, *Angela's Ashes*. Coming from a country (Canada) that is not even 150 years old made my entire historical European trip worthwhile, but I must say I would go back to Ireland in a New York minute if given the chance!

I rented a car and drove from Dublin to Limerick to Cork and stopped at every castle I came upon. I was awestruck and pleased when I would get lost and find myself in the back streets of major highways. I found many hidden pleasures in the cities I entered and could have stayed in Ireland forever if possible.

I flew back to Liverpool and had a whole other experience that I'll remember forever. I had a European train pass and could have gone anywhere in England and Scotland, but I got a little held up (for five days!) in, of all places, Liverpool! There I walked into a pub and sat at the bar and ordered a beer. A group of men and women were sitting nearby, and we struck up a conversation. They said my accent was wonderful and enjoyed talking with me about their country as I enjoyed talking with them about mine.

One of the fellows at the table caught my eye. I would never have guessed that I could experience lust at first sight; it had been many years since I felt the feelings I was experiencing, and this young man had me the minute our eyes met. I found out later he was only twenty-seven years old! I was forty-five and wondered what he would see in an old lady like me! But he seemed as enthralled in me as I was in him, and we spent five lively and lovely days together, enjoying each other's company. I have to admit, I did look good at forty-five. I was slender, my hair was golden blond, and I have a nice white smile! So maybe it wasn't so weird a twenty-seven-year-old would want me! We wrote each other for a while after I returned to Canada.

I did not like Athens. It was dirty, dark, and had an air of doom. I stayed at one of the best hotels, but the outside of every business and building I found bleak and uninviting. I didn't see one Western chain in Athens, which I found very odd as well.

One exciting thing about my stay at the hotel was while I was tanning on the rooftop, I noticed several individual men sitting in varying spots sporting dark suits in the blistering hot courtyard. It was surreal as I glanced here and there and saw these official looking characters looking way out of place of this bistro/pool area on the roof of this hotel.

I figured these men must be undercover security guards, but with just me and a few other hotel guests, it seemed like a lot of overkill. I asked my server what was going on, and he whispered to me that the Prime Minister of Lebanon, Rafiq Hariri, was assassinated in Beirut along with twenty others in a car bombing in February of that year (2005). He went on to say that at the very hotel I was staying and on the rooftop at that very moment was his temporary replacement, his son, Saad, and a girlfriend! I was quietly told Saad and his mistress were not too far from where I was sitting! I looked over and saw the couple and realized that the dark-suited men were there to prevent another assassination. I decided to retreat to my own room for the rest of the evening, exciting as it could have been.

The best part of Athens for me was Plaka Square, which ranged from the extreme expensive boutiques to bargain basement flea markets! If (no when!) I ever go to Europe again, I'm going to concentrate more on the wonderful shopping that is available. The fashions are beyond Western styles, and I just wish I had more money to spend on clothes!

Finally, on my last couple of days in Athens, I took a tour to Opa! parties and enjoyed listening to the Greek music and watching their custom dances. Even though I was traveling alone, I never felt alone on this holiday. The people were all so accommodating and friendly, and I brought home many lovely memories of all of my excursions!

*   *   *

Upon my return from Europe, I gathered up my granddaughter, and we moved into our brand spanking new condo with all of the touches I asked for upon construction. I decorated the condo with my jewels of souvenirs to make my new home have an eclectic of travel themes. I even added some cobalt blue ceramic tiles with several inserts of iron tiles of ancient maps to my kitchen walls, which made the place my own and very special to my travel memories.

Once we were settled in our home, I decided now was the time to hook back up with my Mother. I took Amanda to my mother's work as a surprise, and the three of us we went to lunch. Later, I often telephoned my mother to ask her over to my new condo for dinner. I wanted to show off my new place and hoped she would begin to visit and become the mother she never was and Great-Grandma for Amanda. I was still very naive. Each time I asked my mother over, she turned me down with one excuse or another. My dream to gain my mother's love was failing miserably. Was this her malignant narcissist trait of jealously—even of her own daughter's new pleasures? I don't know, but it reminded me of her bitterness around the time of my engagement and marriage to Gary.

December 13, 2005, was my MN mother's sixty-fifth birthday. She called all of her children to say she was having a birthday party for herself at a local restaurant and she wanted us all to attend. She was so insistent that everyone come I wondered if she had some sort of announcement to make, but no, she just wanted to be surrounded by her children for show in front of her cousins whom she had also invited. Maybe she just needed the feeling of a loving family. If so, I felt very sorry for her because she was at odds with all of her children at one time or another and creating drama that would put one of us in a tailspin of confusion and pain. The party all looked very lovely, but she barely spoke to me if at all, and I had to wonder why I was even invited if not just for her show.

For Mother's birthday, I bought her a $200 spa treatment. I was hoping she would use at least part of the day to learn how to put makeup on, although I didn't tell her that. I think she could have looked very beautiful if she did some adjustments to her makeup regime. Her boils had long disappeared, and she even had her face laser treated to rid the scarring. Unfortunately, Mother's style was to heap one color of brilliant turquoise from eyelash to eyebrow, and it did not flatter her. However, Mother told me she would use the spa day for other things, as she did not like other people putting makeup on her face. Whatever. I knew by then you can't change Mother and maybe it was a little selfish of me to think she would use my gift for my reasons.

*   *   *

Christmas time was approaching, which is one of my favorite holidays. I love to cook and I love to entertain. Holidays were a difficult time for me now without my Trevor, and it was the first Christmas without Gary in over twenty-three years. Amanda always spent Christmas with her maternal Grandparents and her Mother so I was alone. I thought I'd invite my mother and brothers and their families for a Christmas feast. Maybe we could stop all the drama and silent treatments and learn how to love and support each other as any good family would.

When I called my mother to ask her over for that Christmas feast she flat out said no. She said she wanted to invite a couple of her friends over for dinner. Friends instead of family? This was also strange since she did not like to cook. She had a good idea, though. She said why don't I bring everything over to her house and cook there for the family and her friends! What the hell! She was still refusing to come to my condo for some reason, and to offer me to cook for her friends whom I did not know was out of the question for me.

It always embarrassed me to be around any people Mother hung around with knowing she filled their heads with bullshit about me and my character. To not know what she was saying to people was torture, so I avoided her friends any chance I got. I was sick and tired of the dirty looks and uncomfortable conversations with her friends.

I was in a pity pot as I realized she would never love me and only use me for her purposes. My younger brother, Dylan, of course, went to Mother's with his family for Christmas at her insistence. Dylan always did Mother's bidding without argument or question. Gus, my older brother, was heavy into his drugs, and I do not know where he spent that Christmas. Since I refused to cook at Mother's house that Christmas for her "friends," I wasn't invited to attend Mother's Christmas dinner. Not that I would have gone anyway. There was no reason for her not to invite or join me that Christmas other than to flex her passive-aggressive drama on me again.

My tears soaked my bed that Christmas year. I have never been alone at this time of the year before no matter how much drama ensued, and I was beginning to awaken to the thought I would never be loved by my own family no matter how hard I tried.

*   *   *

One of the most common themes within my family was being called too sensitive if I retorted to them on a bullying remark. Now that I am older and wiser, I believe I am not "too sensitive," but rather they were very *insensitive*! Most of my family looked and sounded a lot like passive-aggressive bullies.

I first noticed the bullying with my sister, Shivey, who took on my mother's nasty emotional abuse toward others the older she got. She did not seem to like any of our siblings and constantly put down my older brother, Gus, and younger brother, Dylan, and his wife, Deanna. Shivey was the loudest in hating our mother and once said she would dance on her grave, a very sick remark, which I recoiled at even though my own relationship with Mother was always rocky.

I knew if Shivey was bad-mouthing all of my brothers and their wives, she was surely putting me down as well. If you remember an earlier chapter when she "outted" me for calling the welfare at the suspicion of sexual abuse between my cousins and young niece, that was Shivey creating malignant drama and trouble among the siblings, and if you remember, I lost my brother for some ten years with him believing it was all me causing the trouble. Psychopaths and malignant narcissists are pathological liars. The welfare was called only because of the information given to me by my sister!

Years earlier, when my niece, Cathy (Gus's oldest girl), ran away from home, she stayed with Shivey. I remember Shivey very inappropriately telling my niece what a bad person her father was. It is true Gus had become a drug addict and was extremely selfish. Rarely was there any food in his household of four, and Gus would often stay out late into the night drinking and doing drugs while his family was left with little to eat at home. But the fact that Shivey would talk to an impressionable sixteen-year-old girl about her father's weaknesses was tasteless in the least—evil in its worst. It reminds me of the traits of a malignant narcissist, or worse a psychopath. Shivey always seemed to have an air of superiority around the rest of the family and demanded things be her way or no way—she felt innately *entitled*, much like my mother.

The difference between my mother and my sister is that Shivey laughs at her evil antics, seeming to find great pleasure in hurting others behind their backs and even to their faces, which is a more common psychopathic trait. Malignant narcissists seem off-handedly or thoughtlessly evil toward others where psychopaths thrive and enjoy their evilness. The line is thin between a psychopath and a malignant narcissist, but I suspect that with the experiences I've had with my sister, she is a psychopath and pathological liar and much of her bookkeeping activity borders on the criminal.

When Shivey's mother-in-law passed away, she and her husband rushed to the elderly lady's bank account and depleted it before her husband's family had a chance to share in any money left by their mother. I remember my sister laughing at her husband's family's stupidity, and again, I paused and went "hmmmm" to this hurtful behavior. Darren rarely saw his siblings after their mother died, and I know it had a lot to do with Shivey's relationship-destroying ways. She did keep one member of Darren's family around, Rose, who was the wife of Darren's brother. They divorced during the time my sister was friends with her. Hmmmm.

Shivey also sat for hours trying to figure out how to gain money for doing virtually nothing. She ripped off one of her landlords for some $10,000 and was later sued and lost but I seriously doubt the landlord ever saw a dime of his claim. She started a bachelor of business administration program and took the maximum amount of student loans, stating either she was single or her construction husband was unemployed, and needed living expenses as well. Then she would drop courses to avoid full-time educational commitments. Eventually her loans equaled some $100,000, which she swore she would never pay back. Our government is way too lenient with student loans and grants (and other freebees). She did finally get her degree, but the government was never paid back to the best of my knowledge.

Shivey telephoned me one day to say she was going to have a party to celebrate her undergraduate degree. I was very excited for her and happy that she invited me. She invited the entire family as well as many of her friends and husband's co-workers. Big mistake. When Mother is around, the world must circle with her or she is put out and angry. She will sit and stare and wait for people to ask her if everything is okay, and she would weakly say, "Oh yes, I'm okay. I just didn't know Shivey was having so many friends outside of the family over."

Unfortunately (or fortunately), I became very ill the weekend of the party and ended up spending several days in the hospital. I missed the party completely. From what I heard from Shivey, Mother acted out such a drama she and Mother had it out—almost to the point of a fistfight! I remember my mother coming to the hospital (which really surprised me), and she just said the party wasn't for her (not her cup of tea) and so she thought she would come by to see how I was doing. I knew, however, that if the party went well, I would not have seen my mother while in hospital that weekend.

Shivey was livid with Mother for months. This was *her* day, and to hear her say it, Mother ruined the important event. And I believe her because it was like an old record player going on over and over again. It was nothing new for Mother to steal the thunder.

I cannot write this memoir without sharing other incidences I have had with my sister, which will be described in a future chapter. My story will go on to show how my sister's cruelty toward me knew no bounds, much like my mother before her.

*   *   *

My younger brother, Dylan, was our mother's favorite child. However, she could not stand his wife, Deanna, and made her feelings well known within the family. Even though Dylan was our MN mother's golden child, she used him mercilessly by insisting he to run over to her condo to perform chores and errands for her without so much as a thank you. He had his own demanding wife, with three beautiful children, and I always felt a little sorry for him. It was expected that anyone visiting Mother would put up with her nasty comments about someone else in the family and perform jobs she could do herself but chose not to. Dylan's wife was also verbally abusive toward him, and he later became a chronic alcoholic.

The silent treatment was my sister's favorite punishment toward those she felt lesser than herself or if she chose to create a drama event. If you remember from an earlier chapter, she was giving me the silent treatment when I was phoning Shivey to ask her to my own son's wedding. After Trevor's death, she would boast and say how he was her favorite nephew and yet she had no hesitation in punishing his mother (me) by not returning calls, and thus neglecting his wedding day. She did not attend the wedding at her own choice, but now she places the blame squarely at my feet for what evidence I do not know, but I'm sure she made up something false to tell the rest of the family and friends.

Both my mother and sister (and later Gus) have very bad habits of projection. This is a typical psychopathic and malignant narcissist trait. Psychological projection or projection bias is a psychological defense mechanism where a person unconsciously denies his or her own attributes, thoughts, and emotions, which are then ascribed to the outside world, such as to other people. Thus, projection involves imagining or *projecting* the belief that others have those feelings or thoughts. For example, my mother projected her feelings about my biological father onto me, stating I was the same person he was, a liar, cheat and thief. She was constantly telling me I was feeling or thinking things I was not. It made my head shake at some of the things she would come up with.

Another widely known virtue of the malignant narcissist is jealousy. I know Shivey to be an extremely jealous person just by the things she would say about some of her friends or their husbands' family. I received a letter from a long-term girlfriend who had finally had enough of being Shivey's supply for abuse. This is what she recently told me in a Facebook message:

> I came to understand years ago that Shivey is just a deeply unhappy person with a strongly competitive, jealous type personality. She chooses friends that she can feel better than and when she can't, she turns into a "frenemy." Someone who pretends to be your friend but is actually wishing for bad things to happen to you and who never has anything nice to say about anyone.

Malignant narcissists must have all of the attention in a group or else some kind of drama is going to creep up and often explode. One day, my P Father showed up with my uncle Hilliard in an RV. It had been a long time since I had seen my Father and was happy to have him and his brother spend Easter with us. It was also my father's birthday, so it would be a double celebration.

Unfortunately, my MN mother had already said she was coming to the coast that long weekend, but she usually spent very little time with me and more time with her friends from the days when she lived in the area. I didn't worry about having the long divorced couple together at my dinner table, as I have seen them many times before together without incident.

That weekend, Mother sat very quietly at my kitchen table while we all talked and cooked and enjoyed each other's company. She participated and even laughed a time or two. I always loved the companionship of my Dad and handsome uncle and couldn't be happier. Sadly, when my Dad and uncle left, my mother used the coincidence of them both being at my home at the same time to blow up at me like a nuclear bomb. She blamed me for allowing my Dad to stay in the RV for the long weekend when I knew she was going to be there. I was dumbstruck. She didn't say a word while my dad was there; there was no fighting or problems to speak of. I just didn't get her anger at me for something I was simply put in the middle of! The oddest part of her argument was she *never* stayed at my place more than a few hours before she was off to her friends' homes and yet this time, she stayed every minute my father was there!

My mother brought up this incident of my cruelty toward her for this incident for years afterward. I was such a sick weakling around my mother and wished I had more courage to speak my mind around her. Instead I often sent her emails expressing my rage and disappointment in her. She kept these emails to her dying day and passed them down to Shivey who now keeps them; for what I do not know—everything I ever said, even in my email temper tantrums were true. I shake my head in wonderment at why Shivey now needs these letters to have and to hold.

*   *   *

After a few months of adjusting to my new life in Vernon, I obtained a high-level position with a personnel agency. They liked that I had previously owned a successful business of the same type. I lasted for just two days when I realized I did not have the confidence to carry on. I quit. I went home and wondered what I could do with my life if I had no more self-esteem. I decided to get a junior position in a grocery store as a cashier. This way, I would be slowly bringing myself back out into the career world after the death of my son. I would be with people all day long and hopefully gain some strength and self-confidence back.

I learned from my younger brother, Dylan, that Shivey laughed her head off at my predicament of going from being a business owner, columnist, and motivational speaker to the so-called *lowly job of cashier*. Who does that? Especially a sister? A psychopath or a malignant narcissist would. They swim in glee within the downfalls of others.

*   *   *

I didn't realize this at that time, but my mental health was going downhill. I was barely able to get up to take Amanda to her preschool in the mornings. I was back on antidepressants, and while they were doing me no good, I didn't think to go off of them. I was still listening to doctors who knew science but did not know spirit. Even though I could do my job as a cashier with my eyes closed, to get ready for work was an extreme chore. My spirit was low, and I knew I had to take some action for the sake of Amanda, if not for me.

In September of 2005, I decided to phone Mary to invite her to my home for several months, and I would teach her parenting skills in preparation for her to regain her daughter. She agreed readily. Unfortunately, this idea became such a disaster it deserves a chapter all on its own.

Chapter 14—Meltdown

Your children need your presence more than your presents.

—Jesse Jackson

Time was moving on, and I wondered why Mary had not straightened out her life by now and come to collect her daughter. I still suspected she did not have the maternal instincts a mother needs to be a true mom. She didn't know how to cook or keep a clean home or have structure with her daughter, such as giving her meals at mealtime and bed at a decent bedtime. In addition, Mary seemed to need the company of men, lots of men and lots of moving.

However, I did not expect I would be raising my granddaughter forever, and my self-esteem was so low I felt I was just not good enough to be a substitute mother for Amanda. Not only that, when we agreed to take Amanda, Gary and I were still a couple; I did not anticipate at that time we would separate, and to think I would be a single parent again wore me down hard. I've been an unwed mother before, and now that I was older, and weaker, I could not see myself raising a child to adulthood by myself.

The bottom line was I thought of myself as a failure as a mother based on my own son's early death (however irrational that thought was) and worried my grief and inability to sometimes even get out of bed would be harmful to Amanda. I had no idea how long my grief would last. According to my online support group, losing a child to death was unlike any loss of a loved one, and most of the members were still feeling intense grief years after the death of their child. The reason, I now understand eight years after the death of my son, is that the older the child was, the more memories one has of the good times they may have had with the child. I did not have a lobotomy to remove my emotions, and so my memories were constantly flashing in my mind, causing a deep sadness and spontaneous crying. I did not want Amanda to be witness to these breakdowns, and I literally felt too physically weak to be a single mother again.

And so I invited Mary to come to Vernon and live with me for a few months. There I would give her a chance to see what a child needs to be raised, having her basic needs met. I was looking forward to having the chance to grieve on my own and not be responsible for another child I might screw up. I was hardly able to look after myself!

Mary arrived in early September 2005. She shared Amanda's bedroom, and I tried to make her feel as comfortable as possible. One of the first things I knew Mary would need was a job. If she was going to support her daughter, it would be a great start to begin using some of the skills she obtained from the secretarial courses she was taking when I first met her. However, it became apparent very early on that Mary preferred to be on my computer almost constantly rather than begin her search for a job or spend time with Amanda. I told Mary I would be unable to support her and she would need to get a job first and foremost to contribute to our food and utility bills. If she wasn't ready or didn't have enough confidence to work in an office, Mary had a lot of experience working in fast-food establishments and Vernon had a shortage of unskilled labor so obtaining a position should have been very easy for her.

One of Mary's excuses for not looking for work was not having a car. Our city had a great transit system, and if she really wanted to look for work, it would not have been that difficult. I really found it impossible to go out just to take care of my own business, let alone drive Mary around to find employment!

Finally, I became so frustrated I insisted Mary come with me each morning as I dropped Amanda off at her daycare, and then I proceeded to leave her in the city to look for work until it was time for me to pick up Amanda again. Mary obtained work almost immediately at Burger King, much to my delight.

Now all that was left was to show her how to cook some nutritious meals, shop for groceries, do laundry, and to keep her and Amanda's bedroom clean. Mostly, I just wanted to show Mary how easy it was to have structure and how well Amanda responded to it. I modeled that if Amanda ate everything on her plate, she would get a dessert. Dinner was a very successful and enjoyable time for Amanda, and I wanted Mary to witness and hopefully carry on the tradition of supper first, dessert after, when she regained custody of Amanda.

I also ensured Amanda had a bath every night and allowed her to have Tupperware and other plastic toys to play with for an enjoyable splash before our strict bedtime of 7:30 p.m. One thing I noticed about Mary was that I rarely saw her take a shower herself! This became a problem because her hair was very thick and matted. She usually pulled it up into a bun, and I feel terrible for even saying this out loud, but I think fruit flies would actually live in her hair! When Mary would use my computer, which was kept in my bedroom, I almost always walked into a mess of these pesky flies around my desk! It took a while for me to realize the flies were coming from Mary's hair, and I finally put a stop to her being allowed in my room! If this twenty-six-year-old woman didn't bother to take care of her own hygiene, how could I expect she would keep Amanda clean?

I didn't want to deprive Mary of a computer, and so I let her set up a wireless system and use Amanda's computer in their room. I was not very technical, but Mary was able to set up the internet system without difficulty.

Another important lesson Mary needed to understand was how well children responded to bedtime rituals. Amanda and I always read a book together and then said our prayers before I kissed her and walked out of the room at about 7:45p.m. I never had a bedtime problem with Amanda and hoped Mary would watch and learn how easy it could be to have her child asleep at a decent hour, a happy and relaxed girl.

Mary's shifts were odd hours, and I would sometimes have to drop her off and pick her up from work. But if she was home, I would have her watch me make Amanda's lunch for the day and make sure she saw the foods that Amanda both enjoyed and were good for her. I tried to be as consistent as possible in showing Mary these simple tasks, but she was very resistant at almost every turn. Either she was too busy on her computer or she had a date or she just didn't care.

I was beginning to really resent Mary and felt used by her. It did not look like she had the least bit of interest in learning how to run a household with a child involved. In addition, I noticed she was a pathological liar. She would lie for no reason about general things that did not require a lie. Other times, she would lie for her benefit. For example, she told me for many weeks that there was no bus that came to my neck of the woods. (It took me a long time, way too long, to figure out that was bullshit, and so I found myself driving her to work more often than I should have.) I caught Mary stealing from Amanda's piggy bank, and by this time, I was giving up hope. Unfortunately, I really let Mary have it several times over her antics and lazy ways, and I regret with all of my heart that Amanda had to listen to me admonish her mother.

Some days, when I was really feeling poorly, my anger toward Mary reached boiling points to where I was actually screaming (not a normal behavior of mine). If I was a well person emotionally, I would have never done this in front of my precious granddaughter. It had been a long time since I was able to get away, and in November, I decided to give Mary the benefit of the doubt and allow her to stay in my home with Amanda while I went to visit a male friend who lived some three hours away. Mary had been living with me for almost three months by now, and I saw no reason why she couldn't be responsible for her daughter overnight. I left a large salad in the fridge as well as come chili con carne in a can and other easy preparation meals (I wanted to make this weekend as easy as possible for Mary to manage).

On Saturday morning, I took the long drive to *Randy Kister's home (we had been dating off and on since I moved to Vernon, but having Amanda made it difficult for us to get together). That evening, I telephoned Mary at 6:00 p.m. to see how things were and got no answer. They may have been out for a walk or something, although it was quite cold at that time of year, but I had to trust Mary would do well by her daughter after three months of watching me take care of her daughter.

I called her again at 7:00 p.m. and got no response. I tried again at 8:00 p.m., 9:00 p.m., and midnight—nothing! I was beside myself with worry and wanted to drive home right then and there, but I had already had a few glasses of wine and could not get behind the wheel and drive the long windy road back home. I suffered the entire night, worrying about where the girls could possibly be. Mary did not have any friends that I knew of, and it just didn't make any sense that she wouldn't answer the phone!

At six the next morning, I got into my car and drove home. I was back at the condo by 9:30 a.m. When I went inside, nobody was home. My heart sank. Did Mary decide to take Amanda and move away? Was there foul play, putting them in danger somewhere? I looked in the fridge and saw the salad had not been touched, but the can of chili was used. Figures, I thought to myself, give Amanda a meal without the salad out of laziness or an aversion to eating healthy.

Could Mary not have given me a phone call to say they were okay? At the least? She knew my cell number, Randy's number, and of course, the condo phone number—there was no reason for her not to call to let me know they were safe!

I waited.

And waited.

Tears started to flow around six o'clock that Sunday evening when I realized that they were gone for at least twenty-four hours now. Mary had no car, and she was averse to taking the bus, so I was frantic with worry and conjured up all sorts of horrible images that made me almost physically sick. If they were not back by 9:00 p.m., I was going to call the police.

Finally, at approximately 7:30 p.m., Amanda's bedtime, Mary and Amanda walked in the condo with a large bald tattooed man standing behind them. It was all I could do to hold myself back from becoming violent with Mary as I asked her where the hell she was all of this time! She explained that she had met this man on Plenty of Fish, an online dating site, and that he lived in Kelowna, a one-hour drive from my place. He picked them up and took them back to his place for the night! Mary had never met this man before and yet she took her five-year-old daughter to his home to spend the night!

OMG! With my own history of being sexually molested, it was always at the forefront of my mind to be cautious when it came to men and my granddaughter. Mary seemed to have no judgment at all, and to me this lack of insight was dangerous for my granddaughter.

I realized at that point that Mary would always be selfish and unable to be a good example for her daughter, even putting her in dangerous situations. I was fed up with trying to get her to parent her child safely and told her she would have to leave; I couldn't stand the sight of her a minute longer.

I gave her two weeks to find another place to live. Mary can be very resourceful when it served her purpose, and she contacted a charity organization, telling them she just moved to Vernon, she was a single parent, and needed furniture for an apartment *for herself and her daughter*! I was so eager for Mary to get out of my place I put down the security deposit for her apartment. She would have to learn how to be a mother from a distance now, albeit a short distance—she only moved about a mile away from us. I was not able to contain my anger at Mary's lack of parenting skills or willingness to learn the difference between what is right and what is wrong. One thing was for sure, Amanda was *not* going to live with her in the new apartment.

As the weeks went on, I brought Amanda to visit her mother as often as possible. Mary never took a bus to the condo to see her daughter; it would always have to be me to take Amanda to her. In addition, she rarely phoned her daughter, stating she couldn't afford the minutes on her cell phone. It was not fair for Amanda's life to be uprooted again by not having her mother living with her, but I did everything I could to make excuses for her delinquent parent. Making those excuses reminded me of my own mother who *never* tempered my father's absence to save my feelings. She screeched loud and clear about what a bum he was. A bum, psychopath, criminal, cheat, liar—you know the routine. I was raised with those hurtful remarks, and I was not going to do that to Amanda, no matter how tempting it was.

I could sense some resentment with Amanda at this point. I think she blamed me for breaking her and her mother up (she did hear some of our arguments, and I regret that to this day). It was all I could do to zip my lip and do what was best for Amanda's emotional well-being knowing how devastated I was to hear my Mother speak so ill of my own Father. Children are just the innocents that adults are supposed to protect, and they do not need to be involved with the problems of grownups. I knew that all too well. So by protecting Mary for Amanda's sake, I sacrificed my own relationship with Amanda.

Mary gave me stories about how well things were going in her life; she got a better-paying fast-food job and was managing her home very well, she boasted. It did appear to be kept clean when I came by, and I allowed myself to hope that she had learned something about how to be a worthy parent and would concentrate on getting her daughter back by doing the right thing(s), such as stay at one place for longer than a month or keeping a boyfriend for a period of time; I wanted Mary to make her daughter her primary concern in all of her affairs. I wanted the moon.

One day, Mary said she had the weekend off and asked if she could have Amanda spend the night with her. She made it sound like it was just going to be the two of them and they were going to have taco chips and salsa for dinner and watch videos. I allowed myself to trust Mary once again (this is a common theme in my life when it comes to liars—I tend to believe the best of people, which has gotten me into trouble all too often).

When I picked Amanda up the next day, she told me a man was staying with her mother! This was a different man than the guy she took Amanda to that weekend I was not home. Since Mary only had one bedroom, I asked her where Amanda slept, and she said her boyfriend stayed on the sofa and Amanda stayed in the bed with her mother. I don't know. I just gave up. There would be no more overnight visits because I just could not trust Mary to do right by her daughter.

*   *   *

My nerves were shot. I felt myself slipping into an even more severe depression and could hardly get out of bed. I did what I had to do such as feed, bathe, and tuck Amanda in at bedtime (and give her many hugs), but that was about all I could do, and even that was too much. Amanda deserved better than me, I thought. I even asked if someone from the daycare could pick her up, as just getting out of the door in the morning was becoming impossible. I could not work at all by this point, even as a cashier. I was living on the alimony Gary paid me every month and a couple of hundred dollars the Ministry of Social Services paid me to keep my granddaughter. Mary was supposed to give me her Federal Child Tax Benefit every month, but I found out later that she was chipping off a good portion for herself and giving me less than her daughter received in this government benefit. So not only did Mary not pay any child support for her daughter she was ripping me off of the money the government was paying her as a so-called single parent!

I was fast realizing that the idea of being wholly responsible for Amanda was too much for me. I couldn't do it. Trying to support Mary in gaining back her daughter proved fruitless, and I was an emotional basket case in a downward spiral of hell. I did not want to be responsible for my granddaughter's full-time well-being. I did not want to hurt her by not being available to her emotionally. I did not anticipate being a single parent when Gary and I took Amanda on, and I was fast-realizing I was unable to continue raising my precious granddaughter. The idea of putting her into foster care was out of the question, and thus I felt I was between a rock and a hard place.

I had one avenue I could try. Mary's parents did not seem too involved in Amanda's life (other than the time she stayed with them while I traveled to Europe in 2005). *Ann, Mary's stepmother (her own mother had abandoned Mary when she was a toddler), and *Barry were hard-working people, with Barry working two jobs and Ann operating a horse farm, giving lessons, trail rides, boarding horses, etc. For a couple in their mid-forties they were extremely hard workers. They lived in the Fraser Valley, about four hours from my condo, so having Amanda spend weekend respites with them, which would have been some help, was not realistic. No, I knew any decision made about Amanda's upbringing would have to be a permanent situation. She had been shuffled around far too much to consider anything less than a full-time parenting situation that would be permanent and secure. This precious five-year-old deserved way more than she was getting from her mother or me.

I made the call to Ann in January 2006. I told her how I had tried to get Mary to take the reins and be responsible for her daughter, but I could not see that ever happening after her stay at my place in Vernon and her continued living situation now that she was living on her own again (or with other men). I humbly told Ann just how bad my personal emotional situation had become, and I needed her and Barry to take Amanda from my loving but failing arms. I was not fit, I admitted in my tears, and I would never put Amanda through another move away from me and her mother if I didn't think I had to.

Of course, I knew this would be an awesome task for Ann since she was full of activity with the farm duties and Barry's two jobs kept him busy. Amanda was in kindergarten, and I was hoping they could take over responsibility after spring break. I wanted to take Amanda to Disneyland over the break as a sort of final good-bye but show her how much I still loved her and would miss her.

I asked Ann to think about it with Barry over a few days and to let me know as soon as possible. I should also mention that I promised that every holiday including the summer months, Gary and I had discussed that we would take Amanda to give them a break and to continue our bond with our granddaughter. Gary loved to camp, and he would take Amanda on camping trips with my sister's family for a few weeks in the summer, and I would have her the rest of the summer, taking her to our sun-drenched beaches in the Okanagan, which she had grown to love so much. I would also pick her up on long weekends to give them a break and support.

A few days later, Ann telephoned me and agreed they would take over the responsibility for Amanda. I cried profusely over my huge loss but knew that Amanda would be far better off with two parents—running around with a farm full of animals and horses—than stuck in a condo with a grieving Nana. I knew it would be an enormous adjustment for this little girl, but I prayed she would eventually bounce back and be a healthy happy girl in the end.

The transfer of this little girl was supposed to take place after spring break; however, I could not make it until March. I felt myself slipping further and further into a depressing despair, and I could not fake being emotionally well for even just a few short weeks! I was crying all of the time, and it was becoming impossible to hide my emotional breakdowns from Amanda. I had the loss of Amanda to cry and worry about now as well. I had to tell my little granddaughter that Nana could no longer care for her! I tried to make it sound as much fun as possible, but Amanda's eyes showed me her own heartbreak and fear of moving to a new strange home.

My guilt was overwhelming, and I felt like such a failure I knew it was going to take some time to get over this new loss and I wondered how long it would take Amanda to adjust to her new home and family. I was so emotionally sick Amanda ended up moving to the farm on February 16, 2006 (I will never forget the date)—before spring break.

I decided to go off of all antidepressants at that time because they were clearly not doing anything for me at all. I was sick to death of doctors simply trying different medications on me, and so without telling my doctor, I stopped taking the pills cold turkey. This is a *huge mistake*, and I do not recommend anyone go off "brain" medication suddenly, for the consequences can be deadly.

Since we had agreed that either Gary or I would take Amanda on holidays, I upheld my promise to take Amanda to Disneyland that spring break and drove the four hours to pick her up and take a flight from Vancouver to Disneyland.

*   *   *

> *Death is not the greatest of evils; it is worse to want to die, and not be able to.*

—Sophocles

This next section is going to be one of the most difficult to write. I want to be as honest as I can, but I must also protect my granddaughter from certain events she does not remember, events I do not want her to remember. I have omitted what I consider to be harmful information and unnecessary for the purpose of my memoir.

*   *   *

My Father was still living in Vancouver, and I knew he had an endless supply of anti-anxiety medication he managed to manipulate doctors to give him. I telephoned him and said I was in bad shape but had promised to take Amanda to Disneyland and asked if he would "sell" me some of his pills so that I could get through the five-day vacation. He readily agreed and gave me one hundred Xanax for $100. (I know, it was a highly dysfunctional thing to be involved in, but I didn't have the nerve to ask doctors for that kind of medication and yet I knew I needed it to get through the week.) I was taking Amanda on a trip, but my emotional well-being was still very poor.

When we arrived at our hotel, we settled in. Amanda loved ordering room service so that was one of the first things we did. I brought her Barbie dolls and coloring books and crayons with us just in case I couldn't get out of bed and she would need something to do (something to do in Disneyland? That ought to give you an idea of how low I was at that point).

The next morning, well, around noon, I finally got myself put together to take Amanda to the *happiest place on earth*. Even though I had those little pink pills, little did I know walking into the gates of Disneyland would create a disaster within my soul that nobody and no pill could help. Suddenly I had flashbacks of Trevor, Gary, and I going to Disneyland twice when he was young. Disneyland was Trevor's happiest place on earth! We had such a good time on our vacations a flood of sickly grief overtook me almost completely. I say almost because the worst was yet to come.

I held my knees up and my tears in as long as I could. We walked toward the little children's area so that Amanda could meet Goofy and Mickey Mouse. I lasted less than two hours before I had to get out of Disneyland to the safety of our hotel room. Thank God, Amanda didn't really have a sense of time although I am sure she would have loved to stay longer. When Trevor, Gary, and I were at Disneyland, we were in there from morning to night. Two hours was hardly ample sightseeing or playing. But Amanda didn't know that.

I fell asleep after feeding Amanda, and she occupied herself with her dolls and the television until she fell asleep without her prayers. The next morning (afternoon), I decided to try again. I took more of those little pills to keep myself in check. This Disneyland "day" was no different; in fact, I was in worse shape than I was the day before if that is possible. We went into the "It's a Small World After All" ride three times. It was darker in there, and I could cry silently to myself without being noticed. Every time Amanda looked at me with such glee in her eyes over the ride, I faked a great big smile for her. When she looked away, I put my head into my hands and wept uncontrollably; I was petrified she would see my shoulders shaking.

Clearly Disneyland was not a good idea. Amanda saw very little of the park, but we did manage to get her face painted (while she was enjoying the character doing this to her, I took the precious time to hide behind a building and buckle over with internal pain and weeping). On our way out, I bought her a huge lollipop, which she thought was the greatest thing ever.

In four days, Amanda and I probably spent no more than *five hours* in the Disneyland Park and we visited no other Los Angeles attractions such as Universal Studios or Knotts Berry Farm like I had planned for her. On our last day I felt like I had no life left inside of me. After another short visit to Disneyland, we went back to the hotel and sat in the lobby and ordered drinks with pretty umbrellas and talked about how much fun our trip was (gad), and I was relieved to see at least she was smiling. Inside I was dying.

Have you ever had to hold back a huge wailing crying fit? It can be done because I was able to manage this feat until we got back into our room and I went into the bathroom and ran the tub so Amanda couldn't hear me.

I finally gave my head a shake, washed myself up, came out of the bathroom, and announced we would order room service again with an excited tone of voice for my granddaughter. I told her she could pick out anything she wanted. Amanda was always (and remains to this day) a good eater and loves foods that are healthy. Together we ate, and I tucked her in with our usual prayers and hugs.

I decided to telephone my girlfriend, Veronica, in Vancouver. I was crying and told her about how this vacation had turned into a nightmare. I told my best friend I just hoped I could make it until our flight left for home. Veronica was very upset and worried about my condition, but she was helpless. I also telephoned my Father. No one knew what hotel we were staying at, and for some reason, I never mentioned it. It was not on purpose; it just never came up. I talked to my Dad for a while, but he seemed busy with his own business at that time. He was drunk. I called Veronica back and talked to her again. I could tell she was getting frustrated with me. Veronica could not fix what was going down, and I can imagine how difficult it was for her to hear me on the phone that night. I was not of right mind and she knew it.

I believe I had a psychotic episode that night. Meaning, I was not in control of my thinking or actions whatsoever. I learned later that one must *never* just go off of antidepressants like I did a few weeks before, and this likely added to my breakdown. I took more anti-anxiety pills to try and calm down but that failed. I had only one drink in the lobby earlier, but I think I had some wine in the room and mixing wine with the pink pills was another contributing factor to my meltdown. Amanda was fast asleep, but I kept taking the pills while watching TV to try and calm myself down.

* * *

I woke up in the hospital. I learned from the doctors I was found in my room unconscious by security officers of the hotel. The doctor asked me if I took an overdose of pills. I said I didn't know; if so, it was not on purpose! I also didn't know how anyone could have found me, although I was grateful they did. As I mentioned earlier, nobody knew where I was staying, so how come the security of the hotel came to my room at 2:00 a.m. to check on me? Was the guy serving us drinks concerned about my pathetic appearance and did he say something? I have no idea. All of my pills were gone. Was this another divine intervention thing going on? I was completely confused.

One of the first things I asked the doctor was where my granddaughter was. He kindly told me the police drove her around through the night looking for "bad guys" until a flight left for Vancouver early in the morning. The police officer that came to see me said Amanda had a great time once she knew I was okay, just a little sick. They said my husband picked Amanda up from the airport in Vancouver. Everyone just told my precious, delicate granddaughter that her Nana got sick and had to stay in the hospital for a few days, but I would be okay. Thank you, security guards, medics, and LA police department! The flight attendants who kept Amanda happy and comfortable on her way home are also owed a huge amount of my gratitude.

I was told I would have to go to a different hospital for three days to ensure I was okay. I'll call this hospital "hell on earth" because that is exactly what it was. I refused all medication by now, realizing that being on the antidepressants for so long only numbed my brain, and when I went off so suddenly, it was like a tidal wave of emotion hitting at the core of my being. The death of Trevor, the loss of Tyler to adoption, the loss of Ximi, the end of my career and my marriage, and the nasty and insultive behavior of my mother and sister were too much. I was finally "feeling" now that I was off the antidepressants and the pain came at me like daggers.

As I suffered in this place of *hell*, I was all too aware of my surroundings. Other patients were on heavy doses of medication and likely did not realize just how horrible their living conditions were. For one thing, the nurses were not nurses; they were male guards in guard uniforms. The place was filthy, and the food was inedible. I shared a room with an anorexia patient who could not get out of bed but to go to the bathroom, a bulimic girl who hogged the washroom as she did her business over twenty times in a day, and a seriously drugged-up little girl who threw her plate of supper all over the walls on my first day there. The entire time I spent in that warehouse for the sick, not one housekeeper came by to clean the food off of the walls or sanitize the washroom, which was smeared with feces.

Worse than my environment was the rejection and anger my ex-husband had toward me when I was finally able to phone him. I can hardly blame him for putting so much fear in him and the possibilities that could have gone wrong with Amanda when I was unconscious. What if she had found me dead? Gary and I usually got along very well even though we both knew our marriage was over, and it hurt me to see him so angry with me.

Another blow was the loss of my best friend, Veronica. Veronica and I had been friends for over ten years at that point, and to hear her anger and dismissal of me while I was in this place was almost too much to bear. I knew I had no family to speak of, but to lose the closest people to me?—people who really knew me and knew me well were now rejecting me because I put Amanda in harm's way. I never felt so alone in my life and my biggest fear was I was going to lose Amanda permanently. How do I explain this to Ann and Barry! I will have officially lost *everything*.

* * *

I am very fortunate to say my relationships have since been rekindled, and I feel very blessed for that. Ann and Barry were, of course, extremely concerned and weary of me at this point, but in the six years since that incident, I am very happy to say we are working really well together to keep Amanda happy and well adjusted. I thank Ann and Barry for giving me a second chance with Amanda, where I could prove my worthiness as her Nana. Any time someone appears to understand me or the pain I have endured throughout my life, I feel so grateful for having them in my life. I never take my friendships for granted. I never will.

* * *

I could not stay in my room at this *Los Angeles psychiatric hospital* because of the intense bad odors, and so I found a large holding area where patients could walk around or play cards. I met some very nice people who were schizophrenic, and he was a nice guy (LOL, just kidding). Seriously, there were some very nice people, and I could not have made it through those three days if it were not for my ability to communicate with people who could function in spite of their large doses of drugs. One lady I will never forget was about fifty or sixty or seventy—it was very hard to tell; she had what appeared to be a permanent wide smile on her face. I'm not kidding; it was like her face was paralyzed into a very strange smile. I honestly do not think she had any other expression. I couldn't talk to her because she was mute. Mute with this big odd smile. I have never seen anything like it, and I worried about her. How did this happen to that poor woman? She looked like someone out of a horror film.

The last day I would spend in this place, a fellow I had grown fond of, a great big black guy with some serious mental health issues, was singing a church hymn over and over again. I'll never forget it, as it saved me for that day. He kept singing "This little light of mine, I'm gonna let shine . . ." Most of the residents were getting angry with him about his singing, but I thought it was beautiful, and it was days before that song left my own mind. I decided then and there I would make my light shine again one day.

Finally I was released. A driver picked me up in the early morning to take me to LAX, but my flight was not leaving until the afternoon. I found a restroom and tried to clean up a bit. An older shabby-looking woman beside me said something, and I turned to her (because I didn't hear her) and said, "What?" and she said, "Oh, I thought you were homeless too." Did I look that bad? I must have. I had been to hell and back and just hours away from the safety of my home where I could hide myself from the world.

*   *   *

I felt like the most hated woman in the world as I drove up to my condo. I ruined everything; my vacation with my granddaughter, my friendships, and my own self-respect. I don't think I could have hated myself more as I carried my luggage up to my suite. I had no idea what I was going to do from that moment. Of course, I fell back into my old pattern of feeling like ending my life. What was there to live for? I could not think of a thing, and so I began to think of ways I could end my life.

I had my ideas but I found myself at my computer instead. I started writing. I wrote and wrote and wrote. I wrote everything going on in my mind. I wrote for three solid days. I barely took a nap or ate. I found that as I wrote, my feelings of utter hopelessness and wanting to die left me. So I didn't stop. I was afraid that if I stopped writing, I wouldn't be safe.

Finally, on the third day, I printed out my fifty-page document and took it to my doctor. He said I should go to the hospital for an evaluation. The doctors at the hospital suspected I had a post traumatic stress psychotic episode when in Disneyland. They did not feel I needed to be in the hospital but that counseling would help me greatly. Unfortunately, my ex-husband's extended health plan did not really have a good counseling plan. The very most they would do is give me a contact who would give me other contacts within the community. Or I could hire a registered therapist, but the cap on that was only $300, and that would only give me two sessions, not nearly enough for what I needed.

I contacted the Vernon Mental Health Association and made an emergency appointment. The gal who saw me was very kind to me, much kinder than I was to myself. It brought me to tears to have this person understand my pain and tell me so. She was amazed at my story (I told her the entire works) and said there was a residential program I could attend to try to get to the bottom of my inability to cope with stressful situations and emotional breakdowns.

If I give myself a break here, I have to say I've done pretty damn well considering the events that lead up to my complete breakdown in Disneyland. I'm not sure the average person could take what I have suffered through in my lifetime. I'm always in awe of people who have problems so much worse than mine like the homelessness and those in poverty and war and those still living a bloody nightmare with a psychopath and the physical and verbal abuse that goes along with that. Yes, there are people far worse off than I am, but I do not diminish my own sufferings and realize that in order to really rid myself of my demons, I must work on myself to lose the tapes playing in my head that I am a worthless person who deserves nothing, especially happiness.

I entered the program full of hope. A woman who was in my group "murdered" her two dogs by carbon monoxide poisoning and, at the end of the six-week program, said to me, "Just who do you think you are? Do you think because you have a dead kid you are better than the rest of us?" I gave my head a little shake as I looked at this woman. Of course, all of our issues were different, but that doesn't mean one problem doesn't hurt as much as another! What she was doing was (1) projecting her own thoughts and feelings onto me as if they were mine and (2) being jealous that my situation of depression did not involve killing anyone or any pets but that I lost a beautiful son I raised with such passion. She was jealous! It is this type of soul who reminds me of a sociopath. It is these types of people I try to stay far, far away from.

I completed this group and left feeling good that I had dealt with many of my issues and was able to feel whole again for the first time in years. And I was able to work through my issues with *no* medication (although the doctors really tried to push it on me during my stay).

While I was busy trying to fix myself, Shivey phoned me and said she wanted to raise Amanda with her boyfriend. What a weird request, I thought. With the way my sister ruined my relationships with people, I could just imagine what she would say to my granddaughter about me! Besides, she is the last person on earth who would have a say where Amanda would live! She would naturally stay with her maternal grandparents!

This infuriated Shivey into a rage against me. She was so angry over her inability to get her way she contacted the Ministry of Social Services on me and said I was an unfit grandmother. She wasn't finished; she actually took her daughter, Christine, and her new granddaughter over to Ann and Barry's farm and tried to convince Ann that it would be a difficult long haul to raise Amanda and it would be better if she raised her! The nerve of my sister never fails to amaze me. Ann told me later that Shivey said some not nice things about me, which I expected she would do. Luckily, Ann is not a stupid woman and saw through my sister's nastiness.

I am so happy that Ann gave me a chance to retain my relationship with Amanda. She could have written me off as a nutcase, and I would have lost my granddaughter's affections.

Today Amanda is a happy, healthy, very well-adjusted girl who competes in horse shows and wins gymkhana awards over girls years much older than herself! Her newest goal is to be in the top two barrel racers in British Columbia. I have no doubt she will reach her goal. Amanda gets excellent grades and has many friends who share her passion for horses.

Amanda has a horse, three dogs, and a cat that sleeps with her. Ann has spent thousands of dollars keeping Amanda in various horse and pony clubs and finding her the perfect horse for her to compete with. Meanwhile, Amanda helps out and is learning the value of work for what she is so privileged to have. These values have given her a very healthy self-esteem. She also has Ann, Barry, Gary, and me to support her as she grows up. She is eleven now and is a beautiful person inside and out. We all love her, and the wonderful thing is she knows it.

*   *   *

Love all, trust a few, do wrong to none.

—William Shakespeare

I recently watched a reputable medical program (*Dr. Oz*) where three doctors in agreement stated an article written in the *Medical Journal of America*, the virtual bible for doctors, that antidepressants' true drug affect does *not* work. In fact, there is virtually *no* benefit and a large risk for young people taking this drug—suicide, a major side affect for our youth on antidepressants! The doctor's stated that information about drugs are "filtered" from the drug companies and that most of the information provided to doctors come from these drug companies—not the medical journal.

If mental health drugs do not concern you, maybe this will: it concerns statins, a class of drug used to lower cholesterol levels. It has recently been found that there is *no benefit* for *women* on these drugs. I didn't know much about statins so I looked it up. The following comes from *Wikipedia*, which has the following information about Statin drugs:

> Statins (or HMG-CoA reductase inhibitors) are a class of drug used to lower cholesterol levels by inhibiting the enzyme HMG-CoA reductase, which plays a central role in the production of cholesterol in the liver. Increased cholesterol levels have been associated with cardiovascular diseases (CVD), and statins are therefore used in the prevention of these diseases. Randomized controlled trials have shown that they are most effective in those already suffering from cardiovascular disease (secondary prevention), but they are also advocated and used extensively in those without previous CVD but with elevated cholesterol levels and other risk factors (such as diabetes and high blood pressure) that increase a person's risk.[2] Statins have rare but severe adverse effects, particularly muscle damage, and some doctors believe they are overprescribed.

The best selling of the statins is Atorvastatin, marketed as Lipitor and manufactured by Pfizer. By 2003, it had become the best-selling pharmaceutical in history, with Pfizer reporting sales of $12.4 billion in 2008. All of this and yet it is now proven that these drugs are also of no to little benefit to *women*!

According to the doctors (who were shown to be highly respected in their respective fields before anything was even said), this is the scenario we are seeing at an alarming rate in North America:

1. The FDA approves drugs although they do not limit the drugs administration to its original purpose.
2. The pharmaceutical companies broaden the usage of the drug without regulations.
3. The pharmaceutical representatives (sales force) convince doctors of new diseases (and offer only the *benefits* for the drug downplaying the side effects).
4. The doctor passes along or convinces his or her patient of the disease they must have based on their symptoms and that a particular drug

is made to "fix" the disease. In fact, most drugs may only fix only the symptoms, not the disease at all.

Why can't the medical community just realize that some people have had real situations in their lives that cause them to cope poorly or cause them to be sickly (such as poor diet and lack of exercise)? Sometimes just a little understanding and a kind word can help heal the sick.

I think even the mental health community are afraid of the people they encounter on a day-to-day basis. I blame the pharmaceutical companies for fear-mongering and making up mental health names and manufacture drugs to "fix" the so-called disorders or diseases. This only serves to instill alarm for doctors to push drugs onto their patients. It certainly dis-empowers the patient from taking responsibility for their issues. That is my humble opinion, and it will take a lot for me to believe otherwise at this point. I will always believe in the power of counseling and self-examination over drugs any day. To me mental health is spiritual health and should be handled accordingly. As these doctors were saying on the program, "It is a placebo effect that makes doctors and patients believe they are healed with most mental health drugs."

I've had two doctors tell me patients *want* a diagnosis (or excuse) to explain their problems away. Can't be done, grasshopper. We need to learn how to help ourselves (if our parents didn't teach us basic life skills) and, if not, seek professionals who can help us see our way through the rough or even severely rocky patches of life we all face at one time or another.

* * *

I sometimes wonder when my rocky life's journey will end. I learned in late 2006 that my son's biological father had died in 1999, and I found out in May of 2007 that both of my biological parents were diagnosed with lung cancer! After researching the odds of surviving this cancer, I learned that there was only a 5-percent chance of survival after five years. Even though my father and mother had not lived together for some forty-five years, both of my parents were dying of the same disease! The next chapter will illustrate I had steep mountains to climb while dealing with more loss and a frantic yet futile effort to make amends with my manipulative mother and father even during their final days.

Chapter 15—Learning to Live Again

Although the world is full of suffering, it is also full of the overcoming of it.

—Helen Keller

Amanda was safe, sound, and happy living with her maternal grandparents, and Gary and I were upholding our end of the bargain by sharing in the love by taking our granddaughter for holiday visits. Amanda had just left my home after spending most of the summer of 2006 with me, where we played at the beach and had lunch and dinner picnics almost every day. Gary took her on a wonderful three-week camping vacation with Shivey's family during that same summer.

I was healing after the residential program I attended and felt like I might be finally experiencing inner peace. I remembered the song "This little light of mine, I'm gonna make it shine" the man back at the psychiatric hospital in Los Angela's kept singing. I remember his positive attitude in such dire conditions and was determined to do let my light shine as well: if I have to live, I insist on living well!

As a grade 9 dropout and unwed mother living on welfare who worked my way up to a wonderful career and landing a handsome husband who made a wonderful stepfather for Trevor, I felt that maybe I could pull myself back up from nothing once again.

I sold my condo for a nice profit and moved to the larger city of Kelowna, about one hour away from Vernon. It was clear my mother and I were never going to be best friends, and I stopped trying. In Kelowna, I purchased another brand-new condo and used the extra money from my profits to travel to Cuba. I learned a lesson that trip—don't stay at an all-inclusive resort as a single woman! It was hard to make friends to hang around with since most people were either couples or families. As a *fifth-wheel vacationer*, I was very lonely in Cuba, but the highlight of my vacation was seeing the ancient city of Havana! I have always loved culture and history.

When I got home, I decided to try to track down Trevor's biological father, whom I learned years before was homosexual, which explained so many things to me. I also learned he had turned to drugs such as crack and cocaine. However, I wanted to let him know his son had died in a car accident. When Trevor was an older teenager, he contacted his half sister, but that relationship never developed. Kelly, Arthur's daughter, who was two years older than Trevor, seemed interested in meeting her brother, but at that time, Trevor was still involved with drugs and nothing came of it, although the siblings did talk on the telephone. Years before, Trevor went on one dinner date with his father, but he decided at that time that Gary was his real father in every respect, and so he did not try for a relationship with his homosexual Father, which I think bothered Trevor somewhat.

I googled "Arthur Nolan Fisher, Vancouver, BC" and was surprised to get an immediate hit, although it was a little bit of a frightening find. Arthur's name was listed on the AIDS Memorial Wall of Vancouver! Was he dead? Well, he must be if he is on an AIDS memorial wall! I e-mailed the Memorial Wall people and gave specific details about Arthur and asked if this was the same Arthur Fisher that was listed as a deceased person by AIDS. I got an e-mail back, confirming they were the one and the same person.

I had a good cry for Arthur. I knew he was gay since Trevor was eight years old, but I always loved him deep in my heart. He gave me my son, and Arthur was such a handsome man I couldn't help but melt when he was around. Apparently, Arthur died in 1999, four years before Trevor's car accident. It was very sad for me to learn Arthur was dead. I tried to find Kelly at this point, but I could not track her down. I finally left it alone and said a little prayer for Arthur and Kelly and decided I had to move on and not dwell in that sadness for long.

* * *

I had somewhat of a relationship with my Father, and since he was in Vancouver and I was four hours away in Kelowna, I was safe from his manipulating ways, so I talked to him on the phone at least once a week. If you remember,

I wanted a relationship with my father because he was the only one in the family who did not bully me or put me down in any way (besides my younger brother, Dylan).

My father was very abusive to his second family, but for some reason, he became best friends with my brother, Gus, when he became an adult. They were so close they shared women and drank heavily together. Later they lost touch until my father moved to Vancouver and became a property manager for a social housing organization. When reunited, my brother and father continued to drink and share women as if no time had lapsed.

My father managed to keep me as his one daughter who would talk to him even after the incident of him being in the same work camp as Trevor years before. I did not hang around with my brother and did not "party" with my dad. My father had not been in jail since that last time at a work camp Trevor was sent to for shoplifting so many years before. Dad always lived on the outskirts of the law, and I worried about the residents he was lording over and their belongings. If Dad ever had a chance, he would steal things from their apartments, and I knew this.

None of my dad's second family would have anything to do with him since he had hurt them so profusely in his psychopathic ways, which I'll describe a little later on in the memoir.

*   *   *

I experienced the danger of my psychopath dad in the summer of 2006. He came to the Okanagan to check himself into the psychiatric ward of Kelowna General Hospital. The doctors in Vancouver were fed up with giving him so many painkillers and Xanax that my father thought by coming to Kelowna, he would get a new set of prescriptions from a new set of doctors. I never did go visit him in the hospital because he had already told me he admitted himself only as a way of getting more drugs. He wasn't really sick.

One typically hot summer day, I had a date, and we went boating on Okanagan Lake. I had my cell with me, and it rang. I picked it up, and it was my father, calling from the hospital, asking me to pick him up two packages of cigarettes and bring them to the hospital as soon as possible. I was annoyed that he was interrupting my date and said I would not be able to come that day; I would try to come the next day, however. Suddenly and without warning, my dad laid into a barrage of curse words at me for not being there for him when he needed me. He began manipulating me, telling me how he was always there for me when I needed Xanax (reminding me of the time he sold me 100 of his pills before I went to Disneyland with Amanda) and the times he visited me in the hospital after Trevor died. I hung up on my dad for the first time.

Later on, when I got home from my date, there was a message on my phone from a nurse at the hospital my dad was in. The message was very urgent and warned me to stay away from the hospital, as my father had gone into a psychotic fit over my not coming with cigarettes. The nurse asked me to call her as soon as I got this message, which I did.

When I called the hospital, the nurse seemed very worried about me but would not tell me exactly what my father was saying or doing. She did say they were completely baffled at my father's violent outburst since they had not seen this side of him before; he seemed so charming (a typical psychopath paradox).

I told the nurse he was a diagnosed psychopath and to expect the worst from time to time, especially if he felt crossed. I also told her why my father was in the Kelowna Hospital rather than the closer hospitals to his home in Vancouver to get drugs. The nurse again warned me to stay away from him based on what he said during his fit. After my conversation with the staff member, my Father was promptly discharged from the hospital and had nowhere to stay. He did not call me, still furious that I didn't rush to his side with cigarettes, but he had a sister close by, and my Aunt Thelma allowed him to stay with her for just one or two days; after that, she told him he had to leave.

My sixty-six-year-old dad hitchhiked back to Vancouver, without his drugs and burning with rage over his perceived thought I was disloyal to him.

*   *   *

Meanwhile, my life was improving drastically. I obtained a human resource management position with a local manufacturing company. I had regained one of my losses—a career I loved! The only hard part of this position was the long hours, but I had nothing to do with my time anyway, and so those long hours just filled the silence I felt at home.

Sometimes, however, I would work such long hours I forgot to eat. I was losing weight rapidly, and when I look at some of the pictures taken of me during this time, I was nothing but skin and bones.

Then I met Frank.

Chapter 16—My Concrete Angel

All God's angels come to us disguised.

—James Russell Lowell

In early 2007, I joined an online dating site and saw the profile and photo of a man who looked very attractive to me. We e-mailed each other and soon made a date. He was going to come to my condo to pick me up, and we would go have dinner together. At the last minute, I changed my mind. I phoned Frank and told him I was sick and unable to go out with him that night. I thought that with my job, I just did not have time to date. Fortunately, Frank is a very persistent fellow and insisted he at least drop by to give me the flowers he purchased for me.

When Frank came to the door, the very first thing I noticed about him was his eyes. They were a soft but brilliant blue that matched perfectly with his blue shirt. He was very tall and had pure white hair (but not bald!) that accentuated his angelic eyes. I was in my pajamas, but I felt compelled to invite him in for a glass of wine, which he readily accepted. He stood in my kitchen, and I was on the other side of the kitchen bar, sitting on a stool. We drank wine and talked like we knew each other forever.

Frank is the eldest of ten children, was raised in the harsh cold winds of Northern British Columbia, and is a very responsible man. I have now met most of his siblings and know his mother well since she comes to visit Frank's home, and Frank visits his mother at least once a month (she lives almost two hours away in a city called Kamloops) to help her out around the house she continues to live in at the age of eighty!

I love this family because of the support and respect they have for each other. When he was in his early twenties, Frank traveled to Australia and New

Zealand. There he met his wife of some twenty years, and she immigrated to Canada to be with him. After their three children were grown, the couple divorced. For twenty-five years, Frank worked as a butcher at the same company, Save-On-Foods. I like stable men, and I liked that he had only been divorced once! So many men I encountered on the dating site had been married many, many times.

Frank was ten years my senior at fifty-seven but very attractive and active. I noticed he seemed to have a speech impediment and a constant need to clear his throat. When I asked him about it, he said that three years earlier, he was landscaping his yard and trying to get a tree stump moved (by himself!) when his neighbor offered to pick it up with his back hoe. Frank was very grateful, and as the operator was lifting the heavy tree stump and root, he let it go onto Frank's trailer. Frank was standing close to the hitch of the trailer, and when the tree stump landed in the trailer, the hitch zipped up and almost knocked Frank's head off, splitting his throat! (Frank always said it was one way to get "ahead.")

I loved Frank's sense of humor and enjoyed his company very much. I was thankful he wasn't killed in that accident, and while he spent many months in the hospital and recovering, he was now back at work and doing fine.

Toward the end of our first date, there is a discrepancy of stories on what happened next. To hear Frank say it, we were in my living room and I suddenly threw his 200-pound frame down to the ground and had my way with him—curtains wide open! The real story (my story) is that we both fell into a heap of lust and enjoyed each other for the rest of the night until morning. That man has the stamina of a twenty-five-year-old!

Frank took me to see his sailboat at the West Bank Yacht Club he belonged to, and we went out a few times with the sails down. I noticed he was a little bit odd in that he said hello to every person who passed us by, garnishing some strange looks. I thought Frank might be socially clumsy but I liked him just the same.

While I worked long hours, Frank would bring me food to eat to my office, and he was constantly at me for working too hard and too long. I did have a very demanding boss, but since this was my first human resources job in six years, I really wanted to make a good impression.

Frank and I were different in so many ways. First, I made more money than he did. Second, I am very particular about sanitation, and when he got off of his shift, I knew he probably had raw fish or meat tissue on his shirt from his job in the meat and fish department, and it grossed me out to hug him hello!

The most important difference between Frank and I was that he was union and I was management. What he talked about his work environment, it made me mad at him, wishing he had a better attitude. As an HR manager, I knew that a positive work attitude was important, and Frank had a lot of problems with his harassing managers. He was often visiting the shop steward to lodge one complaint or another.

And so after three weeks of dating, I tried to break it off with him. Frank came over to my condo, and I was sitting on my bed, sorting some photos. I said to him we were too different, and I wanted to end the relationship before it got too serious. As I said this to Frank, I saw tears in his eyes, real tears that he was trying to hold back. It broke my heart. I am a sucker for a man with a tear in his eye, and when he told me what a crappy day he had at work and now to find out I was breaking it off with him was a lot to take.

I changed my mind. I said, "Okay, we will give it a try." I did say that we couldn't see each other as often because I really wanted to concentrate on my job. Frank agreed to pull back a bit. However, that didn't stop him from phoning me many times in a day! I must admit I loved that he cared so much about me and that he took care of my basic needs, such as eating in between work.

I moved into Frank's house (as a friend) in 2010. Together we built a garden and adopted two Maltese/poodle cross pups. We were a family of six with our dogs, two cats, and us. For a while the situation worked out very well.

* * *

Little did I know how much I would need Frank in the upcoming months and years. And little did I know how horribly he would betray me in the end. I honestly believed God sent me an earth angel to help me through what was coming my way. I was wrong which will become clear in my epilogue.

Chapter 17—Step This Way, Please . . . No, This Way

We must embrace pain and burn it as fuel for our journey.

—Kenji Miyazawa

I learned my mother and father, who were divorced for some forty-five years and lived four hours apart, were both diagnosed with lung cancer in May of 2007. I cannot make this stuff up!

I immediately called my mother and asked her about her condition. Mother was very dismissive toward me and would not provide many details, other than to say the doctors were incompetent and she was going to live to a ripe old age. She was currently taking radiation treatments in Kelowna (my city), and I invited her to come to my place the next day after her radiation treatment. Much to my surprise, she agreed.

Mother arrived with Dylan and a girlfriend of hers. We sat in my living room and discussed the prognoses of Mother's cancer. Mother said the doctors put her on a regime of radiation "to cure." She was getting the most radiation her body was allowed. If I remember correctly, that meant thirty treatments in thirty days. While my mother was her usual distant and cold disapproving person toward me, I was happy she finally made the effort to visit me.

After another radiation treatment, Mother actually drove herself to my work, and I gave her a tour of our plant and offices. Mother was on oxygen (she also suffered from emphysema, and her breathing was getting worse day by day). We went to lunch after her visit to my work, and it was a chilly meal, but I appreciated her effort to be with me and to see where I worked. I always wanted to make her proud but was rarely successful.

I immediately researched lung cancer and learned that the prognosis was less than 5 percent of people with lung cancer lived beyond five years. I tried to talk to my mother about her condition and what she was expecting, and she called me negative and to never talk of the cancer like it was a death sentence. I understood her feelings and refrained from bringing it up again. I would let her tell me what she wanted me to know as time went on.

Gus was still on crack cocaine, and Dylan was a chronic alcoholic with a very demanding wife, so neither was very available to be with Mother during this time. Besides, it really was difficult to be with my mother, she never made visits with her children easy. My sister lived several hours away and while she did make several trips to Vernon for Mother's doctor appointments, I knew I would be the one to pitch in and help my mother in any way I could since I lived the closest.

I love to cook, and so once a week, I would conjure up several variations of pasta dishes she could easily heat up for herself during the week. One incident, which is actually quite funny if you look at it so, was that I mentioned to Mom not to heat the pasta in the microwave because anything with flour in it tends to turn to cardboard in the microwave oven. I suggested she just reheat the pasta dishes over the stove. The next week, when I brought more meals to her, I asked her if she would like some pasta for lunch. In her most dripping hostile tone of voice, she said, "Fine, but heat it over the stove—if you heat it in the microwave, it turns to cardboard!" I looked at her with an expression of disbelief but let it go and put the pasta in a sauce pan like I always have!

Mom only lived about forty minutes away from my condo, so I also visited her on most weekends. Mother was always hypercritical and demanding, and cancer did not change that part of her. While she sat at her kitchen table with a full view of everything I was doing in her kitchen, I could feel her eyes burning into the back of my head. If I put a dish that had "touched" soapy water in the sink, she would make me take it out and rinse it thoroughly before putting it in the machine, stating that dish soap ruins dishwashers. At forty-eight, I still felt like a child around my mother. And she still scared the shit out of me.

She had me do errands for her and watched me closely as I tended to some basic housekeeping chores to make sure I was living up to her standards (or not stealing something, maybe). Mother had two friends who came in weekly to clean her condo from top to bottom, which I thought was amazing since a two-bedroom condo with only one resident who practically lived at her kitchen table hardly needed that much cleaning. But Mother seemed proud to have these "real friends," and it almost sounded like she was saying people loved her so much they would clean her home even when it didn't need cleaning. People were doting on her and she was in her glory.

While I was growing up, our house was never spick-and-span clean since it was the children of the house who did most of the housework, especially me. Mother never liked housework, and so to see her so picky now while others were doing the work caused me many bitten lips.

Mother showed me how to play a card game called Skip-Bo, and I did enjoy playing this game with her. I would heat up some pasta for us for lunch, and we talked about, well, nothing really, but at least I was there and she did seem to perk up when I (or anyone) was around. When I would talk to her on the phone, which was daily, she always sounded down and not well. When I would visit her, she seemed so much more active than I would have expected. It was very strange, the difference between the telephone conversations and actual face-to-face visits. I think she really needed company, any company. Mother is an extrovert, and as a qualified Myers-Briggs testing administrator, I know that extroverts get their energy from people, while introverts are energized by being alone. Mother definitely felt better when people were around her.

I wished my brothers would visit more often. Shivey continued to come up (whenever I was not around to avoid me; she was still giving me the silent treatment for whatever reason) and take her to her radiation or doctor appointments.

Mother's radiation came to an end, and she ended up with pneumonia, a common side effect of this cancer treatment. The doctors dosed her up on prednisone, and she jumped into an almost manic energy and wanted to go to her favorite spot, the Legion, where she could dance. And so, my mother went dancing with her oxygen tank and Frank and I in tow. Once again, I was sitting at a table full of her friends, and not one would look at me in the eye and I felt that same old sensation that they disapproved of me for some reason, even though I had never met any of them in the past. Mother's malignant gossip and character assassination hits about me would never end, I guessed. I was very uncomfortable after a period of time, and I finally asked Frank to take me home.

One weekend in late November, I brought Frank with me to spend the weekend at my mother's place. Mother was on her best behavior, and nary a rude comment or hostile demand came from her lips in front of Frank. We took Mother shopping for Christmas gifts and decorations, and Frank hauled up her artificial tree and decorations from her storage unit and put it together for her to decorate. Frank was *very* good to my ailing mother, but I do not remember her saying thank you even once. Mother was the type of person who felt entitled, and therefore thank-you's were unnecessary.

* * *

In late 2006, my father finally cooled down enough to call me to say that he had lung cancer. I was very leery of his claim (he was a pathological liar, after all), so I asked if he was going to have radiation, and he said the doctor at the Vancouver Cancer Clinic didn't mention it. I didn't believe him. I felt strongly that my father was lying to me to gain my sympathies, and I did not give his cancer claim another thought.

Manipulation was an ongoing issue with both my psychopath father and malignant narcissist mother throughout my lifetime. I knew how it worked by now and didn't get upset over his "condition." I did say he could call me anytime, however, and he did. Looking back, he must have thought I was very cold, considering he was given a death sentence and I was acting as if nothing was the matter. Well, you play wolf one too many times and people eventually just do not believe a word you say. And I didn't.

One day in or about May of 2007 (the same time I found out my mother had cancer and was undergoing radiation treatment), he called and said the Red Cross brought a hospital bed to his studio apartment and a nurse was coming in regularly to check on him. I started to wonder if he was in fact telling the truth about having cancer. I asked him for his oncologist's phone number with the pretense of getting information about why they were not giving him radiation to try to stop the cancer growth. Dad readily gave me the number of Dr. Wo, whose office was at the Vancouver Cancer Clinic. I called the doctor and asked him about my father and his condition.

I was floored when he told me that Dad had a seven-centimeter malignant tumor on his left lung, and the prognosis was not good. I asked why they were not giving my father radiation, and the doctor said a very strange thing; he said to me, "Okay, we can give him five days of radiation then." Why did it take my phone call to get treatment for him? Why was he only getting five days of treatment and Mother was getting thirty days? I guessed that the doctors saw my dad lived one step in skid row, still smoked cigarettes, and was not a good candidate for the treatment, but they were going to go ahead with some treatment to satisfy my inquiry.

I felt terrible for not believing him when Dad first said he had cancer about six months before. In July 2007, I left my job due to overwork and stress and became available to assist my father who was rapidly deteriorating. Frank and I drove to Vancouver to visit him during the summer, and he did not look well. In addition, he had become a hoarder of junk! His apartment was filthy, and almost every floor space up to the ceilings were packed with stuff and, interestingly, Boost, a drink filled with vitamins in case he couldn't hold down food. There were *cases* of this stuff filling an entire closet.

I tried to tidy things up for him, but he didn't seem to want anything touched. My Dad, who had spent most of his life behind bars, wanted his things to be left exactly where they were, and I was not to get rid of anything. All of my father's possessions were acquired at yard or garage sales or stolen from his tenants in the day when he was a property manager for a low-income housing corporation. There was not one thing of value in his small bachelor apartment.

Frank and I stayed outside and sat on a couple of broken-down lawn chairs and talked to Dad through his patio doors as he lay on the sofa. I have never seen my father this beaten down in my life. To me, he was always larger than life and very handsome. What was before me was not recognizable. We didn't stay very long and left after a brief afternoon visit.

I took the opportunity while in Vancouver to visit my uncle Hilliard, who by then had lost all of his short-term memory due to alcohol abuse, and took him out for a beer at his favorite establishment at his insistence. He kept asking where Ivan was (his brother), and every time I would tell him Dad was very sick, he would ponder the thought and a few moments later ask the same question again. Frank and I decided to take Uncle Hilliard to Dad's apartment, where they could talk. I could see the shock on my uncle's face as he looked first at the rapid deterioration of my father and then the condition of his suite.

These two men, once *the men about town* in North Vancouver who could get any girl they wanted, were now both broken in their own sad ways. I cried all the way home, realizing the end of an era that I enjoyed so many years before. Oldies country and rock-and-roll music, house parties where quarters would miraculously appear from children's ears, and the White Spot Restaurant, where servers would bring food to the car on a long tray—the place my Dad would often take me when he was allowed a visit. All of these good memories flushed through my mind, and I was left with the realization that I was going to be alone in this, watching my dad die before my very eyes.

* * *

Mother's health seemed to be improving. She said the doctors said that her cancer was now the size of a scar after her successful radiation treatment. I was thrilled for her. But wait! Did I hear her correctly, "the size of a scar" means it was still there! I didn't have the time to worry about that then; my Dad was fast-approaching death, and I wanted to make his last few months as pleasant as possible. He had no one else to lean on due to his appalling treatment of others, especially his families, but I could not bear to see a man die alone, let alone one I called Dad.

*   *   *

In October, my dad called me, crying, saying that they had come to take him to palliative care at Vancouver General Hospital! He asked me to talk to the nurse who was there with him at his place. She confirmed it would be best if he had some time in the hospital and he would likely only be there for about a week. A week? What the hell does that mean? Is he going to die in a week? I knew this was not a good sign; I never heard of people getting out of palliative care! The nurse tried to calm me and said no, he was not going to die in a week but he did have pneumonia and needed to be hospitalized and palliative care was the best place for his care since he did have terminal cancer that was spreading to his bones.

I was still getting alimony and could manage driving the four-hour trip on Mondays and come home on Fridays to assist Mother at her place. I think I went into autopilot around that time because if I could actually feel my emotions I knew were stirring around in my head, I would have collapsed with fear and amazement of the coincidence of both of my parents having lung cancer and would soon be gone.

When I phoned Mother to tell her Ivan (my Dad and her ex-husband) also had lung cancer, I could hear a pin drop with the silence on the other end of the phone. She certainly didn't care, other than to worry my time would now be spent in Vancouver and she would be alone. She also thought the coincidence was amazing.

Out of my father's five children, Gus was on crack; his ex-wife and three children from his second marriage were treated pathologically cruel by him and had no interest in his condition, which left me to be the one to tend to his needs. Mother was not in as bad shape as my father. After her radiation treatment and the pneumonia had passed, she was actually feeling pretty good and back dancing at her regular haunt. So it was time to focus on my Father.

*   *   *

When I learned my Father was going to be in palliative care, I packed my bags for a long visit. My concrete angel, Frank, came with me. We decided we were going to clean my father's apartment up and make it look and feel like a home for when he did get released. I lost my senses I guess because I've never heard of anyone coming home from palliative care, and yet here I was going through the extremely difficult chore of sorting and disposing of my father's belongings (junk) and cleaning his filthy apartment.

Frank and I spent days taking things out and cleaning. I must admit the apartment looked wonderful when we were done, right down to the waxing of his floors and shining of his very old fridge. I left everything I knew he cherished, such as his birch-tree coffee table, photos, and things he made in prison. When we were done, the place looked very livable and comfortable.

Then we went shopping. I bought my dad underwear and some "real" pajamas he could wear in the hospital, as well as some of his favorite snacks and magazines I thought he might enjoy. I really didn't have the money for the countless hotels, car rentals, hospital parking, meals in restaurants, and necessities for Dad, and I started to use my credit card for these things, putting myself into some serious debt, which would come back to haunt me in the future.

I took pictures of my dad's fresh and clean apartment on my digital camera and posted them in my laptop so that I could show my Father what he would be going home to. I think I was still in denial. We were outside on the balcony of the palliative care unit, so Dad could have a cigarette as he watched the slide show of his home. I was shocked at my father's lack of appreciation. He went into a small rage when he asked where this was or that was. We lied and told him it was there; we just forgot to take pictures of them. I had never heard of hoarders before, and now that I know something about the disorder, I realize it would have been a psychological nightmare for my father to see his "things" gone.

Days turned into weeks in palliative care. I was beginning to wonder if we had been lied to about his condition. I asked to speak to the social worker of the department, and he explained to me that Dad would not be going home and would most likely need to go to a hospice where he will die. I told the social worker that my mother also had lung cancer and lived four hours away, closer to my home, and if would it be possible to transfer my dad to a Kelowna's hospice. I even suggested he could get a hospital bed and stay in my living room if need be. The answer was no. The reason I was told was that Dad had at least six months to live and the Kelowna hospice would not take a patient with that long to live. Six months to live? He looked like he could die at any moment to me!

My father was on enough pain medication that could kill a horse. However, since he had abused pain medication for so many years, his tolerance for pain medication was far more than people who were not used to the drugs. At the time my father went into palliative care, he was even on methadone, a synthetic heroin that was so powerful he no longer needed his Tylenol 3s. Every time I turned around, it seemed the nurses were giving him another bout of pain medications, as well as his beloved Xanax. I know that toward the end, his upper back was extremely painful and had a brown tinge to it. It hurt me to see him in so much pain in spite of all the narcotics he was on.

∗　　∗　　∗

Six months to live? Anyone with one eye could see that my dad was on death's door *now*, and I did not believe that the social worker was being straight with me about the reasons my dad could not be transferred to Kelowna. I never did find out the real reasons behind the decision. The thought of having to spend six months more in Vancouver wore me down. I was afraid for my financial well-being, and not being in my own home was difficult.

I telephoned Gus, who continued to use crack cocaine, the brother who was so close to Dad back in the day when they shared woman and wine. He said he would come down and help me cope with Dad. My father was becoming very manipulative and demanding, so much to the point where Frank actually phoned my dad from our hotel room and gave him a stern talking to, saying he had one person on his side during this time and if he continued to manipulate me, he would lose me as well. When I learned Frank had done this, I was very angry. I lived with manipulative parents all of my life, and this was not the time to threaten my dad. However, I was never one to look after *myself*, and today I am grateful that Frank cared so much about me by taking action.

Dad's manipulative ways stopped and was once again kind to me, making my job of caring for him just a little bit easier.

I also called my half sister, Shenay, to let her know our father was dying. I was happy that she later called my father at the hospital and had her last words with him. I know my father was very grateful for that telephone call. I did not know the phone numbers of my other half siblings but knew Shenay would let them all know. No one else called. I cannot blame any of them. My father caused a great deal of pain within that family, and he used up any sympathies they may have had for him by hurting them as much as he did in his lifetime.

There was a suspicious fire at my stepmother, Sunny, and her husband, Michael's home and they were sure Ivan had a hand in it. My father was in Cranbrook at that time and was stalking them, even showing up at their favorite bars. One night, my father was sitting close by them when he pulled out a frightening-looking knife. Sunny was sure she was getting "subliminal" messages from her ex-husband and worried constantly about what his next move would be.

My father used to live in Kelowna years before, as did my sister, Shenay, who was a hairstylist. One summer, my father robbed a bank in Kelowna, and his name (Groseclose) was all over the news media. My sister shared the same last name, as she was not married yet, and she was constantly asked if she knew this "Ivan Groseclose" who got caught robbing a bank. I remember my sister's fury at Ivan for humiliating her in front of her customers and friends.

Another incident I know about is that after Shenay got married in Alberta, she asked my husband and I if we would take all of the wedding gifts back to her house in Kelowna while they enjoyed a honeymoon. I was her bridesmaid and master of ceremonies, and we enjoyed a very good relationship. She told me where the key was, and Gary and I packed up all of her things and brought them to her house and set them on their bed. We put the key back where we found it discreetly.

When my sister and her husband returned home, they found they had been robbed. I cannot remember what was taken, but I know it included many of the wedding gifts. My father was not invited to the wedding out of respect for Shenay's mother, Sunny, and we all believe he was furious for not being able to attend his second daughter's wedding. He was the number one suspect in this robbery.

* * *

I was surprised that not one nurse helped my father have a shower during the two months he was in palliative care. I asked over and over again (as his daughter, I just did not want that responsibility!) for help, but Dad never had a shower at that hospital.

Gus finally showed up, but he was out of his head stoned. He was very angry and took his anger out on me, screaming at me in the hospital for not telling him sooner how sick Dad was. I retorted that he was impossible to get a hold of and it was not for lack of my trying.

I then confronted him on coming into the hospital in a stoned condition, and he didn't like me saying anything at all that was untoward his precious ego. I learned later he was asking my Dad for money out of his meager pension! Finally, my brother left, and I never saw him again during my Dad's dying days. He either hitchhiked or took a bus home. I remember that he later told me it was the worst trip home he had ever been on, and I don't doubt it. He went into treatment soon thereafter.

When Frank learned that Gus had screamed profanities at me in the hospital, he decided to give him a call. This was a very nasty call where Frank called Gus a loser, bum, coward, and every other name he could think of. Gus never forgave Frank and often said later that if he ever ran into him, he would bring him down. That would be impossible since my brother's body had shrunken so much to weight loss because of drugs and Frank was such a large strong man. Well, my brother just had a big mouth and didn't like being confronted for his actions, or inactions as it was. Looking back my brother had a lot of anger problems throughout his adult years, and I feel for his family over his selfishness and anger when confronted with his bad behavior.

*   *   *

The hospital was waiting for a call for a bed at a Vancouver hospice. One day, my Dad told me that he lost his eyeglasses and he couldn't see very well without them. He had one broken-down pair with one lens and no new prescription for a new set of glasses. He also said he needed a pair of good slippers, a certain kind for swelling feet that may be difficult to find. That day I was wearing two-and-a-half-inch high heels and had no car, as Frank went back home to fulfill some of his shifts at work. Most of the time, I had a rented car, but for some reason, I didn't on this particular day.

It was raining that dark and gloomy day in Vancouver (one of the reasons I moved from the area), but I walked all along Broadway Street, trying to find an optometrist who would provide glasses without a prescription, save for one lens. There must have been ten eyeglass shops along my journey, but it would have been against the law for them to fill my order without a prescription. Finally, after walking for approximately two hours in the pissy rain, in those high heels, I finally found a gentle and compassionate soul who would provide some glasses for him. She told me she would use his old lens to make a pair and I should come back in two hours and they would be ready for him. God bless her!

Meanwhile, I had to search for these slippers that would make my father's ever-swelling feet comfortable. This proved to be impossible. Store after store did not have a pair of lousy slippers I could take back to palliative care for my Dad. Finally, the time was up, and I walked back up the sidewalk toward the optometrist's office and picked up my Dad's fresh glasses and made my way back to the hospital. I was crying at this point. Frustrated, cold, and damp to the bone and weary that I could not find a simple pair of slippers for my Father. I prayed to God and my angels that they would help me, but I suspected I would be unable to find the slippers.

When I walked into the lobby, I made my usual stop to get Dad a special coffee before heading back up to the palliative care unit on the twenty-sixth floor. On my way, I looked at the gift shop and wondered, *Hmmmm . . . would this place carry a size 13 slipper?* I couldn't believe my eyes and ears when the staff went out of their way to find what I needed. After thirty minutes of searching at the very back of a shelf, a perfect slipper that also happened to be size 13 was sitting there, just waiting for me to purchase them! They cost $45, but I didn't care; as long as my dad had something to walk around in and eyes to see with, I was happy.

When I walked into my dad's room, he looked terrible. I was very worried about his condition and still wondered why the doctor said he would live for six months, hence the reason for no transfer to Kelowna. A doctor was seeing my father when I came in with my treasures. The oncologist took me aside and said the lung cancer was not the concern; he now had stage IV bone cancer, and with my father's heart condition, it was very likely he would die of congestive heart failure. I think the doctor told me this to stop me from making any more purchases for my father.

I'm very teary as I write this part of my memoir. I was alone to deal with something I never thought I would have to. Flashbacks of my son's death was haunting me in my sleep, and my coping skills were right on the edge of being zero if I did not give my head a shake and a push on, as I learned in my treatment program.

*   *   *

One of my father's biggest fears was being cremated. He begged me not to do this to him after he passed. Of course, I promised I would not have him cremated, but I honestly could not see how I could afford to bury him beside his own father as he wished. He was even talking about a funeral, and I couldn't help but drop a tear thinking, *"Dad, no one will be there for you. You used up all of your tickets on that matter."* Interestingly, about five years prior, my father took out a small life insurance policy to ensure he would be given a proper burial. He made about three payments (which were only $5 a month!) before he stopped. Dad was never very good about paying his bills, and now he was going to suffer the consequences of that, even if he didn't know it. But it broke my heart that I would be the only one to make this cremation decision that was so painful for both my father and me.

I also feared the idea of cremation. When my son died, he had third-degree burns to 80 percent of his body and had to be cremated to get him home with us. I made the decision at that time that I also would be cremated to punish myself for what I did to my precious son.

Now my dad was begging me for a body burial. The stress of not being able to carry out this wish of his was unbearable. I was lucky Frank made it down to Vancouver on his days off and ever so thankful for his support. Without Frank, I do not know if I could have made it. That is why he truly is my concrete angel, and I really do believe God put him in my life to help me deal with the death of my father.

*   *   *

The call finally came. A room was available at a very nice hospice close to where my father used to live. I say "used to" because at this point, I knew he was never going home. On the day of the move, I packed up my father's things in and around his hospital room (he was still hoarding as I found an entire suitcase and drawer full of that Boost drink as I was getting him ready to move from the hospital). It was December 6, and I stopped at a 7-Eleven store to get my dad a phone card so he could call me when he needed or wanted to. When I went back out to the car, I saw my dad with his passenger-side door open and one foot on the ground. He was wearing his cowboy hat, and as I watched him looking around at his surroundings, it looked like any other day, only now he was dying and I think he knew it. I felt very sorry for him.

I purchased digital picture frames for both my Mother and Father and filled them with photos I thought they would enjoy flashing before them. I made sure my Father's room was equipped with everything he would need and went on the tour of the hospice with him and a waiting nurse. I was glad that my Dad's affairs were finally settled and he would be in good hands with the wonderful nurses at the hospice. It was the weekend, and I wanted to get home to see how my Mother was doing. I asked Dad if he would be okay, and told him that I would be back on Tuesday at the latest. He said yes, I should go and not to worry. He seemed to really like his room and the rest of the Victorian-style home, and I left him with a kiss on the cheek.

On December 10, 2007, four days later and the day I was planning to drive to Vancouver to check back in on him, I received a telephone call from the hospice. I certainly didn't expect a call that soon and was curious. The nurse on the telephone said my father had passed away that morning. He got up to go to the washroom and collapsed on the floor. He was still alive when he was found, and the nurse said she and another gal sat holding my father's hand as he lay on his bed until his life and spirit left him. When they said he was not alone when he died, I was very grateful. However, my heart was sick that I left him just days before! I learned a long time ago that often, dying patients will leave this earth after their loved ones leave the room because they want to go alone. This is how my father died on December 10th, 2007, four days after entering the hospice.

*   *   *

The hospice people put me in touch with a crematorium. I had to go with the cheapest company due to my lack of funds. I remember sitting in a restaurant of the hotel Frank and I were staying at with the representative, and he explained the process. He said he could not be cremated for a couple of days, but he would have my Dad's ashes shipped up to Kelowna as soon as they were ready. I was going against my Dad's wishes, and there wasn't a damn thing I could do about it. It broke my heart. Psychopath or not, I loved my Father.

My Father had two sisters and a brother still alive, and not one of them offered to help me pay for any part of my Dad's death. I guess he ran up his bill with them as well over the years. What they didn't understand, nor my siblings, was that they were not punishing my father for his psychopathic ways; they were punishing me and leaving me holding all of the responsibilities. It hurts that they would think it was okay to let their Father be completely alone in his death and me with the bills.

My aunt Thema, who also lived in Kelowna, agreed to hold the ashes for me. I could not bear the thought of having my father's ashes in my small condo until we could find a place to dispose of them.

Meanwhile, Frank and I were responsible for the task of totally emptying my father's apartment and cleaning it. We gave almost everything he had away to other tenants and did a sweep cleaning of his unit before turning the keys into his landlord.

*   *   *

The next spring, Aunt Thelma and I decided that on my father's birthday, we would spread his ashes in Mission Creek in Kelowna. My aunt and a couple of my cousins attended, as well as a sober brother Gus (he went into a treatment center and became clean soon, almost as soon as my father passed away). The biggest surprise to me was that my sister, Shenay, also came in from Alberta to attend this very small ceremony led by a Salvation Army minister. I was not surprised at how few of Dad's living relatives came to say good-bye to this psychopath who had caused so much pain to so many people.

I was the unfortunate recipient of a very nasty e-mail from my half brother, Gilbert, when I invited him to the ashes ceremony. Like Gus, he showed himself to be an extremely angry man, and I think his anger was misdirected, as I have never done a thing to hurt him or his family, other than to care for our mutual Father. I am so sorry he wrote this letter to me and wish he would let go of his hatred toward our Father—and me, his sister. My arms are always open. I am guilty of nothing but being a human being for another human being who was dying.

*   *   *

For several weeks before my father died, my mother was complaining of a sore upper back, which had me worried. She said she twisted it somehow, and it was nothing to worry about. If that were so, why did she phone me almost every day to tell me how sore it was getting and that she couldn't roll over in bed at night even to go to the washroom? She was clearly in painful distress, and I almost fainted with worry. I knew firsthand how selfish or involved in drugs and alcohol my siblings were, and I could see that I would be left to care for my mother by myself as well!

Chapter 18—The Mother of Manipulators

Simply having children does not make mothers.

—John A. Shedd

The day after I returned from clearing up my Father's affairs and cremation Mother called to once again complain about her increasingly sore back. I was spent. I decided I would not do it alone again. Mother's constant phone calls telling me about the pain in her upper back was really worrying me. I sincerely thought she must be at the end by the way she sounded. I sent out Facebook messages and regular e-mails to every member of our family and told them I thought Mom was very sick, maybe even dying soon. I said I just returned from cremating my father and was alone and I would not be the lone hero for Mother. I demanded they help.

A couple of days later, I got a phone call from my mother. She was screaming so loud I could hardly understand what she was saying. She said my brothers came to her saying I was saying she was on death's door. She shrieked that I was a "negative energy" and wishing her to be dead! Of course, my mother was merely doing what she always does, projecting her own thoughts and feelings on me, as if I really was a *negative energy*. Talk about the pot calling the kettle black! She went on with her rage on me, "I don't want you anywhere near me when I am dying. You are such a negative force you will probably kill me with your dark thoughts!" Not only that but, *"You are out of my will. I knew years ago when you sent me that evil e-mail putting me down as a mother that you were never going to get a dime from me when I die. Now you can know it—you will get nothing!"*

What about the aching upper back she was chronically phoning to tell me about? How she couldn't go to the bathroom at night? I had just watched my dad die of lung and bone cancers over the last three months, and I knew the symptoms. She said "I told you I had only twisted my back!" Right. If it was something so insignificant why did she have to sound so sickly and leave her pain at my feet when I had just returned from losing my Father days before?

One thing I am never very proud of is that I was a coward around my mother. I could never stand up for myself to her face. It is true that I have sent my mother many e-mails telling her my feelings about things she did that hurt me so. This last conversation I had with my mother was no different. The only thing I could sputter out was *"I'm sick of being your fucking scapegoat! Go to hell!"* And I hung up. I then sent her a very long hurtful e-mail telling her exactly what I thought of her. My nerves were shot, and I may not have said much of what I did say if I were not so full of rage over her attack on me.

One thing I said to her in my e-mail was that I did not care about money as much as she seemed to think and that I would not be manipulated by her telling me I was cut out of her will. I don't know what kind of money she had, a condo with a small mortgage, a couple of insurance policies, and some RSVPs and money in her account from her employer who was continuing to pay her full wages for over two years? I didn't know what I was going to miss, and I really didn't care. It was she and Shivey who were the money-oriented people in the family—not me.

My malignant narcissist mother was manipulating me with her back-pain stories, knowing I was in a great deal of pain over my father's death, and when I told of her complaints of severe upper back pain to the rest of the family, I surprised her. She may have thought I didn't care (in her own mind), and when I raised all the family together to let them know I thought she was dying, she was humiliated by her own lies and manipulation of me. She was not dying. It would be another two years before she would pass away!

And no, I was not there. In February of 2009, apparently, my mother was told that she had only six months to a year to live. She could try chemotherapy, which she did, and I highly suspect it was the chemotherapy that ended her life so abruptly.

Prior to her death, she made all of my siblings, Gus, Shivey, and Dylan, swear they would not tell me she was dying. And then she proceeded to cut me out of her will as promised. Mom and Shivey were always smart cookies when it comes to money and finances, and apparently wills. Mom had all of her assets put into

Shivey's name so that her will was empty. This was a brilliant move because if there was nothing in the will, I could not fight for my portion at probate.

Interestingly, also listed as a beneficiary to her will was Crystal Palace, a television church organization my mother watched regularly. She was an avid watcher of Robert Schuller every Sunday morning, and she made sure the money in her will was split up to include his congregation. Now, if I am in the will along with my siblings, but the will had nothing in it, wasn't she giving her favorite church show anything as well? Why she would mention them in an empty will is a conundrum I cannot understand.

*   *   *

Mother had another two years to live and she did not change her mind or opinion about me and I was not invited to any family functions at Thanksgiving or Christmas. I never saw my mother again. Meanwhile, my past was about to catch up with me to add fuel to the already burning family dynamic.

Chapter 19—Liar, Liar,
Pants on Fire!

It is hard to believe that a man is telling the truth when you know that you would lie if you were in his place.

—Henry Louis Mencken, *A Little Book in C Major*, 1916

In about 2008, my ex-husband, Gary, called me to say that Shivey called him to ask him to sign off as a professional witness for my molesting stepfather's Dave's passport. He was planning a trip to Thailand! The fact that my sister was using my ex-husband to perform a favor for her only added to my belief she was doing it to try to hurt me. Why didn't she ask one of her own friends to sign off on my stepfather's passport? No, this woman had to make sure I knew she was still *best friends* (in her mind) with my husband after our separation to add to the many daggers of years gone by.

Thailand? Dave is a long-distance truck driver, and as far as I know, he has never taken a vacation overseas since he was in the army some fifty years ago. He can usually be found in a bar getting drunk, so when I learned about his upcoming Thailand vacation, red flags startled me into action.

I had heard much news about North American men visiting Thailand in the thousands to take advantage of the young prostitutes. Girls as young as eight years old are used by older brothers, uncles, and even fathers to support their families.

I found this excerpt in the Internet superhighway, and you can find the same information everywhere:

Victims of Child Sex Tourism

Child sex tourism make its profits from the exploitation of child prostitutes in developing countries. Many children are trafficked into the sex trade. In Thailand, for example, Burmese girls as young as thirteen are illegally trafficked across the border by recruiters and sold to brothel owners.

The lives of child prostitutes are almost too appalling to confront. Studies indicate that child prostitutes serve between two and thirty clients per day! Younger children, many below the age of 10, have been increasingly drawn into serving *tourists* (author's emphasis).

Child prostitutes live in constant fear; they live in fear of sadistic acts by clients, fear of being beaten by pimps who control the sex trade, and fear of being apprehended by the police. It comes as no surprise that victims often suffer from depression, low self-esteem, and feelings of hopelessness.

Many victims of child sexual exploitation also suffer from physical ailments, including tuberculosis, exhaustion, infections, and physical injuries resulting from violence inflicted upon them. Venereal diseases run rampant among these children and they rarely receive medical treatment until they are seriously or terminally ill. Living conditions are poor and meals are inadequate and irregular. Many children that fail to earn enough money are punished severely, often through beatings and starvation. Sadly, drug use and suicide are all too common for victims of child sexual exploitation.

Child Sex Tourists

Child sex tourists are typically males and come from all income brackets. Perpetrators usually hail from nations in Western European nations and North America.

While some tourists are pedophiles that preferentially seek out children for sexual relationships, many child sex tourists are "situational abusers." These are individuals who do not consistently seek out children as sexual partners, but who do occasionally engage in sexual acts with children when the opportunity presents itself. *(This sounds an awful lot like my stepfather!)*

The distorted and disheartening rationales for child sex tourism are numerous.

Some perpetrators rationalize their sexual encounters with children with the idea that they are helping the children financially better themselves and their families. Paying a child for his or her services allows a tourist to avoid guilt by convincing himself he is helping the child and the child's family to escape economic hardship. Others try to justify their behavior by believing that children in foreign countries are less "sexually inhibited" and by believing their destination country does not have the same social taboos against having sex with children. *Still other perpetrators are drawn towards child sex while abroad because they enjoy the anonymity that comes with being in a foreign land* (author's emphasis). This anonymity provides the child sex tourist with freedom from the moral restraints that govern behavior in his home country. Consequently, some tourists feel that they can discard their moral values when traveling and avoid accountability for their behavior and its consequences. Finally, some sex tourists are fuelled by racism and view the welfare of children of third world countries as unimportant.

You can imagine my fright for these young girls because I know Dave as a sexual predator—he came after me when I was in my puberty years as I spelt out in detail in an earlier chapter. Why my ex-husband continued to side with my sick family and even *help my stepfather* knowing what Dave did to me makes me want to throw up.

Dave was taking a trip *by himself* to Thailand! What possible reason for this trip other than to take advantage of the young girls forced into prostitution? It was time for me to jump into action. I didn't want Dave to have a passport. If I could save just one young girl half the world away, I would do it. I called the Elizabeth Fry Society, a nonprofit organization who provides counseling and financial assistance to victims of sexual assault. A nice lady named Jane came to my home for an appointment to talk about my experiences as a survivor of my stepfather's sexual abuse.

I learned during our conversation that I would be eligible for group counseling to help me deal with the sexual abuse that occurred over thirty-five years ago. This would be good for me, I thought, because my mother and family continued to disbelieve me, and maybe now I could get some solid counseling to at least begin to believe in myself over the issue.

Unfortunately, there was a glitch. In order to become a part of the Historical Sexual Abuse (HSA) program; I would have to press charges against Dave! This had not occurred to me. I thought my window of opportunity to press charges was long gone. Apparently not.

The RCMP were called by Jane, and I made my statement in front of the Elizabeth Fry counselor. I found out that since the incidents took place in Delta, British Columbia, who had a different police department than the RCMP, I would have to give statements to the Delta Police. I was shocked at how so many people cared! Jim Coleman was the sergeant who called me to say he was coming to Kelowna (a four-hour drive) with some of his investigators to interview me and any witnesses I may have. Witnesses? When the hell are there any witnesses to sexual assault?

However, I did tell my mother when I was eighteen what Dave had done to me. She didn't believe me, but it does lead credence to my story since I was still telling it. I told many people over the years, especially people I trusted, such as my stepmother, Sunny, and all of my siblings. Unfortunately, while Sunny remembered my telling of this disgusting story when I lived with her at the age of sixteen, she remembered no details, and her statement was not useful.

I walked into the RCMP offices where the Delta Police were waiting for me to tell my story. I sat in a comfortable chair, and a male and female officer interviewed me at length. I didn't know this at that time but Sergeant Jim Coleman from Delta was sitting in another room, watching me through a camera. It didn't matter. I just told the truth as I remembered it.

After the interview, they said they were going to interview my mother, who still held hostility toward me since I was a child. If it was not so sad, it would be funny to hear what she would have to say to the police. I do not know the details of what she said to them. The police then talked to my two older brothers and Shivey, who lived in Abbotsford, quite some distance away. I was very impressed with the thorough exploration into the event that took place so long ago. However, I was very disappointed with my siblings who all denied knowing anything about the abuse. Even my older brother, who was not a child of Dave, had nothing to say in my support, although I know I told him years ago and many times since. He was one of the loudest people in my life who said I need to, "*Let it go.*"

I was afraid, however, that I was going to hurt my younger brother and sister with the police interviewing them about their own father having sexually assaulting me. I knew I was going to pay dearly for this claim of mine. And I did. I do know my mother told the police she didn't remember anything but that I was a liar, and she didn't believe it for a minute that Dave did this to me. I imagine they got the same reaction from my siblings. My mother did quite a job discrediting me throughout our lives, and even though I have never deliberately hurt my siblings, they were always weary about me. Mother was an expert at passing along her paranoid belief that I was a liar, just like my biological father.

The investigating went on for some time because Dave was making himself scarce and never available for an interview. Finally, Jim Coleman called me to say that the investigation was over, and no charges were going to be laid. My heart sank. That meant that Dave would be able to get his passport to Thailand, and there wasn't a damn thing I could do about it. It also stopped me from having access to most of Elizabeth Fry Society's programs, although I could and did go to the Historical Sexual Assault program, which lasted for six weeks.

I did get a lot out of the program and was surrounded by ten other women who suffered the same, if not worse, much worse abuse than myself. I was surprised at how many women were sexually abused by their mothers! I was surprised to see an eighty-year-old woman in our group still suffering the effects of her abuse as a child. Sexual abuse leaves a whole in one's soul that does not go away. I think I was well over the sexual abuse by Dave, but the fact that my Mother was still calling me a liar ate at my soul bit by bit. What mother does not protect her own daughter? A malignant narcissist mother doesn't.

Jim, the Delta Police sergeant e-mailed me to say he had one more idea up his sleeve and he would let me know how it went later on. It turns out he asked Dave to take a lie detector test! Dave agreed but never showed up, and the case came to a complete halt because the police department could not force him to take it.

Shivey, whom I was beginning to believe is as much of an MN as my mother (actually, with her slippery financial criminal ways and laughter at her own evil antics I suspect she just might be more of psychopath), told me that Dave *did* take the lie detector test and passed with flying colors! Did Shivey think I was stupid? I was in constant touch with the police and Dave absolutely *did not* take that test! She may be able to get away with her lies to others, but this was one lie I was not going to let her get away with in my memoir. Charles (Dave) Craig, born Friday the 13th (yes, like Mother) in June 1941 *refused to take the lie detector test regarding molesting me as a child!* If I could say that louder I would. People, keep your pre-teens well away from that man. If he can get away with molestation of vulnerable girls—he will.

Shivey also told me that Jim showed the divorced couple (who lived hours apart) the complete tape of me making my molestation claim and Mother saying, "Were we really that bad of parents?" I do not believe for a minute that (1) the police would show my divorced parents my statement, and (2) that my mother said that type of statement. I didn't believe for a minute what my sister was claiming. Malignant narcissists are liars by their very nature and make up things to suit their own purposes, and I am sure she spread that bit of bullshit wherever she could.

It was over. I no longer had any say about Dave and his sexual desires with young girls. I had nothing left but the six-week HSA program, and then I was supposed to let it all go. Unfortunately things have a way of eating at a person especially when your entire family turns their back on you. I am still sore and sad at the entire event, and although I am glad I finally made a statement to the police, I remain left out in the cold when it comes to family love. Was it worth it? Yes. I'd do it all over again if it meant that at least Dave's name is on a police record as having been accused of sexual abuse on a minor. If he ever dares to try again with any other girl, he will be in a lot of trouble—if he gets caught.

I have no doubt that is why Dave had to travel all the way to Thailand—to get his sexual jollies from young beaten-down girls he couldn't find closer to home. I wouldn't doubt it if as a truck driver he picked the youngest looking waitresses along his travels to put his grubby hands on at those truck stops he warned me so profusely about many years ago.

*   *   *

Stand up for what you believe in, even if you're standing alone.

*   *   *

Chapter 20—The Greatest Sin
In My Family—Feeling

"There can be no transforming of darkness into light and of apathy into movement without emotion."

—Carl Gustave Jung

It was Trevor's forth anniversary of leaving this earth for a better place. I called my ex husband and asked him if he wanted to share in the cost of putting a memorial in the newspaper which he readily agreed.

Immediately after the memorial was published I received an anonymous email (not so anonymous, it was my sister Shivey who knows my email address and would be the only one to stick a knife into me as I bled on the date of my son's death). The email stated that I was not moving on as I should. *That I was causing harm to my granddaughter by not forgetting and moving on.*

I couldn't believe it. I went into my own little rage after getting this cowardly email and sat down and wrote a poem and sent it via email reply:

Let Me Just One Day a Year

Show my heart, which I don in tethers,
as I remember the life of my son.
Produce my soul for all to see,
my pain, no . . . my agony.

Let Me Just One Day a Year

Weep as a loving mother will do,
as I remember the years that we had.
Or reach up from the floor where I fall,
whilst looking to you, so small.

Let Me Just One Day a Year

Touch the air with blinded eyes,
as I remember all that once was.
Never again to be the mother needed,
Or enjoy the fruits, of which I seeded.

Let Me Just One Day a Year

Hold the thoughts that fill my soul,
with memories of laughter, joy, and song.
Forever blemished with a new reality,
the impact, the fire, and then eternity.

Let Me Just One Day a Year

Fill this page with all my rage,
and reveal to you my sins.
Let me strike you down with my sword,
as I watch you suffer against the board.

Let Me Just One Day a Year

Be nothing more than what I am,
childless,
senseless,
hopeless.

Let Me That...

Just One Day a Year.

Typical of my sister and other family members are lack of compassion. In my son's memorial website not one family member wrote a word of condolence—ever. I often wonder if the DNA in our family was not completely unbalanced. Here I had a psychopathic father and malignant narcissist mother (and quite possibly sociopathy in other family members) . . . people with seemingly cold cold hearts, and then there was me.

I am a bleeding heart no doubt. I feel. I am sensitive. I use to write letters to the editor when I would see an injustice toward a person or group. I'm an underdog person. I freely cry at movies. By all accounts I'm light years different than the rest of my family.

I began to wonder if it was not me. Maybe I am the mental case the doctors tried to label me as years before. Maybe everyone else was right, I am *too* sensitive.

But this little voice I have within keeps telling me I am okay. I am right to remember my son, and feel compassion and love toward others. I am right to never want to deliberately hurt a soul. I am always sorry after I lash out. Sorry to the point of debilitating guilt. The way my family reacts to tragic events has always baffled me and the following story only adds to my bewilderment:

* * *

My ex husband, Gary, phoned me to tell me my 19 year old nephew, *Mark, lost his leg at work! This is my sister Shivey's second son; her firstborn died of SIDS years before. Mark was employed with a recycling plant and part of his job was to stomp on plastic milk bottles before the crushing chopper came through and finished the shrinking of the recyclables. Apparently no one else was around and the machine malfunctioned. My nephew got stuck in the process and as the jaws came at him he was unable to turn the machine off, or pull either leg up to avoid disaster. Finally, just as the metal jaws were reaching him he managed to pull one leg up before his other leg got eaten off by the machine.

My heart was sick for my young nephew. Mark was always a sweetie and I love him dearly. I lived several hours away but had flowers and balloons sent to his hospital room and an inspirational email to my sister to pass on to Mark. Not too long after I found out that two weeks after the accident my mother and sister went on a vacation to Hawaii for three weeks—paid for by mother!

I've seen this type of manipulation by my mother before. Even in times of extreme family distress my mother would demand (or manipulate) all attention back on her and it was no surprise she would insist my sister keep their vacation date which she was paying for. Or maybe my sister didn't need that much prodding: she did go dancing on the night of her firstborn's funeral after all.

While Shivey was away vacationing I decided to take the drive to her home town and visit Mark at her house. He was living with my sister and her boyfriend and I when I drove up and knocked on the door I was shocked to see he appeared to have no unhappy emotions about the loss of his leg at all. His whole affect was off, in my view. Maybe he was on strong pain killers, I do not know. But I do know if I had just lost my leg I might be a bit upset over it. I would have expected some kind of feelings of fear or loss over his leg. It had been only two weeks! I am always surprised at people who can stuff their feelings in so deep that on the surface you wouldn't think a thing was wrong. I often wonder when stuffed feelings will seep out.

Or maybe it's just me. Maybe I'm a big baby and I shouldn't let these little things in life get in my way.

*   *   *

I sold my second condo in Kelowna and once again had money left over to play with. I purchased another condo to flip but this one was a bit different; while it had a fantastic view of Okanagan Lake and the city it would need a lot of renovations. That was okay, I had extra money from the sale of my last condo—and I had excellent credit. The plan was to spend lots of money on the condo and sell it for a nice profit as soon as possible.

I also thought a far away vacation was in order.

Chapter 21—Egypt

No one realizes how beautiful it is to travel until he comes home
and rests his head on his old, familiar pillow.

—Lin Yutang

I decided to take a long vacation to Egypt, a place I've always wanted to visit. Frank could not join me as he had to work. So after a lengthy Internet search, I settled on renting a condo in Sharm el Sheikh for seven weeks and was going to travel by air to see Alexandria and Cairo during my vacation. I was going to go to Egypt alone, which is something I would never recommend to any woman.

My trip was very lonely. First, there were very few people staying at the same condo complex I rented. I was usually the only person at the pool. Second, I have been to too many Third World countries before, but I have never been to a country with a completely different religion. When I went on my tours, I could not believe the bullshit that was being said regarding the Christian religion! I understand now that if almost everyone living in the country is Muslim, they would be tempted to skew the history of Egypt to suit their own religion. I may not be a card-carrying churchgoer anymore, but I have studied Christianity at length, and what I was hearing almost made my pores bleed with frustration.

Sharm el Sheikh is only some twenty years old. It is a tourist town and attracts workers from all over Egypt and other parts of Africa. A young Muslim man leaving home is very unusual, and there had to be a good reason for him to be separated from his family. Every single worker was a transient from some other place, and as a person who lives in a tourist city myself, I know they do not have the vested interest to keep tourists coming back. The young Muslim men (I say "men" since I saw maybe a total of five females during my entire stay) did not appear to enjoy tourists, and I found myself being ripped off at almost every venue I visited.

Why was it forty-five Egyptian pounds to take a taxi to the market one day and ninety Egyptian pounds to come back to the condo? When I would go to the shopping market, I was almost always besieged by the taxi driver or vendors. I was harassed everywhere I went, and it was getting exhausting. It was far more insidious than visiting the market places in Mexico or Cuba or anywhere I'd been before. Not having any English-speaking tourists to play with made my trip very lonely, and I spent most of my time in my condo.

I took a snorkeling tour on the Red Sea and not one person on my ship spoke English. There were a lot of Russian tourists, but no Canadian or American ones. Being alone on a trip can be very enlightening. I had nothing to do but sit and watch people, and what I witnessed made me cringe at times. Apparently, Russian tourists are very unwelcome due to their love of vodka (Muslims do not drink alcohol at all). While I was on the ship, I saw employees make many rude gestures toward the female Russian tourists behind their bare backs. I don't understand the Arabic language, but it was not hard to understand their disgust of the patrons. Unfortunately for me, I am blond and fair and easily pass for a Russian, but luckily, I speak English and I fared better with the staff. I think, who knows what went on behind *my* back.

One worker, a young man of about twenty, sat with me often engaging me in conversation (such as it was). He wanted to learn more English, and I was more than happy to accommodate him. I do love to help people, and this young man was innocent enough. Besides, I was bored lonely. This young man, after spending several hours talking to him as a friend, later brought me a "very special coin." He said his coin comes from the days of Cleopatra, and since her time, there were no Egyptian coins made at all.

It is true that I never did see a coin in my travels thus far, and so I was very intrigued. The young man said he would sell it to me for two hundred Egyptian pounds. When I took the coin from his hands, I was very excited; indeed it was unlike any other Egyptian pound I had ever seen—it was a coin! At first, it was easy to believe as I saw a regal-looking woman bearing a crown on one side of the coin. Then I looked a little closer. Being from Canada, a commonwealth country, all of our coins bear the Queen of England's head, and what this man was trying to pass off as an ancient coin was nothing more than an English pound coin!

It bothers me when I would spend so much pleasant time with someone only to be taken advantage of at the end of our journey. It showed me how naive I really am and wished I wasn't so stupid sometimes. I knew at that point of my trip that I could trust little of what they said. I was getting worn out with the lies and harassment. Many men living in Egypt, men in their early twenties, really wanted to emigrate to the West and had no scruples coming onto a fifty-year-old woman to try to get a free pass abroad.

I also gained a new perspective on my health that day when I went snorkeling. I jumped off the ship like everyone else on the boat to experience the millions of varieties of fish and sea life but found myself almost instantly out of breath! I thought I was going to drown when I started to go straight down in the waters and the staff had to throw me a lifeline to get me back to the boat. I had no air. No breath. I have been a good strong swimmer for all of my life, and I wondered if it wasn't the sea, a very salty sea that wore me out so instantly. I would learn when I returned home that was not the case. I was sick and didn't know it.

*   *   *

One day, at my condo in Sharm el Sheikh, I saw a woman whom I later learned was from England. She was blond and very pretty, about ten years younger than me, and very friendly. Finally! Someone I could talk to. Apparently she had been to this condo complex before and befriended a young man named Mohammed (or Hammy as he liked to be called). They were married in a civil union (which means they are not really married but could sleep together), and he was going to travel back to Cairo to ask his parents if he could marry this middle-aged woman under the laws of Allah. He was gone for several days so *Janice and I had lots of time to talk at the pool. She was very excited to bring Hammy to her homeland in England and begin a life with him.

Now I'm not the brightest bulb in the room myself, but I could see a setup a mile away. This twenty-three-year-old and extremely handsome young man could not possibly be serious about marrying a woman twice his age! He wanted a ticket out of Egypt, and she was it. However, I kept my feelings to myself since Janice seemed so happy and excited about her new man.

Hammy finally returned to Sharm el Sheikh and bore the bad news to Janice. His family forbade him to marry her and that he was to return home to Cairo immediately. Janice was devastated, and I really felt for her. She packed up her bags that very night and left for England a broken-hearted woman. I later heard this was a familiar scenario for women traveling to Egypt. It could have been worse, his family could have said yes and who knows how things would turn out once the odd couple arrived in England.

* * *

I was alone in this faraway land once again. I felt my spirit was very heavy and weak. I wanted to go home. I retreated to my own suite and laid in bed, watching many of the DVDs the owner of the condo left for his renters. Lying down was bliss. Sometimes I would go to the pool to add to my tan, but mostly I just wanted to stay inside and rest.

A few days after Janice left, I was surprised to hear a knock on my door and to find Hammy standing there, looking sheepish. I wondered why he was still in the condo complex, as his and Janice's suite was now rented by someone else and he said his family demanded he return home immediately. He said he heard (from whom I cannot guess) I wasn't going out and that if I wanted, he would be my escort to an Egyptian party in a local outdoor mall of Sharm. I really do not know what his motives were because I was more than twice his age and so far had not had good experiences with the Muslim men in Egypt. However, since I had visited with Hammy many times while he was with Janice, I thought him to be safe enough and decided maybe a night out to experience real Egyptian culture would be just what the doctor ordered. I said yes.

This was the best experience I can say I ever had! Not only did I ride a camel around the Egyptian mall but I sat on the pillows in a comfortable typical Egyptian open tent and watched a true to life African concert with music and dancers abound. One of the African dancers who looked like the leader of his tribe came and pulled me up to dance with them! Hammy took pictures with my digital camera, which I later saw much to my delight! I was in my glory, dancing to the African sounds and smiling faces surrounding me. Hammy kept his eyes on me and made sure I enjoyed every single minute of my time at the party. He did not disappoint. I ate lamb and other dishes of the country and, at one point, cried in utter joy of the laughter and noise at the party that Hammy was so gracious to chaperone me to.

When Hammy walked me to my suite in the early hours of the morning, he kissed me on my cheek and told me he too enjoyed himself and thanked me for my wonderful company. He did not make a move on me and didn't ask me for any money, and I knew that he simply was a nice boy who wanted to do something nice for someone else. When I closed my door, I happily went to sleep with my memories of that night, which I will cherish forever.

*　　*　　*

My flight was leaving for Alexandria the next evening, and I spent the entire day packing and fixing myself up for this journey. I love history and was excited to go to the place where Cleopatra lived and died and to learn as much as I could about the ancient city.

I was not disappointed. Things were different in Alexandria. For one thing, the taxi drivers and vendors seemed to love visitors to their city, and all of the people I ran into were generational people who lived in this wonderfully historic place with pride. I hired one taxi driver who took me everywhere I wanted to visit and more. My guy spoke English very well and loved to talk about his city, and I took in every word with wonder. When we went to a very large marketplace, he escorted me on our walk and made sure I got the best deals on my purchases and souvenirs. He told me he was married and had two children and boasted about his family with a great deal of pride. This man had no animosity toward people from the West, and he made my trip very enjoyable.

I was only in Alexandria for three days, and on my last day, I took a cab to a high-end hotel looking over the Mediterranean Sea. I wanted to have lunch where I could have a 180-degree view of an ancient palace on one side of me and the sea on the other. My waiter was very intrigued by me and my own culture and engaged me in some wonderful conversation where we both learned about each other's respective homelands. He was shocked to learn I lived in such a large wealthy country that was only less than 150 years old!

I was sad to leave Alexandria and wondered how I would cope for the next five weeks at my lonely condo in Sharm el Sheikh! I decided to find a travel agent and cut my vacation short. I told the travel agent I wanted to leave in one week's time rather than spend the entire seven weeks in a place I was mostly uncomfortable in. After I got my new tickets, I took the small jet back to Sharm el Sheikh and waited out the few days I'd have left in my rental condo. I was going to fly to Cairo in only a few days and spend three days visiting that city before flying home.

Before leaving Sharm el Sheikh, I decided to take a quad tour in the desert! I was very excited, as I love to ride in the open air and to experience a quad adventure safari in the hidden parts of Egypt, where I discovered the beauty of Egypt's oasis and deserts. There our group met Bedouin tribes who remained living in the hot sands of the deserts and learned about their seeming prehistoric lives. The amazing sunset over the Egyptian desert had me mesmerized as I drank a refreshing soda drink. Again, the women did not show themselves, and I was disappointed I could not get their perspective on life in the desert.

I noticed many camel carcasses, and the live camels I saw were skin and bone. It broke my heart to see these animals so neglected, but I said nothing to the tour guides and thus did not get an answer to my question as to why these people did not care for their livestock.

Another haunting sight was to see thousands, if not hundreds of thousands, of empty plastic bottles of water strewn throughout the desert. It was as if the people did not care about pollution at all. I'm not an environmentalist by any stretch, but this sight was disturbing to my good senses.

However, I enjoyed the rest of my tour immensely as I looked around the desert, wondering if Moses walked here or there. It was a wonderful tour, and I was glad I took it. However, something was very wrong with my health, and I could not maneuver my big quad alone over the sand moguls. My body was very weak, and once again, I was out of breath within minutes. Finally, a tour-guide worker took over my quad, and he drove with me on the back.

These tour guides were wonderful and nothing like what I experienced on the boat in the Red Sea where tourists did not seem welcome but for to making fun of behind their backs or cheating them into thinking an English coin was an ancient Roman one! Thank you Quad operators for a most enjoyable day!

*   *   *

It was time to pack my bags and head to Cairo, where in three wonderful days, I would be back on an airplane home. By the time I got to Cairo, I felt utterly exhausted and defeated. I was afraid of the men of the country and worried about being alone in this large city for one day, let alone three.

I was staying at the Hilton Hotel, and my room overlooked the Nile and a marketplace that was fun to watch from my room. I did not venture out even once during my stay, and I almost starved to death trying to get service in the restaurants downstairs! I was sitting alone and waited for over an hour for the young man to ask me what I wanted to order. The server never even looked my way, even though I was out in the open. There were groups of men to my left and groups of men to my right, and the waiter quickly came to their bidding but was most obvious in ignoring me, a lone single woman. A Western woman who was not veiled.

Finally, I got up and found the restaurant manager and told him I was being deliberately ignored and I needed to order so I could go back to my room. He said he would take care of me personally and I went back to my seat. Another thirty minutes passed and nothing. No tea. No crumpets. I would have starved had I not finally gotten up and went to the front desk manager to lodge my complaint. At that time I did not know that just looking at a woman who was not veiled and who bared her arms and ankles was a sin even in modern Egypt. This was not what the travel brochures said!

I was so upset I told the front desk manager I would just order food service from my room, and the manager thought that would be a good idea. It was not as if I were not clothed decently. I had Capri's and a blouse with sleeves to the elbow. I had no idea this was an unacceptable dress in Cairo. None of the travel brochures mentioned these little rules; in fact, Egypt was supposed to be very liberal and welcoming of tourists no matter how they dressed. I did not find this to be the case as a single woman without a male chaperone.

So for the next few days, I stayed in my room going nowhere, ordering some food whenever my stomach could take it. I did enjoy watching the people below me in the marketplace, the workers leaving for their jobs and coming back, the vendors selling their corn and other goodies. I was surprised to see so many fathers holding their children's hands as they shopped in the market. It was a nice sight to see and a complete contrast to the problems I experienced.

One thing I noticed about Egypt was the constant honking of horns. When I landed in Cairo late into the night, cars zipping by would honk for no apparent reason. Even my own cabbie honked on an almost deserted road just for the sake of honking! It is a strange custom indeed!

I watched with envy boats carrying hundreds of passengers along the Nile, wishing I could get up enough energy to try that experience. I really wanted to see the pyramids, but by the time I had arrived in Cairo, I was spent physically and emotionally, and I just wanted to rest in the comfort and safety of my hotel room.

Finally, it was my day to go home! I struggled with my luggage to the front desk to check out and was told I would be assisted out to the taxicabs waiting just outside of the lobby. The bellboy asked me for ninety-five Egyptian pounds so that he could pay the cabbie. He told me that ten of those dollars were for the cost of entering the airport parking lot, and another ten was for his tip. I saw him give my cab driver the money and was comforted that there would be no problems at the airport when it came to money like the problems I had in Sharm el Sheikh. I gave the bellboy ten Egyptian pounds for his assistance (which I was told at the front desk would be proper).

My drive to the airport was a comedy show if it were not so unnervingly odd! It was during the day this time (on my way from the airport, it was night, and I did not see much of anything). I was excited to see some of Cairo if only by the passenger seat of a cab. What happened was there was a bottleneck on a bridge, and we were moving very slow. I had just blown dry my long blond hair, and it was flying around with the open windows of the cab, so I was an obvious Western female in the open windowed car.

To my left was a car with a fellow in typical Egyptian dress and his passenger wearing the same type of outfit. He had a very long beard, and I was intrigued with that car for some reason. The passenger was putting his hands up as if to cover his window and I could not figure out why. This behavior carried on for what seemed like hours. That car would inch forward as it could, and then our cab would inch forward beside him again. Every time we were beside that car, up went the guy's hands as if to avoid seeing something he ought not see! I asked my cab driver what that guy was doing, and he told me that he was likely a fundamentalist and was not allowed to look at any women not in full veil! Poor man, I likely drove him crazy sticking beside him the entire duration of the long bridge!

I also noticed that the apartments, the many, many apartments along our route, were very poor in appearance. Clothes were hanging everywhere on the windowsills and balconies of those fortunate enough to have a balcony. What was strange were the hundreds or thousands of satellite dishes on the roofs of these buildings! I also noticed that almost everyone I saw had a cell phone. For some reason, this city looked as poor as poor could be but they certainly had enough technology for everyone!

My last uncomfortable encounter came when we finally reached the airport. My taxi driver asked me for payment in full! And he said he needed money for getting into the airport! I said I saw the bellboy at the Hilton give him the money for my ride, tip, and airport entrance fee and that everything was supposed to have been taken care of—that was the rule of the hotel! I guess he thought I was just some blinking idiot woman and wouldn't catch on to his attempted thievery. At this point, I just didn't care and pulled my own luggage out and walked away. Let him call the police if he wanted or stick a fork in me, *I was done!*

Sigh, I was so glad to be going home.

*   *   *

Because I changed my flights' dates, I had numerous airplane switches, and every time I would board another aircraft or complete another layover, I kept telling myself I would arrive home safe and sound soon. I learned a lot about patience on this trip. When I finally arrived at the Kelowna International Airport at midnight, I was greeted by my concrete angel, Frank.

Chapter 22—Bankrupt
Financially and Physically

*Pain is temporary. It may last a minute, or an hour, or a day,
or a year, but eventually it will subside and something else will take
its place. If I quit, however, it lasts forever.*

—Lance Armstrong

When I arrived back at home, I was ready to sell my condo, as all of the renovations had been completed while I was away. It was always my intention to fix it up and resell my high-rise condo for a good profit as I did twice before in less than three years. I was shocked to learn that in a few short weeks, the bottom came out of the real estate market and my fully mortgaged condo was worth a fraction of what it was when I bought it! I never planned on staying in this condo, as it only had one bedroom and I needed two for when Amanda would come to visit.

Not only that but I put thousands of dollars on my credit cards to pay for caring for my Dad, and the condo renovations! I was in deep trouble.

Meanwhile, I was not feeling well. I felt weak and my joints hurt to the point that even walking on my floors was difficult. I was constantly sick and ended up with asthmatic bronchitis and pneumonia within a few short months. My doctor diagnosed me with fibromyalgia, a disease of the central nervous system that can be debilitating. I often wonder if fibromyalgia is depression turned outward since my symptoms seem to flare up more when I am under stress, and during the years of 2007 through 2009, I was under a great deal of stress. Actually, since I sold my business back in 1999, I was stressed and depressed. All of my losses since that time were huge and added to my feelings of being paralyzed to the point of completely isolating myself from the outside world.

I had other health problems. I had surgery to correct a bottom pelvic prolapse likely a result of the ectopic pregnancy blow-up years ago and my aging body. I noticed that I was running out of breath a lot, and this caused me to feel weak and lethargic. I was getting infections every time I turned around and was on antibiotics more often than not.

I thought if I went back to work, I would snap out of my chronic illnesses and feelings of despair over the failing of my real estate. I needed money, and it didn't take me long to find a position as a staff writer with Ogopogo Media, a company who owned several dot-com domains, such as Kelowna.com. Since I enjoy writing, I thought I had found a dream job and was very excited to start. My responsibilities were to write about our various customer venues such as hotels, wineries, and other tourist attractions in the Okanagan Valley where I lived. This was a brand-new company, and the owners dumped a whole lot of money into this venture. My employer used to sell pool tables to drinking establishments and made a heap of money and wanted to try something different. His partner was a computer geek who set up the sites from his home, and I rarely saw him.

I was discouraged when *Andy, my employer, would read my write-ups and hack them to death for no apparent reason. One day, I described a high-end hotel and used the word *milieu*, which is just another word for *environment*. It's important not to use the same words twice in short write-ups, and *milieu* was a perfect word to use. My boss had never heard of the word before and challenged my ability to write! Needless to say, the job did nothing for my self-esteem. I didn't like writing about hotels or restaurants; I am more of a business writer on the subject of what I know most about—employment and human resource management since my entire career was in these fields. I did not feel comfortable writing for tourism, but I stuck it out for as long as I was allowed.

One day, my boss was at a convention in New York, and it was just me and the receptionist. Our building was undergoing construction in the offices next to us, and the constant banging made it impossible for me to concentrate on writing. I told *Carry, the young receptionist, that I was going to take my laptop home and write from there until the construction noise subsided. I asked her to telephone me if the construction stopped.

There was something about Carry, a twenty-one-year-old gal who came to the company as part of a short-term office skills practicum and then hired on full time with a big title, office administrator. She seemed to be jealous, even angry, when I was given a large office and she was told to set me up on their Mac computer. Almost from the beginning, Carry had little complaints that were more irritating than anything. For example, she was allergic to oranges, and one day, she came into my office and said I was never to bring oranges to the offices again and that she was severely allergic. That was odd. I had brought and eaten an orange almost every day, and it was not until she saw me eating my orange that her "rule" was enforced.

Two staff writers before me were fired. This was another red flag for me, but I chose to ignore it, thinking I was a perfectly good employee with a positive attitude and ability to write, and what could possibly go wrong? Everything.

The day I went home to write due to the construction noise, the boss who worked from his home came into the office and asked Carry where I was. Her response? "I don't know." She told my boss she did not know where I was, and yet I was directly across the street in my condo and I had told her if anyone needed me, I could be reached there. She knew about the construction noise, and she knew I left because of it and yet she kept her mouth shut. Was she hoping to get me in trouble?

When I went back to the office at about 3:00 p.m. to transfer my newly written data into the company computer, a very angry *Len was waiting for me. He asked where I had been, and I told him I was at home working (I did live directly across the street from our offices) because I could not concentrate due to the building construction. It was too late. For hours, he must have been steaming about my whereabouts and Carry allowed him to think I was simply AWOL and she was as much in the dark as he was!

Ahhh, I've been to this rodeo before. The little witch was stirring up trouble for me and I would not fare well at the end of the day. I was fired!

*   *   *

I walked home with my belongings and slumped in my sofa, feeling utterly defeated. I needed that job! How could this happen? I went over things again and again in my mind, and while the problem was likely a simple case of my not being suitable to their office culture, I blew it out of proportion in my mind, analyzed the events to death, and finally decided I was a complete loser and unworthy of a good job.

The tapes my mother put into my head over the years began to play. There is something wrong with me. I am a poor excuse of a human being. I am a liar, cheat, and thief! I stole time from the company (no, I didn't; I worked like a dog at home, and my work spoke for itself). I can't write; I used words like *milieu* and nobody gets that! I deserved to be fired.

* * *

I decided I would have to claim bankruptcy. I could no longer keep up with the interest let alone the principal of my credit cards. I could no longer afford my car payment. I was still getting alimony, but it merely covered my mortgage and strata fees. Until this time, I had a perfect credit score. I used my cards often and paid them back quickly. It was a real blow to know that at forty-nine years of age, I was going to have to start over financially, and it would take many years for me to gain my good credit score back. And my alimony agreement was running out.

I began to isolate myself to my suite and rarely ventured out in public. Frank would bring me anything I needed, and I paid him for the groceries I couldn't pick up for myself. I stayed in my pajamas all day long and stared into the television hour after hour to try and forget about my financial and health problems. It was during this time that Frank and my relationship shifted to just friends and he was dating other women. He still remained my best friend and was there whenever I needed him. I made him dinner often to repay him for his generosity and assistance.

* * *

I was hospitalized in late August of 2009, with double pneumonia and pleurisy. They put me on oxygen, and my family doctor came to see me with bad news. I have COPD. This explained why I was feeling so weak all of the time and why my chest was constantly filling up with mucus, rendering me very sick. I now understood why I couldn't breathe when I went snorkeling in the Red Sea in Egypt!

I was discharged after ten days and was able to celebrate my fiftieth birthday with a girlfriend and my younger brother, Dylan, on September 11. It was a small party at a local pub, but I had fun. It was good to see my brother again since I hadn't seen him in a long time. He lives about forty minutes from me, living back and forth between our mother and his girlfriend. Since his two eldest children were grown he had finally ended his marriage to verbally abusive Deanna.

The morning after the party, I was very weak and unable to breathe. Frank "happened" to come over and called the paramedics for me. I was readmitted to the hospital for the COPD symptoms and remained there until September 30, 2009. Dylan never came to see me, nor did Gus, who I thought was off drugs and alcohol, but at this stage, I had my misgivings. It was sad to be in the hospital without family visits, but I was happy when Dylan would call me on my cell to check up on me and always apologize for not visiting. As usual I would say, "No worries, Dylan, you have enough on your plate, I'm sure." I never did ask for much from my family.

*   *   *

I still had not spoken with my mother after her rage against me for raising flags about her health to the family and my angry e-mail response. I had no idea how her lung cancer was developing, but assumed if something was wrong, someone would have told me. I was wrong.

Chapter 23—Good-bye, Mother

For some moments in life there are no words.

—David Seltzer, *Willy Wonka and the Chocolate Factory*

When I was released from the hospital, I went straight to bed. The next day, on October 1, 2009, I puttered around the house, feeling extremely restless. I went for a walk, came home, and tidied my condo, dusting after my long absence. At about 2:00 pm I picked up a little glass ornament that said MOTHER in large letters with a poem written below. I bought this piece for myself soon after my son passed away for comfort. I imagined he would have wanted me to have it.

I kept holding the glass and sat on my bed when I suddenly burst into tears. I was sobbing over the loss of my son and the loss of my Mother, whom I knew I would never see again due to our family dysfunction and her lung cancer. My crying lasted for almost an hour before I took the MOTHER ornament and put it in one of my jewelry boxes. I do not know why I did this.

Dylan phoned (drunk) later that afternoon and said he was going over to Mom's place. I again wondered how she was doing, but it seemed Dylan never wanted to talk to me about her. I do not know why he phoned me before he went to Mother's condo that day. It was unusual to hear so much from him but he said so little.

At about 6:00 p.m., I received a call from Dylan again. He asked, "Are you okay?" I said, "Yes, why?" He asked again, "No, really, are you okay?" I said, "Dylan, what is wrong?" I dropped the phone when he said our mother had died that afternoon, and he just found her in the bathroom with blood everywhere! He said she was told in February that she was dying and only had months to live. Mother still opted for chemotherapy treatments, which is often a cause of death rather than a cure if a person's immune system is very low. Chemotherapy is very toxic.

I said I will be right over, and he immediately said, "No! Don't come over." I said, "Dylan, you shouldn't be alone right now, and I want to be with the family as they arrive!" Dylan once again very firmly said, "Do not come. I won't be here. Nobody will be here, just stay home." Those were the last words I ever heard from my brother.

The next day, I tried phoning all of the siblings, but no one was answering their phones. The day after, I asked my cousin, Richard, if he would drive me to Mom's condo so that I could find out what was going on. When we got to the condo in the late afternoon, there was no answer at the intercom. I pulled out my cell and called Gus, who finally answered. I asked him what was going on. I said I was at Mother's place and asked where everyone else was. Gus burst out with a raging string of profanity toward me and said to get away from Mom's condo; it was her wish that I not be around! He repeated himself as I argued with him that I wanted to be there with everyone else.

Mother's wish that I not be around *after* she died? That did not make any sense to me. What made even less sense was that my siblings appeared to be bound and determined that I have nothing to do with comforting or engaging in grief discussions surrounding Mother's death. They had nothing to do with the horrible dynamic between my mother and myself. Or did they?

I must repeat here—I did *nothing* to any of my siblings to warrant silent treatment abuse on the day of my Mother's death or the days to come. *Nothing.* If they want to get involved with the anger my mother had toward me throughout my life, there had to be a reason! It was cruel to not be told anything surrounding my Mother's death. I did love my mother and spent fifty years trying to earn her love without success. How do my siblings think they have a right to exclude me from normal grieving meetings among the family? I was dumbfounded. I was sick to my stomach that I was being left out at this very sad time.

My cousin and I drove to the hospital to see what we could learn about my Mother dying in her own apartment, in her own bathroom, by herself! We were told that my mother had already been transported to the funeral home and was no longer in the morgue. Richard and I rushed off to find out what we could about the funeral.

The funeral director was very kind and said my Mother had just arrived and was not prepared for a viewing. I said between my tears that it did not look like I would be welcome at the funeral and I needed to talk to her—even if she was unable to be shown. The gentleman finally agreed and had my mother's body wheeled out to the auditorium. I sat on the front pew with my mother directly in front of me, still lying on a gurney. I had a long talk with my Mother that afternoon. I told her how sorry I was that we could not resolve our issues and I was sorry she could never find it in her heart to show me her love, if she ever had any for me. I needed to say things that I could not say to her face, save for a tongue lashing for my stupidity or ignorance or twisting of words, as she would put things.

When I finished talking with her, I went to her body and slightly touched her heart, and then I turned around and left.

A few days later, I called the funeral director again and asked what the funeral arrangements would be. My siblings were not answering my calls. He told me the date and time (it would be the very next day!), and I hung up, wondering what to do. I did not want to create a scene with my obnoxious siblings by attending unwelcomed, and I did not want to be humiliated for the potential lies my Mother and sister may have been saying about me to her friends and extended family.

I decided to get a rush order of fifty roses, one for every year of my life. I also telephoned the minister who would be presiding over her funeral and gave him a message from me to be read to the guests. It was all very simple and friendly. I was excluded from the funeral, but they could not stop me from grieving or thinking about her on the day of her funeral.

*　　*　　*

Little did I know there was a good reason for my siblings to suddenly turn their backs on me. Money. How could they face me knowing that they contributed to Mother's last kick to my ass?

Chapter 24—You Keep the Money, I'll Keep My Soul

I thank Thee . . . it was I who was robbed, and not I who robbed.

—Matthew Henry

Mother made good on her promise to cut me out me of her will. I was confused, however, when Shivey (Mother's executor) sent me a copy of the will, and it clearly stated that I, along with my other three siblings was listed as the beneficiaries. In addition, Mother gave ten percent of her money to the Crystal Palace Cathedral operated by her favorite minister, Robert Schuller. No other person was mentioned in the will.

I contacted my sister, and she told me that although I was listed in the will, there was no money to be distributed. Mother had put all of her property and other assets in hers, Gus's, and Dylan's name *before* she died! Shivey and Mother were very careful to ensure I could not sue for part of Mother's estate. Wow, she must have *really* hated me.

As I said in an earlier chapter, one thing I could not figure out is was how much the Crystal Palace would get if I got nothing based on the emptiness of this will. If there was no money in the actual will, why did Mother put them down as a beneficiary? It did not and still does not make sense to me. I knew my mother loved her church program on Sundays and am very curious that she would dupe them in her will. I already knew why she would dupe me. She never liked me.

Apparently, Mother forgot about one small insurance policy where I was mentioned as a beneficiary, and Shivey dropped off a check to me in the amount of just over $3,000. I knew Mother's assets were valued at well over

$300,000 and figured the siblings would split the money three ways. For a while, I was very angry and called my siblings the Three Little Pigs. But the truth is, it was Mother's money to do with what she wished. It was none of my business. It still hurt, however.

* * *

Two weeks after my mother passed, I went to her condo, thinking Dylan may be living there until the condo was sold. I was surprised to hear Shivey on the other end of the intercom. I told her I was there to find out where Mother was buried. I wanted to visit her resting place. My sister said Mother was cremated and was going to be taken to North Vancouver and be buried with her mother. I said, "Oh, okay. Bye." With that Shivey invited me up to Mother's place, and we had a talk. My older brother, my angry older brother, Gus, was there as well and would not speak to me (again, why is the question) at first. Shivey told me something that made me go "hmmm" again. She said, "Mother spent a lot of money in her last few months."

I knew my mother was terminally ill and on chemotherapy and wondered what on earth she would have spent her money on. But even more intriguing was why my sister was telling me this. I've always known my sister to be greedy and a pathological liar, and this seemed like an instance of *"I think thee lady doeth protest too much."* (Shakespeare) I didn't care, and I was just happy not to be a part of Mother's manipulation money, but I wondered how savvy my brothers would be to Shivey's cheatful ways. I'd love for them to ask for a copy of Mother's bank account the day before she died, and the day after she died. I think they would be very surprised. I've seen my sister rob accounts of dead people before, namely Shivey's mother-in-law.

Nevertheless, when the siblings saw I was not angry with them over any money and was not there to cause trouble for them, they relaxed, and we did have a good conversation. I found out that Mother was alone at the time of her death and likely started to bleed from the mouth and went into the bathroom. Minutes later, she would go to the toilet where she passed out and died. Alone.

I know my mother and I did not have a good relationship. In fact, we had a horrible one. But as a human being, I was sick to my stomach to think she had four children living nearby who could have been with her in her last days but were not. When Mother was first undergoing radiation treatments, I went out of my way to give her meals and other assistance and put up with her verbal and emotional abuse while doing so. I would have done the same had

I known she was dying. Especially if I had known she was on chemotherapy. She should *not* have been left alone.

But not one of my siblings told me Mother was dying in the months leading up to her death. And not one of my siblings was with her in the end. My mother died alone, and I just pray to God she was not afraid. As turbulent as our relationship was, I would not wish that kind of death on anyone. If I knew my mother was on chemotherapy, as bitchy as she was toward me, I would have slept at her home to keep my eyes on her.

I remember buying a book for my mother in her radiation days called *Through Grit and Grace*, which is about a woman going through breast cancer. Mother did not want the book so I read it. There I learned that chemotherapy can be the cause of death in the cancer process. People have to decide if the risk is worth the danger, and I can see my mother risking everything to stay alive as long as possible. She was a very strong woman. However, she should have had someone with her at all times.

*   *   *

During my short visit with Shivey, she handed me a box. The box was about one-fourth full and had a few photos as well as the ring I bought Mother when I was a teenager working at a restaurant. Mother had taken the ring off of her finger the minute my sister gave her a new ring a few years later, and I never saw my mother wear my gift of the family ring again. I didn't want the ring. I hated my mother at that moment, and I did not want the ring I worked so hard to buy for her, only to have it thrown back in my face with her projection that I had somehow stolen it so many years before.

In the end, I kept the ring, and it is somewhere in one of my jewelry boxes. I don't care about it and wonder what will happen to it after I die. Since it is only Mother's children, it seems rather useless to anyone else.

I kissed my sister on the cheek and said no matter what, we will always be sisters. With that, I took my little box and left. I never saw her or any of my siblings since. I looked in the box later and saw several letters and cards I had sent my mother over the years and cried at how pathetic I sounded. I was literally begging for her love, trying to impress her with my accomplishments when I was just coming of age at twenty-one. Some people might think my mother saved these documents because she loved me. Not possible. My mother did, however, have a paper-hoarding problem and rarely threw anything out.

*   *   *

I sent an e-mail to each of my sisters and brothers during my bankruptcy to ask if they would be kind enough to each give me a mere $5,000 so that I could purchase a car. I didn't hear from any of them. I didn't expect to, but I wanted to give them the opportunity to be kind. They silently declined.

*   *   *

And so it was over. My psychopath Father could manipulate me or hurt anyone no more. My malignant narcissist Mother could never again cause me painful and paranoid projections, or sear my soul with her hostile voice, or backstab me, damaging my good reputation. My angry drug addict brother Gus, alcoholic younger brother Dylan, and especially my sociopathic sister must leave my heart so that I can go on to grow with people who do love me. It is over, and I allow myself that relief while I still wish my parents and siblings only the best wherever they are now.

Epilogue I—Fallen Angel

The new monster picked me up by the hair and dropped me
down at the doorstep of insanity. But this time, I had the courage to
stand up and walk away from him without looking back. My good.

—Cherylann

Unbelievable. Just when I thought my story was done and ready to be published, I was forced into another crisis that potentially had the power to destroy me once again.

Psychopaths, malignant narcissists, and sexual predators (SPs) are unchangeable beings we cannot revolutionize no matter how much we want to or try. It is also impossible to recognize them immediately, and it takes open eyes to protect ourselves and our children from these soul suckers. The only answer to save ourselves from Ps, MNs, and SPs is to remove ourselves from them swiftly and without a second thought. To try to change or hang on to a love that was never there is likened to banging your head against the proverbial wall and only hurt yourself or your children in the end.

I never imagined I would be writing an epilogue introducing a new monster in my life, a man I trusted with all of my heart and soul for five years.

Frank DeSmet never loved nor cared for me at all. He was after my granddaughter. I was weak and sick and tired over all of my adversities, and along came what I thought to be a "concrete angel." Frank. He held me. He stood up for me with my family when they were mean or manipulative when I couldn't speak for myself. He fed me when I could not feed myself. He put me in his car and took me to the hospital or doctors too many times to count. He taught me how to garden and love dogs.

He loved my granddaughter like his own.

I thought.

He was yet another love fraud in my life, and I did not recognize it until it was too late.

*　　*　　*

We do not know who predators are or what they look like. They could have soft beautiful blue eyes or raging bulging green eyes. They can act like your life's savior and, in fact, only want the most precious thing you have—and steal that thing from right under your nose. In this case, Frank stole my granddaughter's innocence. How are we to know who to trust? How are we to protect the most important people in our lives from the monster in the closest? I don't know anymore. I don't know anything anymore, if I ever did know anything.

*　　*　　*

Frank went away for four days. The night before he left, I had a horrible headache and asked him to grab me a Tylenol. I saw him go into his bedroom and open a drawer and pull out a bottle and carefully take two out for me. He then went and got me some water and came back to me with the medicine. How nice. How considerate! How lucky I am to have seen where he went to get the pills.

The next night, Frank was on his four-day vacation—to visit his mother and a friend who lived several hours away. That first night he was gone, I was in bed and that headache came back. I walked into Frank's room and opened the drawer I thought he kept his medication in. My world once again betrayed me.

There, sitting out in the open, on top of his underwear, were two CDs. There was writing on the disks, and I could not help but pick them up because I saw Amanda's name on one of them. Then I saw Amanda's name on the other. The first label said, "Amanda's First Orgasm," and the other said, "Amanda Masturbating."

My knees broke loose, and I fell to the ground. I grabbed the CDs and felt that there was another CD behind each of the two obvious ones. I shakily took them to my laptop and slipped the disks into my drive to see what Amanda's name was doing on Frank's CDs! What I saw was enough to put me into a tailspin of temporary insanity.

I was only able to open about ten photos and one video, which was very black and difficult to see what was going on. They were of my precious granddaughter doing exactly what the labels said the CD was about!

I pulled the CD out and grabbed my shoes and ran out of the house toward the police station. On my way, I realized I did not have a cell phone and would need one because I was not going to go back into that house. I stopped at the mall, and in the cell store, I asked the man to hurry up and charge a phone for me so that I could use it immediately. I told him I could not stand for much longer so please, please hurry. But it was too late. I fainted and went out cold on the floor of the store. Security was called who called the medics. By then I had woken up and told the security what I had found and showed them the CDs. I could not breathe. A young man of about twenty-three came to me and asked if I had any medication to take, and I said yes, I have anti-anxiety medication in my purse and would he get two for me. He did.

As I waited for the phone, I sat in the chair just outside the store with the young man who kept my mind occupied with chitchat. His name was Jacob. I was in a trance. What the hell had been going on and for how long? Was this why Frank was so nice to me? *Of course! No one is nice to me for no reason,* my tapes within my head played. I have betrayed my granddaughter by bringing a pedophile into her life and putting her head full of fear, shame, guilt, and an unwillingness to tell so that she would not upset my sickly life. She did not tell so that she would protect *me!*

How do I know this? I was in Amanda's shoes so many years before. Back in the day when Dave was molesting me; to tell would be to blow my family apart—something I was unwilling to do. I would sacrifice myself for the sake of my family. Did Amanda not tell what Frank was doing to her to save me? Oh my god, oh my god, oh my god!

Amanda would have only been between the ages of eight and ten at the time the CDs were made I later learned. *She is a baby!* She needed protection from the evil men of the world, and I was supposed to be that protection for her! I failed my granddaughter. I failed myself.

My tears will not stop. I am heaving great sobs that cannot be suppressed with kind words. I am back in post-traumatic stress mode, and I want to die. I cannot face this. Yes, I can. For the sake of my granddaughter, I must show her how wrong Frank was to go anywhere near her, and I must show her what I was willing to do to make sure she was safe again.

After about an hour of sitting and staring at the floor as my new friend Jacob talked to me I finally got my phone and headed straight to the police department. Frank must be stopped. Amanda must be saved, and the only way to save that girl is to show her all of my love and support and to do the exact opposite of what my family did to me when I finally came clean about Dave Craig. I must wrap her in my arms and tell her how so, so sorry I am for introducing her to Frank. I must tell her none of this old man's actions was her fault in any way. I must *show her* by taking action. I must put the man who was my concrete angel for so many years behind bars!

I was interviewed by the police for several hours. They got a search warrant and went back to Franks home where I had been living for the last year and tore his room and desktop computer apart. After they watched those videos they told me there was far more in the CDs than what I was able to see before I left for the police station. I wanted to throw up. I had the dry heaves, and I could not stand myself once again. I did as I was trained to do growing up—blame myself. Frank had to be stopped. Amanda had to know that I would never have introduced her to a monster on purpose! *Never!*

Finally, at 10:00 p.m., I was introduced to a woman from Victim's Services. "But I am not the victim," I said, *Amanda is!*" The nice lady talked to me for over an hour explaining how I must not slip into oblivion over someone else's bad (evil) intentions. She calmed me down enough to think. I decided I had three more days before Frank would be home again to find a place to rent, find movers, and beg my ex-husband for money to do all of this (which he readily did).

My girlfriend, Veronica, flew up to my city and helped me pack as fast as we could. I found a place on Craigslist that would be suitable. It is a two-bedroom fourplex that, at the very least, was clean and ready to move in. It was also available for Monday—the day Frank was due home.

Meanwhile the special abuse police in the lower mainland of British Columbia visited Amanda's maternal grandparents, the ones who are raising her. Amanda was very quiet and did not say enough to the police. She was afraid, I knew. She does not know this at this point, but she will have to undergo an invasive physical examination this very week as I write this. She does not know what is to come. I cannot stop crying for my hurting granddaughter. If she is a strong gal, and I know she is, she will overcome the bad experience and make something good come from it. What doesn't kill us makes us stronger people, my dear!

* * *

When was the last time I was so broke, emotionally and literally? It does not matter. My granddaughter is safe. I was able to apologize to her over the phone, and she now calls me to see how I am doing, bless her heart! I put my happy voice on and tell her how lovely my new place is, and I am fixing up a bedroom just for her, painting it pink and putting a purple chandelier on the ceiling for her. Over the years and through my travels I have purchased many pretty ornaments for Amanda and they will complete the new bedroom—when she can come and see me again.

Why do I feel so strongly that this is my fault? Why are the people at the police station and the victim services and the Elizabeth Fry counselors telling me it is not? I know why. This is what predators do. They make one feel they need that person so much and cannot live without them. I feel the guilt because I accepted Frank's kindness to be true. My history of being accused of being a liar, cheat, and thief and evil eyes has once again caught me off guard, and the tapes are playing over and over and over again. I must stop. But how?

To hell with Frank! I will lie down for a while, but I will get back up and learn to trust myself and my judgment again one day. I will find a way to live and live well. I will forgive myself and all of those who have hurt me throughout my life. I will move forward.

* * *

Frank was arrested without incident in front of his home the evening he returned. The police confiscated his laptop computer and took him to the police station for a very long interrogation. He spent three days in jail before being released on his own recognance. He is forbidden to visit any area where children under eighteen years of age play and not to contact Amanda or myself.

His first hearing will be on September 8, 2011, and I will be there to make sure he pleads guilty. I did telephone him one night on my new restricted phone and confronted him on his betrayal of me and my granddaughter. Frank apologized profusely, claiming he needed help. He swore he never intended to hurt anyone and this was the first time he had ever encountered such feelings toward a child. I don't know if I believe him or not. I know he has numerous sister's who all share loving feelings toward him. I know his own daughter told me she was never molested by him, and she had never heard of him doing any such thing to others.

Why now?

Frank told me he has a lawyer and has directed him that he wants to plead guilty to avoid Amanda having to testify or prolong this travesty. Since this is his first offence, it is very likely he will get a very light sentence, along with having to register as a sexual offender.

The moral of this epilogue is this: You cannot easily and freely trust just anyone with your children or grandchildren. You cannot close your eyes and pretend people are giving you too much—because they likely are taking something else behind your back. If it seems too good to be true, it likely is.

My second message is to mothers and grandmothers who know their child is being abused by a lover or friend. I know it is hard to suddenly uproot yourself and/or your family, but it can be done if you call on the right people. Our children are our future. We must stamp out sexual abuse, and the only way it can be done is for the adults to put their big girl's and boy's pants on and do the right thing for our offspring. Equally important, although difficult, predators must be reported! This is another difficult decision, I know. It is hard to one day think your man (or woman) is an angel and the next day find out you have been fooling with the devil in disguise. It is hard, but absolutely essential to take action. I know my own mother chose to look the other way rather than upset the apple cart, and I also know the affect this action of hers had on me in my years to come.

Please, make the right choices for yourself and/or your children. You *do have the power to make the decision to be a hero—or a zero!* If you are living with a psychopath, a malignant narcissist, or a sexual predator, there is nothing you can do to save them, so again, please, save yourself and save your children and run as fast as your legs will carry you.

Running Away Down River Road

Songwriter Lyrics by Sylvia Tyson

Well here I go once again
With my suitcase in my hand
And I'm running away down River Road
And I swear, once again, that I'm never coming home
Yes, I'm chasing my dreams down River Road

Mama said, listen child
You're too old to run wild
You're too big to be fishin' with the boys these days

So I grabbed some clothes and I ran
Stole five dollars from a sugar can
A twelve-year-old jail breaker runnin' away

Here I go once again
With my suitcase in my hand
And I'm running away down River Road
And I swear, once again, that I'm never coming home
I'm chasing my dreams down River Road

Well, I married a pretty good man
And he tries to understand
But he knows I've got leavin' on my mind these days

When I get that urge to roam
I'm just like a kid again
The same old jail breaker runnin' away

Here I go once again
With my suitcase in my hand
And I'm running away down River Road
And I swear, once again, that I'm never coming home
I'm chasing my dreams down River Road

Epilogue II

Pain is inevitable. Suffering is optional.

—M. Kathleen Casey

This memoir was the most difficult project I have ever worked on. Some days, I would stay under my covers and sob as I relived my life with my mother, father, stepfather, siblings, and Frank. I kept pushing myself forward to ensure my story got out, but it did not come without emotional consequences.

As I look back over my life, I have many questions but few answers. Why was my Father a psychopath, and why did he spare me while he hurt so many others within our family? Why did I have a malignant narcissist Mother who could barely stand to look at me since I was a small child? Why did the psychopath and the malignant narcissist get married and bore two innocent children, who suffered over their dark love, one child who turned to drugs to hide his feelings and the other to feel internal pain so much she wanted to die?

Why did my stepfather pick me as his victim for his perverted ways? Why did no one believe me when I told on him? Why did my loving son die so young? Why did I give up my gift of life by suicide—and fail so often? Why did I experience paranormal activity after my son passed? Why did my siblings and other relatives on my mother's side turn their backs on me? Why do so many of my mother's friends give me dirty looks when I do not know them and they do not know me in person? What did my mother and siblings say about me to tarnish my otherwise good reputation, and why? Why did my siblings close the door on me after Mother died when they were just as fed up with her as I was? Why was Shivey so strangely calm and footloose in her behaviors after her own devastating family events?

Why did I allow Frank DeSmet into mine and my granddaughter's life?

But now it is time for me to stop asking myself questions I know I will never get answers to. It is time to move on to the rest of my life and to make my life as happy and fulfilled as I can. I am so blessed to have two beautiful grandchildren and have friends who believe in me, trust me, and love me unconditionally—no matter how often I may have failed them. I ask my grandchildren why I am so lucky to have them as my family almost every time I speak with them, and they say they just don't know. We don't need to know. It just is. Thank God for what I do have, and *thank God it is not me who has turned her back on her family.* In spite of the pain and torment I have endured by my family, I still love them and I always will. It is embedded in my soul! I am just fortunate to not be like them.

I do not believe there are answers to my questions, and so I must say farewell to the questions and take my leave from their presence. I must look ahead to a brighter future that I know is in store for me. My wish is to let this little light of mine shine and bring peace to others who have suffered in their lifetimes, even much worse than myself.

My wish is that by writing my "open book," I have helped others who are scapegoats within their families and suffer deeply for it. My wish is those who are involved with a sociopath gain the courage they will need to let them go and still feel whole and loving toward themselves and others. Sociopaths must be let go from your life completely or you will pay dearly for their sins upon you. Sociopaths cannot love! You cannot make an empty soul or monster love you. This is the most important thing for survivors of sociopaths to remember. If they do not kill you, *you* might kill yourself by proxy! Think of a psychopath or sociopath as someone without an arm instead of without a soul. Just as you cannot grow an arm back, a psychopath cannot grow a soul. And it has been proven that a child molester cannot change his desires for sexual interactions with children.

* * *

I moved all of my furniture from Frank's home before he returned from his vacation and was arrested. Unfortunately, I was unable to bring Duchess, the cat Amanda picked out for me two years ago, because my rental agreement would not allow a third animal, and I couldn't separate my new Maltese sisters, Callie and Sadie, who give me so much unconditional love. I planted a patio garden and am in the middle of making my new home comfortable for when my grandchildren visit.

I love to read and sit in my garden watching my dogs play in the large backyard. Thankfully, the dogs force me to go out on regular walks and to not isolate. They keep me busy taking care of their little needs, and this is a joy for me.

I have high hopes for a bright future and am ready to let go of all of the people who have hurt me, my child, and my grandchildren. I am ready to put my big girl's pants on and learn to take care of myself. I am not bitter. Maybe one day I will find someone who really is capable of loving me. It may, however, be a long time before I will be able to trust again. I believe my prayers will be answered and all good things will come my way as long as I continue to be true to myself.

I feel love and I am so grateful for this emotion! I cannot deliberately hurt anyone or any animal. I despise sexual and verbal abuse and violence. If the members of my family are harmed or angry due to my truth saying in my own memoir, I cannot help them. I did not write my memoir to hurt people; I wrote it for my own sake and to tell it from the mountains that I am a good person after all of these years of thinking I must be a horrible person since my own family do not love me! I have finally learned *I am not what my family have tried to draw a picture of me as.* I deserve to have my say. I finally feel empowered to have my side of the story told!

When people who are capable of love and yet do not receive love back, it hurts. It digs deep within our souls and leaves scars. I am not sure if my scars will ever heal, but my prayer is that I never grow into a habit of carrying a bitterness or unforgiving attitude for the sake of my own well-being. I once heard that if we cannot forgive someone for their awful actions upon us, it is like we carry their bodies with us until the day we die. That is a heavy load to bear! That is a weight I am *not* willing to hold on to. My goal is to move on with visions of a peaceful (albeit small) family, unconditional love, and hope for champion generations after me. As the Nana of two beautiful children, peace really does begin with me, and I pray I can mentor them well so that they can pass on healthy, happy lives to their children and the children after them.

* * *

My husband and I will be divorced within the month. It hurts to have twenty years with someone and to have to let them go. I love Gary for taking such good care of our son with me, for going through the pain of losing Trevor with me, and for enduring the pain of watching me want to die. However, I now realize I picked a man who is incapable of having the emotional attachment I so much need and desire. I wish him only the best in his future and hope he finds true love and lives his life in peace and harmony. Gary stays in close touch with our grandchildren and takes them skiing, skating, and on wilderness camping trips whenever possible.

Amanda's mother, Mary, has still not settled down in any home of her own, always living with others. At thirty-two, she now lives with a new boyfriend she calls fiancé.

Amanda has developed into a stunning young woman of eleven and has become a champion horse rider, winning many first place gymkhanas and horse shows. Some of her scores are off the charts for a girl of her age. Amanda continues to live with her maternal grandparents on their horse ranch in a small community in the lower mainland of British Columbia. She loves all of her many animals and the farm where she plays in delight every day after school and on weekends. Amanda is getting above-average grades and is a beautiful person in her own right—her hugs cannot be matched!

We go on a vacation together every year to faraway places, and she puts a thumbtack on her globe showing her travels. I love her dearly and am so glad to have her in my life my eyes tear up when she comes to visit me. We pack picnics and stay all day long at our beaches here in the Okanagan of British Columbia. The screeching delight of Amanda in the water is like music to my ears. Amanda has many positive role models in her life, and I am so grateful things turned out the way they did after I had to give her to her maternal grandparents. They are truly angels and have done a wonderful job in making Amanda feel like a part of a loving family, which she needed so very much after so much loss at such a young age.

Tyler's adoptive mother now allows Gary and I to see him from time to time. He lives a short distance from Amanda, and have recently been introduced to each other. We (their guardians and I) try to get the half siblings together as often as possible just as their daddy (Trevor) would have had it. Tyler has had many successes in his short thirteen years including playing drums and piano. He loves to wrestle and is in a rugby team. Tyler is a lot like Trevor in that he is a square peg going to the round hole of school and prefers to be tutored at home. I recently heard that he may want to return to school in September of this year, his first year of high school. Tyler is a very bright boy, and I have no doubt he will grow into a fine young man. He looks so much like his father I often stare at him with pride and joy that my son made such a beautiful son in body and spirit. Amanda and Tyler tease each other just like any other brother and sister do, and it brings me so much joy to see them laugh at (with) each other together!

I do not know the whereabouts of my siblings on my mother's side other than what a cousin told me recently; apparently, Gus is living away from our city now since he obtained his inheritance and is very happy. My younger brother, Dylan, moved to California for a job. He was fired for his drinking problem at the company he worked at for over twenty years. Shivey still lives in Abbotsford, British Columbia, and beyond that, I do not know how she is doing or her family is doing. Since Mark lost his leg at his workplace, I have not seen or heard from him. I hope he is adjusting well and has learned to live with his loss with peace and hope for a very bright future.

I tried to "friend" my nieces and nephews on Facebook but was declined by all, except my nephew (son of Dylan) who is about nineteen years old by now. The last time I saw my nieces was when we did our makeovers on their sixteenth birthdays. I do not know what they have been told about me by their parents or my mother, but if they ever want to know the real me, they should contact me directly and get to know me from their own perspective rather than by third-party gossip. I love all of these precious children and wish them all the best for their futures.

My siblings from my Father's second family have not contacted me. I understand they are angry with me for their perceived betrayal when I looked after our father as he was dying. I wish all of them, Gilbert, Shenay, and Danny, as well as their loving mother, Sunny, all of my best and forgiveness for seemingly turning their backs on me for doing what I just thought was right—helping an old man die with someone by his side. All of this family suffered greatly by my Father's actions, and I do not hold any resentment toward them for leaving me and hope they can forgive me one day. I miss them dearly.

I have a long way to go before I can feel whole again. Being raised by sociopaths, losing my son, and learning about Frank's interference with my granddaughter literally sucked the life out of me until I was ready to fill myself back up with the realization I am okay. I am more than okay. My Trevor loved his mother (me!), and to me this is my biggest accomplishment in life. I miss his daily phone calls and bear hugs, but I know he would be very proud of me and how I pushed on in writing this book. At times I broke down and put the laptop away until I could move forward with my story some more. This has not been an easy write, but it is a story that had to be told.

I realize some people will judge me for some of my actions or experiences and am ready to face anyone who doubts one word I have written or why I have behaved as I have in my past. As my book so boldly confesses, I am human. I make mistakes, but I am not a mistake! What a wonderful feeling to finally let go of my guilt and shame and feel the emotion of forgiveness toward myself! If I ask anything of the reader, it is this: Do not let anyone tell you you are worthless. It is the finger-pointer who is worthless, and he uses you as supply to build him or herself up. It is the abuser with a serious mental condition, not the abused! Repeat this to yourself several times in a day, and soon you too will come to believe it. Replace your old tapes with new ones, and learn that you are neither above nor below any other person.

* * *

I've been so busy writing and trying to stay well I have not gone back to work, but I plan to as soon as possible. I miss my career as a human resources manager and having a place to go to every day. I am very good at my job and miss working with people. While my health has not been the best in the last several years, as I come to the end of my story, I can feel myself healthier than I have in years. I think I am ready to walk back out to the world and enjoy all that life has to offer. I want to contribute in any small way possible to repay God for stitching up my broken heart so many times. I want to pay forward!

I hope this book gets read by many survivors of sociopaths who need to know they are not guilty of anything they may have been accused of by the empty-hearted bullies or monsters who freely walk this earth, seeking out supply to inflict their abuse upon.

As I said in the beginning of my story, sociopaths come in all shapes, sizes, and colors. They could be the most handsome man or woman you have ever seen. They will seem to be the most loving and caring person you have ever met. They are the wolves in sheep's clothing that Jesus talked about. The bushy-haired boogeyman is likely just a sad man who has lost everything and who needs a few words of kindness or a meal to feed on.

Let me rewind and remind there is only one cure for victims of sociopaths: No contact. You have a heart. You feel for others, even the psychopath or malignant narcissist. However, he cannot feel empathy or love for anyone. They may be able to fake it for a while, but eventually, their true colors come out and hurt you sorely. Remember this, it is never too late to get out and stay out of their lives. It's hard, I know. It's heartbreaking, I know. Saving yourself by staying away from those evil characters you may love deeply but cannot love you back is the *only way* to begin your healing. The good side of the sociopath is a lie. They do not exist other than in *our* own minds and craving for love.

* * *

Thank you for reading my story, and if I have helped just one person gain strength to keep going in the face of adversity, then this book has been more than worthwhile. May God bless you and reap heaps of love and joy onto you today and forever into eternity!

Someone Is Looking for Someone like Me

Lyrics by Gail Davies

You say that nobody cares where you're going
And that your life don't mean nothing at all
You've heard the saying you reap what you're sowing
So plant a good seed and watch it grow tall

Somewhere a man's got no woman to turn to
Somewhere a woman is lonely and blue
Somewhere a child's got no mama to hold her
Someone is looking for someone like you

You say there's no road you'd care to travel
Nothing to say that ain't been said before
And life's a mystery that you can't unravel
Well love's the key that will open that door

Somewhere a man's got no woman to turn to
Somewhere a woman is lonely and blue
Somewhere a child's got no mama to hold her
Someone is looking for someone like you

Think of all the time you waste complaining
Think of all the good that could be done
Think of all the friends you could be gaining
If you lift your hand to help someone

You say that nobody cares where you're going
And that your life don't mean nothing at all
You've heard the saying you reap what you're sowing
So plant a good seed and watch it grow tall

Somewhere a man's got no woman to turn to
Somewhere a woman is lonely and blue
Somewhere a child's got no mama to hold her
Someone is looking for someone like you
Someone is looking for someone like you

Acknowledgments

I first thank God and his angels for always watching out for me and saving me from myself in times of extreme stress. I was blessed with a son who taught me that love is unconditional and eternal, and I am grateful for the twenty-five years Trevor and I had together, in the good and bad times.

Thanks must go to all of the staff with Xlibris who patiently worked with me in making my memoir a success through their editing the cover and interior of this book.

Veronica Reedwell has been my true friend for over fifteen years and has stood by me even when she had her own issues to work through, and I send her many hugs of thanks.

I thank Gary, my ex-husband, for his patience with me in trying to get back on my feet even after our separation; I appreciate that Gary and I can communicate with maturity on matters of our grandchildren.

Finally, I thank my beautiful grandchildren for just being who they are—I accept you both just the way you are because in my eyes you are perfect, and this book would not have been possible without having you to inspire me as you do. You both make your Nana so proud, and I am looking forward to many more years together. I pray you both live long and prosperous lives and the cycle of abuse will continue to end with us three.

In loving memory of my son

Trevor Thomas

(May 27, 1978-June 28, 2003)

My beloved gift from God for twenty-five years
www.trevor.virtual-memorials.com

Top of the World

Lyrics by the Carpenters
Such a feelin's comin' over me
There is wonder in most everything I see
Not a cloud in the sky
Got the sun in my eyes
And I won't be surprised if it's a dream

Everything I want the world to be
Is now coming true especially for me
And the reason is clear
It's because you are here
You're the nearest thing to heaven that I've seen

I'm on the top of the world lookin' down on creation
And the only explanation I can find
Is the love that I've found ever since you've been around
Your love's put me at the top of the world

Something in the wind has learned my name
And it's tellin' me that things are not the same
In the leaves on the trees and the touch of the breeze
There's a pleasin' sense of happiness for me

There is only one wish on my mind
When this day is through I hope that I will find
That tomorrow will be just the same for you and me
All I need will be mine if you are here

I'm on the top of the world lookin' down on creation
And the only explanation I can find
Is the love that I've found ever since you've been around
Your love's put me at the top of the world

Index

V

W

CPSIA information can be obtained at www.ICGtesting.com
Printed in the USA
LVOW120706261011

252057LV00003B/2/P